The Hospitals of Medieval Norwich

THE HOSPITALS OF MEDIEVAL NORWICH

Carole Rawcliffe

Studies in East Anglian History 2

Centre of East Anglian Studies
University of East Anglia
1995

© Carole Rawcliffe 1995

ISBN 0 906219 39 6

Published by the Centre of East Anglian Studies,
University of East Anglia, Norwich NR4 7TJ.

Printed by the Printing Unit, University of East Anglia.
Cover design by UEA Printing Unit.

Front cover: The care of a patient by two nurses, c. 1283.
Regulations of the Hospital of Notre Dame de Tournai.

Back cover: Seal of the Master and Brothers of St. Giles's Hospital, Norwich, late thirteenth-century.

CONTENTS

Acknowledgements..8

Foreword 9

Introduction...13

CHAPTER I: THE LEPER HOSPITALS OF MEDIEVAL NORWICH.......33

CHAPTER II: ST PAUL'S OR NORMAN'S HOSPITAL...............................61

CHAPTER III: THE HOSPITAL OF ST GILES...91

CHAPTER IV: SMALL HOSPITALS BEFORE THE REFORMATION...135

Conclusion... 153

Appendix 163

Bibliography 167

Index 185

MAPS AND PLANS

1. The Hospitals of Medieval Norwich 7

2. The Estates of St Paul's Hospital 60

3. St Giles's Hospital... 110

4. The Estates of St Giles's Hospital 118

TABLES

A. The Finances of St Paul's Hospital, 1422–1510.. 78

B. The Finances of St Paul's Hospital and Norwich Cathedral Priory, 1363–1534 79

▷

C. The Finances of St Giles's Hospital, 1319–1397 123

D. The Finances of St Giles's Hospital, 1465–1527 124

PLATES

1. Bibliotheque Nationale, Paris, Ms Ea Res, French, c.1500

2. Sprowston Leper Hospital, Norwich

3. British Library, Lansdowne Ms, 451, f. 127r, English early fifteenth century

4. St Elizabeth Window, Church of St Elizabeth, Marburg

5. Seal of St Giles's Hospital, British Library, D.C.F. XXXIX

6. Ceiling of the Chancel of St Giles's Hospital, Norwich

7. The Bell Tower of St Giles's Hospital, Norwich

8. St Margaret and the Dragon, St Helen's Church, Norwich

9. The Cow Tower and Bishop Bridge, Norwich

10. The Cloister of St Giles's Hospital, Norwich

11. Bibliotheque Nationale, Paris, Ms Latin 8846, f. 106r, French thirteenth century

Numbers 1 and 11 are reproduced with the permission of the Bibliotheque Nationale, Paris; and numbers 3 and 5 with that of the British Library

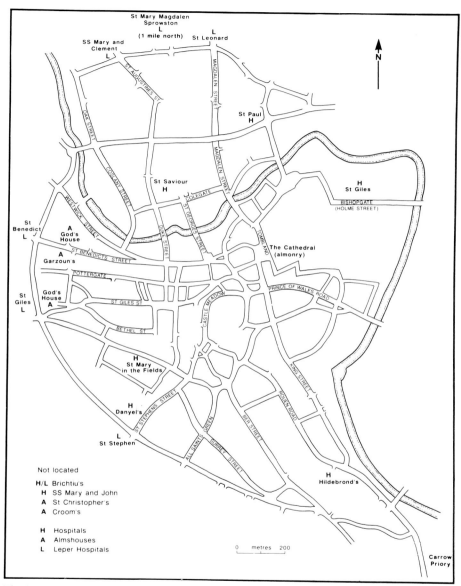

The Hospitals of Medieval Norwich

ACKNOWLEDGEMENTS

This book was written with support from the Wellcome Trust, which provided a research grant for my study of the medieval history of St Giles's hospital (now the Great Hospital), Norwich. I am also grateful to the staff of the library of the Wellcome Institute, of the Warburg Institute and of the Institute of Historical Research, London, for their help. The advice and assistance of Miss Jean Kennedy, Mr Paul Rutledge and their colleagues at the Norfolk Record Office is warmly acknowledged and greatly appreciated. Thanks are due, too, to the staff of the UEA Library, the British Library and the Public Record Office, London. Among my colleagues at UEA, I would especially like to thank Dr Roberta Gilchrist, Dr Richard Wilson, Dr Roger Virgoe and Dr Ian Atherton. Mr Philip Judge drew the maps and Miss Mavis Wesley prepared the manuscript for publication: I am indebted to them both. The Trustees and Master of the Great Hospital have been extremely helpful from the outset, putting into practice the founder's dictum that strangers should be made welcome. I owe a great deal to the late Mr Ken Terry, who placed his knowledge of the hospital at my disposal. Advice and information have been generously given by Mr Brian Ayers, Dr Bruce Campbell, Professor R.B. Dobson, Dr John Henderson, Mr R.P. Martin, Professor Nicholas Orme, Mrs Elizabeth Rutledge, Professor Hassell Smith and Dr Ann Stirland. Dr Steven Cherry and our students taking the Social History of Medicine Units at UEA have encouraged me to think about medieval hospitals in new and different ways, and I am grateful for their ideas. Last of all, a unique contribution was made by Captain Zarco, who enthusiastically explored the Norfolk countryside with me.

Carole Rawcliffe
Norwich, April 1995

FOREWORD

In May 1992, I began work at the Centre of East Anglian Studies on a history of St Giles's hospital, Norwich, during the Middle Ages (since it only later became known as the Great Hospital, I have here elected to use the medieval name). This, the largest and richest of the city's pre-Reformation hospitals, was in most respects entirely typical of its kind: it never possessed the resources of the great monastic hospitals to be found in London or York, but occupied a prominent place among the scores of charitable institutions founded in the towns and cities of thirteenth-century England. Now, however, because of the nationwide destruction of ecclesiastical buildings and manuscripts during the 1530s and after, it appears unique. Not only does a substantial part of the medieval fabric, comprising the infirmary, the nave and chancel of the adjoining church, the cloisters, refectory and bell tower, still stand, but a mass of documentary evidence, dating from the time of its foundation in 1249, has also survived. The hospital archive includes a cartulary, hundreds of account rolls, deeds and other legal records; and its existence makes possible an unusually detailed study of an English medieval hospital.[1] In addition, the city of Norwich itself possesses an outstanding collection of early records, ranging from enrolled deeds and court rolls to administrative material and guild accounts, which contain additional information about the treatment of the sick poor. Over 1,800 wills left by residents between 1370 and 1532 constitute an invaluable source of evidence for changing attitudes to charitable relief, and that part of the archive of the Dean and Chapter of Norwich Cathedral relating to the Benedictine Priory is also extremely important, not least because it holds the surviving accounts of the almoner and of the monastic hospital of St Paul.

During the Middle Ages, six leper houses, six hospitals for needy travellers and the sick poor and some seven almshouses were set up (but did not necessarily flourish) in the city.[2] In order to understand the precise role of St Giles's and its contribution to the care of the indigent, I decided to investigate the history of these institutions as well, and was surprised to discover exactly how much evidence about them could be unearthed. Since, with the exception of a few antiquarian studies, this material has been neglected by historians, the idea of making my research into St Giles's the basis of a wider investigation of institutional philanthropy in medieval Norwich seemed especially worthwhile – all the more so in view of the fact that a comprehensive economic and social history of the city in this period has yet to be written. The initial plan was to incorporate all my findings into a single volume, but it became apparent that a short, readily accessible study of Norwich's nineteen medieval hospitals would be of interest to local historians, as well as to students of medical and social history. The fire at Norwich Central Library in August 1994, and the subsequent removal of the contents of the Record Office into storage (where they remain at the time of writing) brought the final stages of my work on the archive of St Giles's to a halt, but at least gave me the opportunity to complete this book using material already collected.

In order to produce a balanced survey, I have omitted much of the detail about the finances, estate management and personnel of St Giles's hospital which will eventually appear in my history of the institution itself. Nor is it possible in this short space to provide more than a limited amount of background about medieval Norwich or to make detailed comparisons between the hospitals under scrutiny here and other English or continental models. It is, however, important to remember that the men and women who endowed and helped to maintain the charitable institutions of medieval Norwich shared ideals and concerns which were current throughout Christendom, and that similar organisations, with similar problems, might be found elsewhere in Europe. This book was finished before the appearance of Nicholas Orme's *The First English Hospitals, 1070–1570* (New Haven and London, forthcoming), which I understand will provide a wide variety of such comparative material, notably from the South West of England.

The period covered here, beginning with the arrival in Norwich of the Benedictine community at the very close of the eleventh century and ending in the 1540s, is a long one during which the practical and theoretical responses to urban poverty underwent many changes. The teachings of the Church (which were never entirely consistent with regard to the matter of almsgiving) clearly exerted a powerful influence over donors and recipients alike. So also did the more immediate, practical considerations of supply and demand, pressure of population and the availability of resources. During the four and a half centuries under review, Norwich experienced a steady, then rapidly accelerating period of demographic growth, followed by a dramatic decline. Limited recovery in the fifteenth century gave way to decades of stagnation, made worse by two serious fires in 1507. The improvement in urban standards of living and attendant fall in the numbers of truly destitute, vagrant paupers after the first outbreaks of plague in the mid-fourteenth century probably reduced the most pressing need for institutionalised philanthropy. But the trend towards informal systems of parochial relief, which inevitably gave priority to 'deserving' cases in the community over the claims of outsiders, may also be seen as a consequence of the collective uncertainty generated during a time of social upheaval.

It is against this background that historians now seek to assess the nature of institutional provision for the sick poor of medieval England. After years of neglect following the appearance in 1909 of R.M. Clay's pioneering book on English hospitals, the subject has, over the last two decades, been transformed into a 'discipline of relevance'.[3] Much of the credit for this transformation must go to Miri

Rubin's study of *Charity and Community in Medieval Cambridge* (Cambridge, 1987), which sets the town's hospitals firmly in a European context, as well as exploring the theological background and the transmission to the laity of ideas about almsgiving. In the final pages of her book, Dr Rubin concludes that the late fourteenth and fifteenth centuries saw a considerable hardening in attitudes and a more pronounced level of discrimination on the part of donors. This argument is further developed in two subsequent articles, where she explores the practical consequences of the 'decline in consensus and trust' which she believes was increasingly apparent after the Black Death.[4] Her views have been questioned by Patricia Cullum, whose research into charitable effort in medieval Yorkshire has led her to maintain that an altruistic concern for the poor remained a continuous feature of life right up to the Reformation and beyond.[5] So, indeed, it did; but the *focus* of this concern appears to have shifted and grown narrower during these years, perhaps even from the time of the great famines of the early fourteenth century. The evidence for Norwich, which suffered badly during the agrarian crisis of 1314–22, and was subsequently devastated by plague, reveals an unambiguous reaction on the part of the wealthier citizens against philanthropic ventures which could not be controlled personally either by them or their nominees. In other words, relief moved from the general, relatively unselective hospitality of the *xenodochium* (hospital) to the stricter confines of the parish, where the needs and merits of the resident poor could more easily be assessed.

Changes in the personnel, finances and activities of Norwich's two largest hospitals both reflected and encouraged this trend: on the one hand, St Giles's placed increasing importance upon its status as a college for secular priests and choristers, offering the citizenry a prospect of salvation through intercessionary prayers rather than good works, while, on the other, St Paul's developed into a retirement home for respectable women of limited means, who seemed neither threatening nor profligate. The decline of charitable institutions in the medieval city was undoubtedly hastened by difficult economic conditions, which hit ecclesiastical landowners very badly and confirmed lay and clerical benefactors in their belief that schemes for 'self help' ought generally to prove more effective. In most cases a number of factors came into play, and donors would often have been hard-pressed themselves to disentangle their motives. Far more research needs to be done on demographic and social change in medieval Norwich before we can fully understand the relationship between the city's poor and their more affluent neighbours. It is hoped that this essay will stimulate further debate on an important aspect of medieval studies.

END NOTES

1   A rudimentary list of of these records may be found in *The Revised Catalogue of the Records of the City of Norwich*, ed. W. Hudson and J.C. Tingey (Norwich, 1898), pp. 68–79.

2   These institutions are listed in the appendix.

3   R.M. Clay, *The Mediaeval Hospitals of England* (London, 1909, reprinted 1966). A comprehensive survey of recent writing about the medieval hospital and its place in society appears in P. Horden, 'A Discipline of Relevance: The Historiography of the Medieval Hospital', *Social History of Medicine*, I (1988), pp. 359–74. See also, M. Carlin, 'Medieval English Hospitals', in *The Hospital in History*, ed. L. Granshaw and R. Porter (London, 1989), pp. 21–39.

4   'Development and Change in English Hospitals, 1100–1500', in *The Hospital in History*, pp. 41–59, and 'Imagining Medieval Hospitals', in *Medicine and Charity before the Welfare State*, ed. J. Barry and C. Jones (London, 1991), pp. 14–25.

5   P.H. Cullum, 'Hospitals and Charitable Provision in Medieval Yorkshire 936–1547' (York University PhD thesis, 1990). Part of this thesis has been published in *Cremetts and Corrodies: Care of the Poor and Sick at St Leonard's Hospital, York, in the Middle Ages* (University of York, Borthwick Paper, LXXIX, 1991). For other articles by Dr Cullum, see the bibliography.

INTRODUCTION

And before him shall be gathered all nations: and he shall separate them
one from another, as a shepherd divideth his sheep from the goats. And
he shall set the sheep on his right hand, but the goats on the left. Then
shall the King say unto them on his right hand, Come ye blessed of my
Father, inherit the kingdom prepared for you from the foundation of
the world. For I was an hungered, and ye gave me meat: I was thirsty,
and ye gave me drink: I was a stranger, and ye took me in: Naked, and
ye clothed me: I was sick and ye visited me: I was in prison, and ye came
unto me.

Matthew XXV, vv. 32–36

Some English medieval hospitals were monastic foundations; others came under the
management of secular clergy; and some, usually of later date, were set up and run
by guilds, fraternities or town councils. Whatever their origins, all were the visible
expression, in bricks and mortar, of Christian teaching on the subject of charity: all,
to a greater or lesser extent, owed their existence to the trepidation with which
contemporary men and women awaited the Last Judgement. Then, in the words of
St Matthew's gospel, the goats, who have behaved with selfish indifference towards
their fellow men, will be consigned 'into the everlasting fire, prepared for the devil
and his angels'. Although ideas about the purpose of almsgiving and the best means
of achieving salvation changed quite radically during the later Middle Ages, the
eschatological drama described by the Evangelist lost none of its terrors[1] Herbert de
Losinga (d.1119), the first Bishop of Norwich and founder of two of the city's
earliest hospitals, stressed repeatedly that the poor represented the body of Christ on
earth, and would therefore share his eternal throne:

Know ye, brethren, that the Church's poor are themselves among the
saints ... Make them your friends, as the Lord saith, that when you shall
fail they may receive you into everlasting dwellings. The holy poor are
lean with hunger, and shiver with cold, but hereafter in heaven they shall
be kings, and in the presence of God shall sit in judgement upon your
crimes and those of all the wicked.[2]

Perhaps the greatest work of art ever executed for a hospital, the altarpiece painted by Roger van der Weyden in the 1450s for the Hotel Dieu in Beaune, depicts in its open state the weighing of souls before Christ: an image intended to inspire deeds of mercy and to comfort the sick poor who were reputedly shown it whenever one of their number lay dying.

Theologians stressed the symbiotic relationship of Dives and Lazarus, neither of whom could survive apart. Yet, if 'the ryche man and the pore been too thynggys wol nedeful iche to othir', their relationship was far from equal. The humble pauper was already sure of his celestial reward, but the rich man's soul hung precariously in the balance.[3] The 'purchase of paradise' through the intercession of grateful bedesmen offered an attractive proposition to those who feared that they might either be damned outright or else destined for a long term in purgatory. 'The poor, who spiritually have clear sight', were compared to cripples dependent upon the crutch of alms, 'teaching the rich the way to the banquet of heaven, and praying God for them'.[4] St Augustine of Hippo (d.430) had taught that a combination of prayer, masses and almsgiving might hasten the period of purgation when Christian souls were cleansed of sins which had not been confessed or absolved. The definition and acceptance in the thirteenth century by the Church of a formal doctrine relating to purgatory further refined and elaborated this tripartite division of the afterlife.[5] The obit roll of the hospital of St Mary Magdalen, King's (then Bishop's) Lynn, which lists scores of names of local men and women, priests, guild members and merchants for whom prayers were to be said, provides a powerful testimony to popular anxieties on this score.[6]

Since purgatory differed from hell only in so far that its torments were finite, the benefactors of medieval hospitals did their best to ensure that everything possible would be done to shorten the ordeal. Thus, in 1356, Richard Fastolf left an annual rent of £4 to the hospital of St Mary in Yarmouth, which had been founded by one of his ancestors, on the condition that the master, brothers and sisters would 'have my soul and the soul of Petronilla my wife recommended in masses and prayers and other orations, and that they will keep our anniversary for ever'. For added security should they prove negligent, he gave the mayor and bailiffs power to rescind the grant.[7] His wishes were clearly respected, in the short term at least: an indenture of 1386 between the Prior of Norwich and the townspeople of Yarmouth established that a priest would celebrate mass every day in the hospital chapel for the souls of all past patrons, unless feast days were being observed at the neighbouring church of St Nicholas. Each of the patients was, moreover, obliged to attend the eight daily offices of the *Opus Dei*, and to say intercessionary prayers as well.[8]

This document, like so many others relating to medieval English hospitals, is almost exclusively concerned with the spiritual life of the house, which was of understandable importance to its benefactors. Anxiety about the welfare of their own immortal souls did not, however, blind them to the physical and emotional needs of the patients. Prominent among these was the desire for a decent burial,

1. Food for the body and the soul. Hospital patients take physical nourishment from a nursing sister while a priest administers spiritual medicine, in the form of the last rites. The figure of the crucified Christ (the Physician of Souls) and his mother, Mary (the nurse), dominate the scene, offering the promise of solace in heaven. At the front of the picture corpses are prepared for Christian burial.

which served not only to confirm that each departed brother or sister, however wretched, belonged to the Christian community, but also to make less arduous the journey ahead. Although Christ had not specifically instructed his followers to perform this act of charity, medieval men and women came increasingly to value it, not least because funerary prayers and masses promised further relief from the pains of purgatory. Turning to the Book of Tobit (in the Apocrypha), they found the example of the righteous Jew, who had been mocked and persecuted for burying the bodies of his co-religionists, and added 'burying the dead' to the original list of Comfortable Works. This brought the number up to seven: in a society convinced of the occult power of numbers, analogies with the sorrows and joys of the Virgin, the sacraments, the acts of Christ's passion, the deadly sins and the cardinal virtues were easily made.

The guilds of medieval Norwich and all other English cities, towns and villages reassured their members that everything possible would be done to give them a funeral with as many requiem masses, prayers, lights and offerings as funds would allow. The fraternity of St James, for example, enabled men and women of modest means, none of whom owned property worth more than 26s, to pool their resources so that each would, in due course, be 'carried and buried honestly' in Norwich.[9] The city's hospitals, too, were able to offer the sick poor the consolation of confession, absolution and interment according to the rites of the Church, sometimes in their own cemeteries, or else in the graveyard of a nearby parish church. Only a few of the thirteen hospices, almshouses and infirmaries for the poor which are discussed in the course of this book possessed the resources to discharge all the other Comfortable Works on a regular basis. Some did little more than supply rudimentary accommodation to passing pilgrims and vagrants while others housed the elderly. The six *leprosaria*, considered in chapter one, were largely (but not exclusively) devoted to the care of lepers and thus performed a more specialist function. It is, even so, important to remember that, in principle, the medieval hospital was as much concerned with outdoor relief as it was with the provision of beds for the sick or disabled.

To argue that such institutions did little to address the underlying problem of urban poverty is to misunderstand the purpose of the founders, who accepted suffering and destitution as a necessary part of the divine order. The assumption that most English medieval foundations helped only a narrow elite of deserving cases and barely impinged upon the lives of the abject poor does not, however, take sufficient account of the wide range of charitable activities which they performed. Toward the close of the Middle Ages many houses made stringent economies in this area, but their initial contribution may have been considerable. In 1338 the hospital of St Leonard at Skirbeck in Lincolnshire, which was run by the knights of St John of Jerusalem, supported twenty sick and debilitated paupers in the infirmary and fed twice that number in the hall every day. At just over £51, the cost of food and drink accounted for more than two-thirds of the annual budget. Over the next forty years the number of inmates fell to seven, and the master abandoned all his other obligations.[10]

Although the demand for alms may have fallen somewhat after successive outbreaks of plague, men and women living at subsistence level remained vulnerable to bread shortages. The threat of famine was never far away in medieval and early modern England. Bad weather and low crop yields pushed up the price of grain with dire consequences for the poor, whose survival often depended upon a combination of private and institutional relief. For many Christians, the distribution of food was the most important of the Seven Comfortable Works, not simply because it might make the difference between life and death, but also because it had symbolic connexions with Christ's sacrifice in the mass. The authors of the Ypres scheme for poor relief (1525) hoped that an element of social cohesion and mutual regard might be engendered if rich citizens and their children visited 'the poore mennes lytell cottages' with 'a messe or two of meat', and thus learnt that almsdeeds meant nothing without compassion.[11] Hospitals also gave drink to the thirsty. At Skirbeck, as at the hospital of St Giles in Norwich, ale was specially brewed on the premises from the house's own malt supplies. Dusty travellers must also have welcomed a draught of pure, uncontaminated water: in 1297 the London hospital of St Mary Bishopsgate secured the use of a fountain and well 'for the recreation, refreshment and profit of the poor who assemble there'. In winter, blankets, clothes and shoes were handed out by many hospitals, while some allowed the poor to warm themselves indoors. For a substantial proportion of medieval men and women, hunger was a constant companion, made infinitely worse by biting cold.[12] It might be assumed that the obligation to visit prisoners fell outside the remit of the English medieval hospital, but some did, indeed, provide chaplains to work in gaols. During this period the long term inmates of prisons were often debtors, whose predicament aroused compassion rather than contempt. This was not simply because of Christ's pity for prisoners: misguided investments, losses at sea, vexatious litigation or simple bad luck could place the wealthiest of men at the mercy of their creditors. In 1472 the master of St Giles's hospital contracted with the mayor of Norwich to support an unbeneficed chaplain, presumably from his own staff, 'for the relief and comfort of the prisoners and others incarcerated in the Guildhall'. In return for a payment of £200, left by two aldermen for the purpose, he promised that divine service would be properly and regularly celebrated in the adjoining chapel of St Barbara (who had herself reputedly been imprisoned in a tower).[13]

Although few could afford to be so generous, approximately sixteen per cent of the laymen and women of late medieval Norwich whose wills survive made bequests to the city's prisoners; and far more remembered the sick poor, either lying in hospital or living at home.[14] The contemplation of St Michael's scales at the Last Judgement was clearly a powerful incentive to charity, but so too was an awareness of the mutability of fate. Sickness, poverty and disease might be sent by God to punish or test the sinner at any time. The more affluent craft guilds and fraternities, whose members could afford to incorporate schemes for mutual assistance into their regulations, recognised that an accident, blindness, illness or 'sudden and catastrophic misfortune' would all too often result in destitution as well as unemployment.[15] As was increasingly the case with hospitals, however, the level of practical assistance available at any given time was limited by moral as well as financial considerations.

The Sick Poor of Medieval Norwich

Emphasis upon the value of the Seven Comfortable Works tended to soften a harsher, very different attitude to poverty and disease, which took its tone from the Old Testament and in particular from the account of the Fall of Man in the Book of Genesis. All men and women were believed to share in the Original Sin of their first parents, Adam and Eve, and thus to be heirs to a legacy of pain and death. In addition to this burden, which was assumed at birth, each individual had to carry the weight of his or her own sins, and might well be punished for them on earth as well as in purgatory or hell. Sometimes, this punishment was inflicted collectively because of wholesale wrongdoing. The years of famine, epidemics, floods and droughts which caused so much suffering between 1314 and 1322 were, for example, seen in many quarters as evidence of divine wrath. In July 1315 and again in 1316, the archbishop of Canterbury urged that acts of public penance should be performed, and that the people of England should together seek divine forgiveness through 'prayers, fasts, almsdeeds and other works of charity'. The conviction that illness often arose as a direct consequence of some terrible misdeed had led the fourth Lateran Council of 1215 to rule that no physician should treat a patient unless he or she had first confessed their sins, or at the very least had sent for a priest. So seriously did the Church take this directive that practitioners who ignored it were themselves threatened with excommunication. Since debility of any kind was so often associated with divine displeasure, it seemed all the more important to give alms selectively. Those whose poverty or ill health might be represented as a 'test' or 'purification' or even as a sign of grace inevitably seemed more deserving of charity than indigents who had brought misfortune upon themselves, not least because their intercessionary prayers would be more effective. Significantly, some canonists maintained that rich food should never be given to the poor, since it would excite lust and provoke gluttony *(scilicet quia inde pauperes provocantur ad libidinem et excitatur irritamentum gule)*.[16]

Although medieval preachers and social commentators sometimes tended to describe the poor as a single homogeneous group, whose members were to be distinguished one from the other simply in terms of moral worth, the more perceptive among them recognised many degrees and types of poverty. As William

Langland observed in *Piers Plowman*, it took different forms and had a variety of causes, from fire or flood to bankruptcy:

> Ac olde and hore, that helples ben and nedy,
> And wymmen with childe that worche ne mowe,
> Blynde and bedredne and broken in here membres,
> And alle pore pacient, apayed of Goddes sonde,
> As mesels [lepers] and pilgrimes and parauntur men y-robbed
> Or bylowe thorw luther men and lost here catel [chattels] after,
> Or thorw fuyr or thorw floed y-falle into pouerte,
> That taketh thise meschiefes mekeliche and myldeliche at herte,
> For loue of here lower hertes qoure lord hath hem y-graunted
> Here penaunce and here purgatorye vppon this puyre erthe ... [17]

Accidents and illness apart, a combination of factors, such as gender, age and the number of dependents an individual or married couple had to support, meant that the threat of poverty loomed far larger at certain stages in the life-cycle than at others.[18] Young, single mothers with small children and old people living alone might easily be caught in a downward spiral of debt and homelessness from which it was impossible to escape without assistance. Langland also wrote movingly of the plight of women reduced to despair by the struggle of earning enough money to feed their offspring while they themselves went cold and hungry.[19] Yet if not all poverty sprang from disability or ill-health, it often went hand in hand with sickness. Here too, women worn down by the physical and mental strain of repeated pregnancies and elderly paupers were especially vulnerable. An analysis of the Norwich Census of the Poor of 1570 reveals, for example, that once they reached the age of sixty, between one third and one half of the population were likely to be poor (by sixteenth-century standards), and of these elderly paupers at least one in four would be seriously debilitated as well.[20]

From birth to death, poverty made, and still makes, its victims more susceptible to chronic diseases, infections, injuries and stress. Illness, in turn, could reduce the able-bodied to a state of penury from which it was difficult to stage either a financial or physical recovery. It has been suggested that in 1570 a minimum of seven per cent of the residents of Norwich 'might be grossly infectious, repulsive, confined within doors, immobilised, bedridden or unable to see'.[21] According to William Marshall's English translation of the influential scheme for poor relief adopted at Ypres in 1525, one of the principal arguments in favour of public hospitals was that

> the dysfygured syghtes of these vysured [visaged] pore men ar nat now
> sene all roughe and scouruy and ronnynge with matter bothe vgely to
> loke on and euyll smellynge to the nose, and ouer that to some tender

stomakes lothsome ... the comen welth hath nowe lesse hurte and lesse
corruptyon that so many sore folkes be gone the helth of the cytie is
nowe more safe.[22]

The conventional iconographic image of the beggar in medieval and early modern
art conveys a similar impression. Ragged, ugly, diseased and disfigured, he or she
presents a spectacle which is both disturbing and pitiful, not least because the poor
are rarely depicted as individuals, but collectively in groups.[23] (The Master of
Alkmaar's panel paintings of the Seven Comfortable Works, now in the
Rijksmuseum, Amsterdam, provide a good example of this genre.) Sick paupers
must have been even more conspicuous in the streets of English towns during such
crisis periods as the late thirteenth and early fourteenth centuries, when conditions
were far worse and qualified medical help beyond the means of all but the relatively
affluent. Although, by modern western standards, a significant proportion of men
and women from the upper as well as the lower reaches of society bore the visible
marks of injury and disease, poverty was still intimately associated with
disfigurement. Highly stylised literary and artistic sources are not always the best
guide to the experience of ordinary men and women, although in this instance
archaeology is able to provide some important corroborative support.

Osteological evidence from the cemetery of the poor York parish of St
Helen-on-the-Walls indicates that about twenty-seven per cent of the 1,041
individuals examined died in childhood. Since few babies were found on the site
(their graves would have been shallower, and thus less likely to survive into the
present century), a rate of infant mortality approaching fifty per cent seems possible.
It is, however, clear that whereas only thirty-six per cent of adult males died before
the age of thirty-five, a far higher proportion of females (fifty-six per cent) did so.
This seems to confirm the assumption that poor women who survived childbirth
were more likely to succumb to post natal infections spread in cramped and dirty
conditions or else to be weakened by dietary deficiencies during pregnancy. Only
nine per cent of the individuals examined appear to have passed the age of sixty,
underscoring the fact that old age, like poverty, is a relative concept. Moreover,
most of these older skeletons exhibited signs of extreme debility, including serious
dental problems.[24]

An analysis of the dental remains from St Helen's shows that malnutrition was
widespread among both men and women. The unmistakeable and ubiquitous
evidence of periodontal disease (infection or decay of the gums), abscesses
(sometimes numbering two or three per individual), calculus (the calcified remains
of bacterial plaque), enamel hypoplasia (thinning of enamel caused by poor diet or
illness in childhood) and of damaged or lost teeth reveals a population subject to
protracted food shortages, where dental hygiene was virtually non-existent. The rye
or barley customarily used to make bread for the poor was often poorly milled or
adulterated, with the inevitable result that teeth were either worn down or broken.

In addition to painful and debilitating dental problems, many of the men and women buried in this cemetery appear to have suffered from chronic osteoarthritis. This is caused by continuous stress or trauma of the kind experienced by labourers and other manual workers, and must have been exacerbated by constant exposure to wind, rain and cold. The onset of arthritis of the spine, neck, hips, knees or neck would seriously restrict opportunities for employment, and might eventually turn the sufferer into one of the destitute cripples so often mentioned in the foundation statutes of hospitals.[25]

The 1985 excavation report on the late Anglo Saxon graveyard in the north east bailey of Norwich Castle has produced similar findings, including what was then the earliest known case of rickets in England. A lack of vitamin D in childhood, when the bones are still growing, causes this disease, which was common among the urban poor until the middle of the twentieth century. More recent excavations in Magdalen Street, Norwich, have produced further evidence of rickets from the pre–1468 cemetery of the parish church of St Margaret in Combusto, which lay in one of the most deprived areas of the city. Cases of parietal and orbital osteoporosis, both from this site and the north east bailey, likewise suggest that the juvenile population was at risk from anaemia.[26] Although they were unlikely to prove fatal in the short term, low levels of nutrition, especially among the young and during pregnancy, cold, damp and insanitary living conditions and years of onerous physical labour made the urban poor extremely susceptible to contagious diseases. If the principal breadwinner was killed or permanently incapacitated the consequences for his or her entire family could prove disastrous.

Whereas the upper ranks of late medieval English society were probably far cleaner than was once supposed, the poor (who in this context include wage labourers and others living near the poverty line) had none of the resources necessary to maintain a reasonable standard of personal hygiene. Accommodation, where available, might be shared with livestock; methods of waste disposal were rudimentary; and because facilities for washing clothes, bedding, skin and hair were often nonexistent the incidence of lice, fleas and intestinal parasites remained high. These last spread disease and gave rise to many of the disfiguring skin complaints to which contemporary sources, both literary and medical, constantly refer. Since the food and drink consumed by the poor was of variable quality, and might well be contaminated, food poisoning and other digestive disorders were rife. Local juries in Norwich were constantly presenting butchers, cooks and other stallholders for selling 'putrid and ill-salted meat', 'measly pork', animals found dead by the wayside and food which had been re-heated. The high incidence of blindness among the medieval population, and the frequency with which special provision was made for blind priests, craftsmen and paupers by the founders of hospitals, is also worth noting. The famous Parisian hospital, Les Quinze-Vingts, was set up by Louis IX (d.1270) specifically to house 300 such people, who helped to support themselves by begging in the streets. Low standards of personal cleanliness must account in part for the prevalence of eye infections such as trachoma. A parliamentary statute of 1542, permitting 'divers honest persones, as well men as women, whom God hath endued with the knowledge ... of certeyne herbes, rotes and waters' to continue their charitable work among the poor, notes that the latter were especially prone to ulcerated eyes and conjunctivitis.[27] The smoky atmosphere of badly ventilated rooms heated by turf fires can only have made matters worse, while at the same time providing ideal conditions for the spread of tuberculosis, bronchitis and other respiratory diseases.

The living standards of the urban proletariat fluctuated considerably during the later Middle Ages. The long-term effect of the plague of 1348–49 on the population may have been less devastating than the cumulative impact of two further national outbreaks in the early and late 1360s, but the survivors clearly benefited almost immediately from improvements in the quality and quantity of food and the availabilty of better accommodation. Although epidemics (such as that of 1437–40, which hit East Anglia especially hard) and food shortages still took their toll, town dwellers seem to have grown fitter and more resistant to disease.[28] Throughout the difficult years of the late-thirteenth and early fourteenth centuries, however, chronic overcrowding had led to land hunger, famine and, inevitably, widespread destitution. The situation in Norwich can be documented in unusual detail because of the survival of an early fourteenth century tithing roll for the leet of Mancroft, which covered a quarter of the city. Elizabeth Rutledge has calculated that between 1311 and 1333, the number of adult males entered in the roll rose by seventy-six per cent (from 860 to 1,513), and an average of sixty-three newcomers were admitted every year.[29] The great majority of these men were poor immigrants from the surrounding countryside, desperate to find work as servants or casual labourers. Norwich then possessed a densely populated hinterland, parts of which may have contained as many as 500 people per square mile. The effects of such pressure on the local peasantry have been studied by Bruce Campbell, whose analysis of the land market on the Norfolk manor of Hakeford Hall in Coltishall (where St Giles's hospital owned property) reveals a dramatic increase in the number of impoverished smallholders living at, or below, subsistence level. Bad harvests, especially during the agricultural crisis of 1314–22, led to panic selling as grain prices more than doubled and starvation threatened. Since the majority of plots were now too small to support their tenants, the search for alternative employment became imperative.[30]

To this vicious combination of circumstances, which reduced a substantial part of the rural population to abject poverty, were added the demands of manorial lords, the Church and the government. The East Anglian peasantry suffered quite lightly from seigneurial exactions, but there was no escaping the burden of taxation, conscription and purveyance imposed by the Crown. Because of its value as a grain producing area with easy access by sea to the north of England, both Edward II and his son relied upon Norfolk to supply their armies and garrisons on the Scottish border. At the same time, taxes on moveables (which included animals and supplies of grain) were regularly imposed. It has sometimes been assumed that the high tax assessments made on west and north-eastern Norfolk (which in 1334 were among the heaviest in England) reflect a corresponding level of prosperity, but, as J.R. Maddicott suggested in 1975, they may equally well serve as indicators of overcrowding and the existence of a large rural underclass. Corruption made matters worse. In 1298, for example, a Norfolk official was said to have taken corn 'from the poor and impotent' and 'left the able and powerful alone'.[31] These impositions, which pushed up bread prices while forcing many poor peasants off the land, provided yet another incentive for migration to the nearest town or city.

A steady rise in the population of Norwich, from an estimated 17,000 in 1311 to perhaps as many as 25,000 in 1333, brought into the city an unprecedented number of men and women who, if not actually paupers, found it hard to support themselves.[32] Already, at the beginning of the century, the civic authorities had expressed concern about the influx of poor labourers who were unable to offer pledges for good behaviour or pay fines if they broke the law.[33] The provision of food and housing for individuals whose wage of about one penny a day (when they could find work) was barely sufficient for subsistence placed a further strain on available resources. Although some development schemes were started in response to the demand for lodgings, most newcomers appear to have found rented accommodation in existing buildings, which were more intensively let, or in rows of cottages erected speculatively in gardens or on waste land in built-up areas. With a couple of exceptions, no attempt was made to ease the growing congestion by exploiting new sites in the open fields. The rows had clay walls and were therefore less permanent than the multi-storey timber framed terraces occupied by the poor of York. They must also have been colder and damper, especially in a period notable for wet winter weather and gradually declining temperatures. The thatched and clay-walled houses of Norwich could be erected quickly, and thus met an obvious need. But they had neither foundations nor damp courses, remained exposed to the elements and made little, if any, provision for heating or cooking. Waste disposal facilities were minimal, posing an additional hazard to residents. Elizabeth Rutledge suggests that each dwelling would have covered rather less ground than the cottages excavated at Brooke Street in Winchester (which measured just 15 feet square), but that they would have had two or three storeys. Many families supplemented their meagre incomes by subletting rooms, with inescapable consequences so far as public health and sanitation were concerned. In 1311, for example, thirty-six adult males were living in twenty-seven separate properties in Upper Newport (St Stephen's parish), but by 1333 the number had risen to 112, excluding women and children under the age of twelve.[34]

If, as seems likely, the problem of overcrowding persisted until 1349, it is easy to see why the Black Death claimed so many victims in Norwich. The level of mortality in the city has been debated at length, but as demographers produce more evidence to suggest that early fourteenth century English towns were far larger than was once supposed, so too claims that over half the population may have succumbed in some areas again become more credible. For example, Bruce Campbell's findings for Hakeford Hall in Coltishall, which lay just seven miles north of Norwich, indicate that well over half the tenants died between 1349 and 1359, and that total mortality from the plague may have been as high as sixty per cent.[35] The poll tax return of 1377, which in theory was supposed to list all adults over the age of fourteen unless they were beggars or religious, records just 3,952 inhabitants of Norwich. Compared with that for 1381 (giving a total of 3,833 individuals), the earlier return is generally held to have been carried out more systematically. The entire population of Norwich may thus have fallen to about 6,000 and cannot have been much higher. Relatively speaking, the city then ranked in size after York, Plymouth, Coventry and Bristol, and had only a few hundred more inhabitants than Bishop's Lynn.[36] The next reliable estimate, for 1520, suggests that with a population of about 11,000, Norwich had again resumed its position as the second city of the kingdom after London. Even so, the number of parish churches had fallen from over fifty during the early fourteenth century to forty-six; and hospital provision had decreased even more dramatically.[37]

As will become apparent in the ensuing chapters, the decline of Norwich's larger hospitals was the result of a combination of economic, social and religious factors, which do not neatly correspond with these demographic changes. Never, at any time before the Reformation, did the citizens of medieval Norwich expect their hospitals to do more than ease the problems of a small proportion of the sick poor (often drawn from specific, clearly delineated groups, such as pilgrims, the aged and lepers); and although outdoor relief may initially have been provided on a far larger scale than the modest supply of beds might suggest, it must often have been woefully inadequate. Well before the first outbreak of plague, the sheer enormity of coping with such a frightening and seemingly interminable influx of poor immigrants seems to have provoked a negative reaction: a sentiment modern readers might identify as 'compassion fatigue', but which in the early-fourteenth century derived largely from fear, hopelessness and a sense that the labouring poor (or at least those capable of work) were not truly 'deserving'. Even so, the consequences of such a sudden fall in population, the high death rate among the poor and the ensuing reduction in the demand for assistance clearly made the epidemics of 1348–49 and the 1360s a watershed in the history of the charitable institutions of medieval Norwich.

Medicine and the Medieval English Hospital

By the middle of the fifteenth century (and in certain cases well before) most French towns and cities of any size had arranged for the provision of qualified medical help for the sick poor. Some of the wealthier, more successful physicians and surgeons gave their services freely as an act of Christian charity, while the rest were paid by the civic authorities or other interested parties to tend those who could not afford leechcraft. As was already common in Italy, larger hospitals also numbered salaried practitioners (including apothecaries) among their staff. Significantly, the first English hospital to employ trained medical men on a permanent basis was the Savoy in London, which its founder, Henry VII (d.1509), modelled on the great Florentine Ospedale di Santa Maria Nuova.[38] No other pre-Reformation hospital either in London or the provinces followed suit; and although attempts have been made to establish connexions between members of the medical profession and specific medieval foundations, very few offer convincing proof of actual practice. This is hardly surprising, since the institutions in question were not only far smaller but also entirely different from such hospitals as the Hotel Dieu in Paris or Santa Maria Nuova, which specialised in a rapid turnover of acute cases and might receive over three thousand patients a year.[39] The smaller hospitals and almshouses of medieval Europe, which accommodated pilgrims, housed the elderly or nursed the terminally or chronically sick, were, however, remarkably similar, and it is here that we should seek our model.

The emphasis upon spiritual healing and the salvation of the soul so evident in the foundation statutes of English medieval hospitals does not mean that patients could expect little or nothing in the way of medication. The nurses of Norwich's two largest foundations may well have been as accomplished as the city's male practitioners (who treated the monks in the Cathedral Priory at considerable expense), and almost certainly inflicted less pain with the herbal medicaments they prepared from ingredients grown in their own gardens. They may, indeed, have attempted minor surgical procedures and have acquired a smattering of theory from the priests and chaplains with whom they worked. Medieval medicine was so diverse and the connexion between the body and the spirit so close that contemporaries would have found 'the dubious antithesis of care and cure' quite meaningless.[40] But once new demands, over and above the support of the elderly and hopelessly disabled, were made of English hospitals as part of a national policy towards the poor, it became necessary to engage the services of trained practitioners.

During the second and third decades of the sixteenth century leading members of the English medical profession and social reformers began seriously to address the problem of medical provision for the poor. Those parts of the Ypres scheme concerned with treating the 'syckly and weke' so that they could go back to work (and thus regain moral as well as economic worth) made a particular impression.[41] The most novel aspect of draft proposals for the poor law legislation of 1536 (which may have been written by William Marshall himself) was that free medical services should be made available for paupers at public expense. Although, as Margaret Pelling has shown, these ideas found practical expression in Norwich from the mid-sixteenth century onwards, when the city led the field in devising and implementing a centrally funded scheme for poor relief, they were not incorporated into the Act of 1536.[42] Political commentators, anxious lest the confiscation of monastic property should benefit only the rich, continued to agitate:

> I heare that the masters of your hospytals be so fatt that the poore be kept leane and bare inough: the crye of the peple is heard vnto the Lord, though ye wyll not heare ... Let phisicyans and surgens be found in euery such town or cyte, where such houses be, to loke vpon the pore in that towne and in all other ioyning vnto it; and thei to lyue vpon their stipend only, without taking any peny of there pore, vpon payne of losing both his earys and his stypend also.[43]

Thus, although fifteenth-century Norwich, like other English provincial towns, possessed a flourishing guild of barbers (forty-one barbers and four leeches were admitted to the freedom of the city between 1400 and 1450), and a few university-trained physicians are known to have practised there as well, we should not expect to find them at work in hospitals. Here, as was usually the case in society at large, the poor were tended by women.[44]

Norwich's First Hospital?

Very little is known about the care of the sick poor in Norwich before Bishop Losinga founded the *leprosarium* of St Mary Magdalen and began planning St Paul's hospital, although it seems likely that the Cathedral monks ran a hostel where they could be nursed, as well as clothed and fed. The rule of St Benedict, which was followed at Norwich, honoured the poor as Christ's representatives on earth, and made detailed provision for their reception and support. The requirement that one tenth of net receipts should be reserved for charitable purposes was subsequently allowed to lapse, but during the eleventh, twelfth and thirteenth centuries many English monasteries spent heavily on charitable relief. The Constitutions compiled by Archbishop Lanfranc (d.1089) for the Benedictines of Christ Church Canterbury had, for example, instructed the almoner to 'take great pains to discover where may lie those sick and weakly persons who are without means of sustenance' and to provide them with whatever necessities they might require.[45] Eventually, this system of home visits was abandoned in favour of a daily or weekly distribution of alms at the monastery gates. The itinerant poor and pilgrims thus became eligible for doles, while the monks themselves could be more strictly supervised and protected from the snares of the outside world.

The practice of medicine by regular clergy among the laity was seen as a dangerous distraction from their spiritual duties, especially when undertaken for gain, and incurred repeated censure. Even so, despite a ruling of the second Lateran Council of 1139 against monks who 'promised health in return for detestable money', Walter the physician (fl.1198), the almoner at Bury St Edmunds in Suffolk, made such a profit from his patients in the town that he was able to donate a large sum towards the demolition of the 'ramshackle' wooden almonry and its rebuilding in stone.[46] The men and women who queued here for food and drink almost certainly received basic medical treatment as well. Those who were too sick to resume their travels may have been allowed to remain on the premises, even though the monks had already provided the townspeople with two hospitals for the sick and aged (one of which later became a *leprosarium*).[47]

A similar situation probably obtained at Norwich. In recognition of his work among the destitute and infirm, the almoner of the Cathedral Priory (founded in 1096) attracted far more support from the local laity than any of his fellow obedientiaries. An analysis of pre-Reformation deeds in the archive of the Dean and Chapter reveals that, where donors expressed a desire to assist one particular obedientiary rather than simply making a gift in free alms to the priory, eighty-five named the almoner, fifteen the cellarer, eight the sacrist, four the refectorer, three each the pittancer and chamberlain, two the infirmarer (who cared only for sick monks) and one each the precentor, communar and hosteler. Almost all these gifts to the monastic almonry were made during the twelfth or thirteenth centuries.[48] They are couched in conventional terms, referring simply to the benefactors' quest for spiritual salvation through charity, but one early, undated charter specifically reserves the property in question 'for the house of the poor *(domus pauperum)* and the use of the almoner's servants in the said house'.[49] We do not know if this building provided much in the way of long-stay accommodation, but the sick probably found shelter here during the early years of the monastic community.

The problem of poverty seems to have grown more acute during the years after the Normans arrived in Norwich and began altering the urban landscape. The Domesday Book records a fall in the number of English burgesses from 1,320 at the Conquest to just 665 in 1086, although 124 Normans had taken up residence in the 'French borough' beneath the walls of the new castle. Significantly, the city's 480 bordars were then too poor to pay any customary dues, and 297 messuages lay vacant. This exodus had in part been caused by the destruction of property to make way for the castle, but a variety of other reasons, including a fire and the depredations of the settlers, were advanced to explain the general state of decline. Even so, Norwich must still have seemed a bustling and impressive place, with a total of between 5,000 and 8,000 inhabitants (if not more), its own port on the river Wensum and up to forty churches.[50] By the end of the eleventh century it was expanding fast. Along with commercial growth came a steady rise in population and a demand for charitable relief which the almoner alone could not fulfil.[51]

The hospitals of medieval Norwich were thus a post-Conquest development, and were, as will be now be apparent, almost exclusively devoted to the care of the poor or the leprous. A comparison with the infirmary of Norwich Cathedral Priory, which lay just south of the cathedral cloister and only a few hundred yards away from the hospital of St Giles in Bishopgate, shows how very different was the treatment accorded to privileged members of society, whether lay or religious, when they fell ill. Benedictine monks would certainly have placed great importance upon spiritual medicine (the infirmary had its own chapel), but they were no less anxious than the local gentry or merchants to purchase the best professional care available. A total of thirty-eight infirmarers' rolls survive in the archive of the Dean and Chapter for the period 1312 to 1530. Although they are less informative than the remarkably detailed set available for Westminster Abbey for the same period, they present a similar picture of what, by contemporary standards, constituted regular, highly priced and expert medical attention.[52] All the monks were routinely phlebotomised, having their own servant to care for them during the two or three days' rest which customarily followed this operation; and when necessary they could rely upon the services of physicians and surgeons, who were either retained on a yearly contract or called in as circumstances required. In 1347–48, for example, the physician, Master Geoffrey de Suffield, drew his usual annuity of 20s for treating sick monks, a colleague named Master Adam was paid 2s 6d for attending brothers convalescing near the sea at Yarmouth (where the priory had a dependent cell) and Master Geoffrey, the surgeon, received 2s for unspecified services. A total of twenty-three named monks (about half the community) were given medication at a cost of almost £2, but servants and other employees of the house did not come under the infirmarer's aegis.[53]

In addition to the provision of hospitality for visiting practitioners, the accounts record a regular outlay on glass phials used to inspect the monks' urine and arrive at an appropriate diagnosis. Indeed, during the fifteenth century physicians were paid specifically *pro inspeccione urinarum*. Unlike his opposite number at Westminster Abbey, however, the Norwich infirmarer did not rely upon the assistance of local apothecaries for help with the production of drugs, which required a great deal of manual skill as well as expert knowledge. Quantities of pharmaceutical commodities – frankincense, aniseed, dragon's blood, pepper, cloves, senna, cassia, liquorice, pine seeds, sugar (for making electuaries) and olive oil – were all processed on the premises, as, of course, were herbs gathered fresh from the infirmarer's own garden. That he was well provided for the task is evident from the supply of an alembic and other equipment for distillation, along with enough glasses, storage jars and boxes to equip an apothecary's shop.[54] Although the infirmarer felt it necessary to rely upon outside experts when diagnosing his charges, there is good reason to believe that he, too, was well informed about classical medical theory. The library at Norwich Cathedral Priory was one of the best in England: in 1397 Cardinal Easton's bequest of 228 books was transported there in barrels all the way from Rome; and by the Dissolution it housed about 1,350 volumes. Unfortunately, the collection was then destroyed by local tradespeople, but it is known to have included works by Galen, Avicenna and Aristotle, copies of the *Questiones Physicorum* and the *Secreta Secretorum* (a quasi-medical compilation, wrongly attributed to Albertus Magnus), volumes on astronomy and a dietary, the last of which would have been of considerable value when the infirmarer had to cast the horoscopes of sick monks and decide the most suitable regimen for restoring their humoral balance.[55]

It is as well that St Bernard of Clairvaux (d.1153), who had attacked the use of earthly medicine by monks as an affront to the will of God, never lived to visit a late medieval Benedictine monastery. Nor, in many respects, would he have pronounced himself satisfied with the provision of spiritual care in Norwich's larger hospitals. The rest of this book is concerned with the practicalities of life in these institutions, but it should not be forgotten that contemporaries judged their success or failure by a scale of values which often differed radically from our own. Yet the importance of administrative efficiency and proper financial management was always recognised, even if such goals proved almost as difficult to achieve as a place in heaven, on the right hand of Christ in majesty.

END NOTES

1   Rubin, *Charity and Community*, chapter III, provides the best overview of changing attitudes to charity and the poor. A classic study still remains M. Mollat, *The Poor in the Middle Ages*, trans. A. Goldhammer (Yale, 1986). For the practical application of the Seven Comfortable Works, see P.H. Cullum and P.J.P. Goldberg, 'Charitable Provision in Late Medieval York: "To the Praise of God and Use of the Poor"', *Northern History*, XXIX (1993), pp. 24–39.

2   *The Life, Letters and Sermons of Bishop Herbert de Losinga*, ed. E.M. Goulburn and H. Symonds (2 vols, Oxford, 1878), vol. II, pp. 424–27. Losinga's ideas about poverty, not in themselves original, are discussed by J.W. Alexander, 'Herbert of Norwich, 1091–1119: Studies in the History of Norman England', *Studies in Medieval and Renaissance History*, VI (1969), pp. 216–17.

3   *Dives and Pauper*, ed. P. Heath Barnum (Early English Text Society, CCLXXV, 1976, and CCLXXX, 1980), vol. I, part 1, p. 63.

4   *Fasciculus Morum: A Fourteenth-Century Preacher's Handbook*, ed. S. Wenzel (Pennsylvania, 1989), p. 541.

5   J. Le Goff, *The Birth of Purgatory*, trans. A. Goldhammer (London, 1984), pp. 81–82, 283–85.

6   *The Making of King's Lynn*, ed. D.M. Owen (Records of Social and Economic History, new series, IX, 1984), pp. 108–16.

7   H. Manship, *History of Great Yarmouth*, ed. J. Palmer (Yarmouth, 1854), pp. 430–31.

8   Norfolk Record Office, Phi/623.

9   Public Record Office, C43/47/297. Norwich guild returns made in English in response to a government enquiry of 1388 may be found in *English Gilds*, ed. T. Smith, L.T. Smith and L. Brentano (Early English Text Society, XL, 1890), pp. 14–44. Most made some provision for the burial of members. Elderly East Anglian peasants who were in a position to negotiate with kin and neighbours for support in their old age often gave clear directives about their funerals. See E. Clark, 'Some Aspects of Social Security in Medieval England', *Journal of Family History*, VII (1982), p. 312.

10　*The Knights Hospitallers in England: The Report of Prior Philip de Thame, 1338*, ed. L.B. Larking (Camden Society, LXV, 1857), pp. 61–62; *Calendar of Inquisitions Miscellaneous*, vol. IV, no. 180.

11　The sacramental significance of food constitutes one of the main themes of C.W. Bynum's study of female piety, *Holy Feast and Holy Fast: The Religious Significance of Food to Medieval Women* (University of California, 1987). For the Ypres scheme, see *Some Early Tracts on Poor Relief*, ed. F.R. Salter (London, 1926), pp. 70–71. The distribution of food to the rural poor is described by E. Clark, 'Social Welfare and Mutual Aid in the Medieval Countryside', *Journal of British Studies*, XXXIII (1994), pp. 403–5.

12　*Historical Manuscripts Commission Ninth Report* (London, 1883), part 1, p. 29. For doles of fuel to the poor, see C. Pythian-Adams, *Desolation of a City: Coventry and the Urban Crisis of the Late Middle Ages* (Cambridge, 1979), p. 135, and Cullum and Goldberg, 'Charitable Provision in Late Medieval York', pp. 34–35.

13　Norfolk Record Office, case 24, shelf B, no. 25.

14　N. Tanner, *The Church in Late Medieval Norwich* (Pontifical Institute of Medieval Studies and Texts, LXVI, 1984), p. 223.

15　B.R. McRee, 'Charity and Gild Solidarity in Late Medieval England', *Journal of British Studies*, XXXII (1993), p. 204.

16　D.W. Amundsen, 'The Medieval Catholic Tradition', in *Caring and Curing, Health and Medicine in the Western Religious Traditions*, ed. R.L. Numbers and D.W. Amundsen, (London, 1986), pp. 65–107, and especially pp. 88–89; C. Rawcliffe, *Medicine and Society in Later Medieval England* (Stroud, 1995), chapter I; *Historical Manuscripts Commission Eighth Report* (London, 1881), part 1, pp. 352–53; B. Tierney, 'The Decretists and the "Deserving Poor"', *Comparative Studies in Society and History*, I (1958–59), p. 366.

17　*Piers Plowman by William Langland: An Edition of the C-Text*, ed. D. Pearsall (York Medieval Texts, second series, 1978), Passus IX, lines 175–85. See G. Shepherd, 'Poverty in *Piers Plowman*', in *Social Relations and Ideas: Essays in Honour of R.H. Hilton*, ed. T.H. Aston and others (Cambridge, 1983), pp. 169–89, for a discussion of Langland's views on charity.

18　R.M. Smith, 'Some Issues Concerning Families and their Property in Rural England 1250–1800', in *Land, Kinship and Life-Cycle*, ed. R.M. Smith (Cambridge, 1984), pp. 68–85.

19　*Piers Plowman*, C-Passus IX, lines 70–97. See E. Clark, 'Mothers at Risk of Poverty in the Medieval English Countryside', in *Poor Women and Children in the European Past*, ed. J. Henderson and R. Wall (London, 1994), pp. 139–59, for a discussion of this problem.

20　M. Pelling, 'Illness among the Poor in an Early Modern English Town: The Norwich Census of 1570', *Continuity and Change*, III (1988), pp. 282–83.

21　Ibid., p. 286.

22　*Some Early Tracts on Poor Relief*, p. 69.

23　Mollat, *The Poor in the Middle Ages*, p. 233.

24　J.D. Dawes and J.R. Magilton, *The Cemetery of St Helen-on-the-Walls, Aldwark* (York Archaeological Trust, 1980), p. 63. Sixty was, however, widely recognised as the age at which a person became incapable of hard manual labour (Smith, 'Some Issues Concerning Families', p. 84).

25　Dawes and Magilton, *The Cemetery of St Helen-on-the-Walls*, pp. 51–59, 84–109.

26   A. Stirland, 'The Human Bones', in *Excavations within the North-East Bailey of Norwich Castle*, 1979, ed. B. Ayers (East Anglian Archaeology, XXVIII, 1985), pp. 49–58. The report of the excavations in Magdalen Street has not yet been published, but a brief description of the site may be found in B. Ayers, *Digging Deeper: Recent Archaeology in Norwich* (Norwich Museums Service, 1987), pp. 11–15.

27   *Leet Jurisdiction in the City of Norwich during the Thirteenth and Fourteenth Centuries*, ed. W. Hudson (Selden Society, V, 1892), pp. 8–10, 13, 16, 24, 47, 57, 60, 71; B. Gemerek,*The Margins of Society in Late Medieval Paris*, trans. J. Birrell (Cambridge, 1987), pp. 172–73; *Statutes of the Realm*, ed. A. Luders and others (11 vols, London, 1810–28), vol. III, 34 and 35 Hen. VIII, c.8. The thirteenth-century encyclopaedist Bartholomaeus Anglicus lists several common diseases of the eye and writes compassionately about the trials of blindness. His account contains an interesting reference to the use of dogs as guides: a reversal of the divine order whereby the man should have commanded the animal *(On the Properties of Things: John Trevisa's Translation of Bartholomaeus Anglicus' De Proprietatibus Rerum*, ed. M.C. Seymour and others (3 vols, Oxford, 1975–88), vol. I, pp. 359–66).

28   C. Dyer, *Standards of Living in the Later Middle Ages* (Cambridge, 1989), chapter VII, passim, and p. 268.

29   E. Rutledge, 'Immigration and Population Growth in Early Fourteenth-Century Norwich: Evidence from the Tithing Roll', *Urban History Yearbook* (1988), p. 15.

30   B.M.S. Campbell, 'Population Pressure, Inheritance and the Land Market in a Fourteenth-Century Peasant Community', in *Land, Kinship and Life-Cycle*, pp. 87–134.

31   J.R. Maddicott, *The English Peasantry and the Demands of the Crown 1294–1341* (Past and Present Supplement I, 1975), pp. 18–21.

32   Rutledge, 'Immigration and Population Growth', pp. 25–27.

33   *The Records of the City of Norwich*, ed. W. Hudson and J.C. Tingey (2 vols, Norwich, 1906–10), vol. I, pp. 189–90.

34   M. Atkin, 'Medieval and Clay-Walled Building in Norwich', *Norfolk Archaeology*, XLI (1991), pp. 171–85; E. Rutledge, 'Landlords and Tenants: Housing and the Rented Property Market in Early Fourteenth-Century Norwich', forthcoming in *Urban History*. I am grateful to Mrs Rutledge for letting me read this article before publication and discussing its contents with me.

35   Campbell, 'Population Pressure', p. 96.

36   Figures from the poll tax returns of 1377 and 1381 are given by J.C. Russell, *British Medieval Population* (Albuquerque, 1948), p. 142, but the analysis is unreliable, and the author's own statistics should be used with caution.

37   A. King, 'The Merchant Class and Borough Finances of Late Medieval Norwich' (Oxford University DPhil thesis, 1989), p. 27, argues that the population may have reached almost 12,000 by the close of the fifteenth century, but fell somewhat during the early-sixteenth.

38   D. Jacquart, *Le Milieu Medical en France du XIIe au XVe Siecle* (Hautes Etudes Medievales et Modernes, series 5, XLVI, 1981), pp. 120–21; K. Park and J. Henderson, '"The First Hospital Among Christians": The Ospedale di Santa Maria Nuova in Early Sixteenth Century Florence', *Medical History*, XXXV (1991), pp. 164–87.

39   J. Henderson, 'The Hospitals of Late-Medieval and Renaissance Florence: A Preliminary Survey', in *The Hospital in History*, p. 75, notes that Santa Maria Nuova treated more then 300 patients a month in the mid-fifteenth century. See also, K. Park, 'Healing the Poor: Hospitals and Medical Assistance in

31

Renaissance Florence', in *Medicine and Charity before the Welfare State*, pp. 26–45, notably p. 38. For the Hotel Dieu in Paris, see *Histoire des Hopitaux en France*, ed. J. Imbert (Toulouse, 1981), chapter IV.

40   Horden, 'A Discipline of Relevance', pp. 366–67.

41   *Some Early Tracts on Poor Relief*, pp. 66–70.

42   G.R. Elton, 'An Early Tudor Poor Law', *Economic History Review*, series two, VI (1953–54), p. 59; M. Pelling, 'Healing the Sick Poor: Social Policy and Disability in Norwich 1550–1640', *Medical History*, XXIX (1985), p. 117.

43   Henry Brinklow, *Complaynt of Roderyck Mors*, ed. J.M. Cowper (Early English Text Society, extra series, XXII, 1874), p. 52.

44   Rawcliffe, *Medicine and Society*, p. 136.

45   *The Monastic Constitutions of Lanfranc*, ed. D. Knowles (London, 1951), p. 89. For hospital provision in English Benedictine houses, see B. Harvey, *Living and Dying in England 1100–1540: The Monastic Experience* (Oxford, 1993), pp. 17–18.

46   D.W. Amundsen, 'Medieval Canon Law on Medical and Surgical Practice by the Clergy', *Bulletin of the History of Medicine*, LII (1978), pp. 28–29; A.F. Dawtry, 'The *Modus Medendi* and the Benedictine Order in England', *Studies in Church History*, XIX (1982), pp. 25–38 (note 70 should refer to the Norwich hospital of St Paul not St Stephen).

47   J. Rowe, 'The Medieval Hospitals of Bury St Edmunds', *Medical History,* II (1958), pp. 253–63.

48   Norfolk Record Office, DCN 44 and 45, passim.

49   Ibid., DCN 44/126/3.

50   H.C. Darby, *The Domesday Geography of Eastern England* (Cambridge, 1971), pp. 111, 139–40.

51   William de Malmesbury, *Gesta Regum Anglorum*, ed. W. Stubbs (2 vols, Rolls Series, 1887–89), vol. II, p. 386 notes that Norwich was famous for its trade and rapid expansion.

52   Norfolk Record Office, DCN 1/10/1–38; E.A. Hammond, 'The Westminster Abbey Infirmarers' Rolls as a Source of Medical History', *Bulletin of the History of Medicine*, XXXIX (1965), pp. 261–76.

53   Norfolk Record Office, DCN 1/10/6.

54   Rawcliffe, *Medicine and Society*, pp. 149–52.

55   N.R. Ker, 'Mediaeval Mss from Norwich Cathedral', *Transactions of the Cambridge Bibliographical Society* I (1949–53), pp. 1–28; H.C. Beeching and M.R. James, 'The Library of the Cathedral Church of Norwich', *Norfolk Archaeology*, XIX (1917), pp. 109–10.

CHAPTER I

The Leper Hospitals of Medieval Norwich

If they were asked to name the endemic disease which caused the greatest fear and attracted the widest intellectual and medical debate in medieval England, most readers would probably suggest bubonic plague. But the Black Death (as it later became known) was a phenomenon of the mid-fourteenth century and after, by which time leprosy had come to occupy a unique and terrible place in the popular imagination. Even today, the leper arouses feelings of revulsion as well as pity; and in the Middle Ages, when the etiology of the disease had yet to be established, sufferers encountered far worse prejudice.[1] The intensity of this psychological reaction may perhaps have led scholars to overestimate the physical impact of leprosy on the population. The palaeopathologist, Calvin Wells, argued that, at the height of its spread in the twelfth and thirteenth centuries, approximately one out of every two hundred Europeans was infected; but since no meaningful statistics can be produced to document the progress or incidence of contagion such figures must remain impressionistic, even at a regional level.[2]

Only rarely is it possible to achieve more than a rough idea of numbers from English sources: an account of charitable payments made by the executors of Bishop Bitton of Exeter (d.1307) to thirty-nine communities of lepers in Devon and Cornwall confirms, for example, that the disease exercised a strong hold in the south west, with perhaps up to 580 or so known victims then living in the latter county alone. Isolated by land, but vulnerable to sea-borne contagion, Cornwall retained at least one lazar house until the end of the seventeenth century, and is thus hardly typical of the country as a whole.[3] On the other hand, we can be reasonably confident that small, informal groups of lepers, as revealed in this document, must have existed throughout England, offering a refuge of sorts to those who were unable or unwilling to find accommodation in hospitals. The case of the leprous Cornish priest, who continued to inhabit designated quarters in his vicarage at St Neot while another clergyman discharged his parochial duties, serves as a reminder that sufferers with adequate resources might stay cloistered in their own homes, at least until the disease entered its final stage. In this instance, orders for the construction of partition walls, separate doors and a privy, so the vicar could remain in complete isolation, are recorded in the register of his bishop, Walter Stapledon (d.1326), but similar arrangements may well have been made unofficially in households throughout England.[4] The rich and well-connected were certainly assured greater privacy and consideration if only by virtue of their bargaining power. Having relinquished the bulk of his property to his younger brother, the Northamptonshire landowner, Robert de Torpel, appears to have lived 'infirm and afflicted with leprosy' on one of his manors for over twelve years, until in 1147 he entered St Leonard's hospital Peterborough. In return for a substantial grant of land, the monks agreed that he and his four servants would rank as pensioners of the Abbey, and that after his death he might share in the spiritual benefits of their community.[5] Inevitably, though, given the elusive and fragmentary nature of the evidence, attention concentrates upon institutionalised care for the less affluent and terminally sick, which is easier to trace but was by no means the only method of segregation.

Although repressive measures for the removal and confinement of lepers were not introduced until the latter part of the twelfth century, most English cities and towns of any size had already started to build or provide special places where they could take refuge. Between 1075 and 1150 alone a bare minimum of thirty-three such institutions came into existence nationwide, including one at Sprowston, about half a mile to the north of Norwich. The problem of dating *leprosaria*, which were often quite small and poorly endowed, unlike the great monastic hospitals, makes statistical analysis very difficult. But they continued to be set up at an impressive rate during the late-twelfth and thirteenth centuries, and are now seen as a valuable indicator of urban growth and prosperity.[6]

In their survey of the medieval hospitals of England and Wales (1971), Knowles and Hadcock identified a total of 345 leper houses (about twenty-eight per cent of all foundations), and subsequent research continues to find more.[7] Of the sixty hospitals known to have been planned, if not actually put into commission, in Norfolk before the Reformation at least twenty-six were initially intended to receive lepers; and of these no fewer than five lay at the city gates of Norwich, commanding the approaches from the north, west and south. Their history provides a fascinating insight into contemporary attitudes towards an illness which, more than any other, came to be seen as the judgement of God upon sinners.

The Medical and Social Background to Medieval Leprosy

Known since 1874 as Hansen's disease, leprosy is spread by the bacillus *Mycobacterium leprae*, usually through sneezing, spitting and coughing. Experts still disagree about levels of contagion, since not everyone who is exposed to the disease, even on an intimate daily basis, will become infected. The period of incubation may last from six months to twenty years, but on average takes two or three years. After an initial phase, characterised by numbness, tingling or weakening of the muscles, leprosy will develop in one of two ways, depending largely upon the strength of the body's immune system. In cases of high resistance, where the tissues are able to maintain their defences, it assumes a relatively benign *tuberculoid* form. But if resistance is low, or breaks down altogether, the more virulent, degenerative *lepromatous* strain persists unchecked, sometimes after a *dimorphous* stage during which the patient displays symptoms of both types of infection.[8]

Whether caused by *tuberculoid* or *lepromatous* leprosy, the lesions and dry, scaly patches produced during the early stages of the disease could easily be confused with eczema, erysipelas, psoriasis and the many other dermatological disorders common during the Middle Ages. Poor diet and low standards of personal hygiene gave rise to a variety of abscesses, boils and unpleasant skin conditions, as contemporary collections of remedies for domestic use clearly reveal. Yet an advanced case of lepromatous leprosy would be far easier to diagnose: progressive ulceration leading to the loss of extremities and facial deformity (especially round the lips and nose), blindness, infection of the larynx and extensive scarring gave the leper his or her characteristic voice and appearance, so often described in the pages of homiletic as well as medical literature.[9]

Archaeological evidence suggests a fairly impressive level of diagnostic competence, at least in cases where the disease was far advanced. A significant proportion of skeletons so far excavated from English medieval leper cemeteries exhibit clear indications of damage caused by *lepromatous* leprosy. Having, for example, examined eight fragmentary sets of human remains unearthed at South Acre, Norfolk, in 1967, Calvin Wells concluded that leprosy was 'possible in one case, probable in three and virtually certain in three more'.[10] Given that many lepers would have died before their bones underwent any discernible change (especially once the population began to develop a higher level of resistance), we may reasonably assume that the skeletons of up to fifty per cent of men and women dying of the disease would have remained intact (the present day rate). And the burial grounds of medieval *leprosaria* do indeed reveal a significant chronological decline in the ratio of skeletons disfigured by *lepromatous* leprosy to those still unscathed.[11]

From the early-fourteenth century onwards the diagnosis of leprosy, particularly in the towns and cities of continental Europe, was often undertaken by qualified physicians and surgeons, either in a public capacity on behalf of the local authority, or privately at the behest of their patients.[12] Allowing for the limitations of medieval medicine, which lacked the investigative techniques we now take for granted, the criteria adopted on such occasions were meticulous and exact: guide-lines established for the examination of lepers might suggest over fifty separate pointers or lines of enquiry, many of which addressed the symptoms described above.[13] Practitioners were urged to proceed with the utmost caution, assessing the evidence over a long period and never jumping to hasty conclusions, lest they 'withdrawe tho men that schulde not be sequestred or withdrawen'.[14] There is good reason to believe that this advice was scrupulously observed. The three royal physicians assigned in 1468 to determine whether or not Joan Nightingale of Brentwood in Essex was, in fact, leprous as her neighbours affirmed certainly took their duties seriously. After a long consultation, involving 'discreet men of the county' who knew Joan and were also knowledgeable about the disease, they proceeded 'by the science of medicine' to work through a list of over forty 'distinguishing symptoms', finally agreeing that she did not present enough of them to be removed from society.[15]

However implausible they may now appear, medieval medical theories about the cause and spread of leprosy sought to establish a natural, scientific explanation of the disease consonant with contemporary ideas about man and his place in the universe. It was seen as a hereditary condition, which might also be sexually transmitted (notably through coitus with a menstruating woman or one who had previously had sexual relations with a leper), contracted through association with lepers or otherwise brought on by adverse planetary influences or through the retention of superfluous humours.[16] The devastating psychological consequences of a positive diagnosis were clearly recognised, in so far that the physician was advised to comfort his patient and avoid unnecessary moralising. 'If soche men forsothe be noght reproved, thai schal stande in pees', noted the fourteenth-century French surgeon, Guy de Chauliac, who evidently consoled his patients with a short speech about Christ's love for lepers and the promise of heavenly bliss bought through suffering on earth.[17]

The leper stood in desperate need of reassurance, not simply because of the physical ordeal ahead, but, more immediately, as a defence against the deep-seated animosity he or she was likely to encounter from friends and strangers alike. The objective 'naturalist' approach to disease adopted by late medieval medical authorities (in keeping with the classical Greek tradition) helped to soften a widespread assumption, propagated by many theologians from the end of the twelfth century onwards, that if sickness was inflicted by God as a punishment for sin such a terrible fate must betoken a life of unusual depravity. Although by no means lacking in compassion as individuals, leading figures in the Church collectively assumed an ambivalent, often hostile attitude towards the leper, sometimes portraying his disease as a symbol of moral decay or as a real, physical manifestation of wickedness on the part of the sufferer or his parents. Despite its evident incompatibility with the idea of divine retribution, a popular conviction that leprosy was highly contagious, spreading like a miasma on the breath, through close personal proximity and even on the gaze, made matters infinitely worse.

Orders promulgated by the third Lateran Council of 1179 for the segregation of lepers and subsequent attempts by ecclesiastical and lay authorities throughout Europe to restrict their movements have been seen by historians as part of a wider campaign against heretics, Jews, homosexuals and anyone else whose conduct or beliefs aroused fear and suspicion.[18] A rising tide of anti-semitism in Norwich was intensified by the late-twelfth century cult of William the boy martyr (an alleged victim of Jewish ritual abuse); as enthusiasm for the Third Crusade reached fever pitch in 1190 a number of atrocities occurred there and in other English towns; and two more riots directed against members of the Jewish community and their possessions took place in 1235 and 1238. Throughout this period, moreover, the city's Jews faced a constant barrage of threats and hostility from their neighbours, ostensibly sanctioned by official directives issued, in 1222 at a provincial council of the English Church held in Oxford, with the intention of isolating them in much the same way as lepers.[19] In accordance with decrees passed seven years earlier by the fourth Lateran Council, Jews in the dioceses of Norwich, Oxford and Lincoln were henceforward forbidden to hire Christian servants, enter churches or build new synagogues, while at the same time being forced to wear a distinctive badge or *tabula*. As a writ sent by the government to the authorities in Norwich makes plain, these precise restrictions were applied locally with such vigour and lack of discrimination that almost all dealings between Christians and Jews, including the sale of food and other essential commodities, temporarily fell under the ban.[20] Since no other English provincial councils went so far at this time (although later, in 1253, the above measures passed into statute law), we may reasonably assume that intolerance was then running particularly high in the region. It does not, of course, necessarily follow that lepers encountered a similar level of institutionalised prejudice, although the general climate of distrust can hardly have eased their predicament.

The assumption that Judaism would spread like a contagious disease, infecting members of the Christian community unless it were effectively contained, lay behind most of these thirteenth-century prohibitions. Not surprisingly, the same terminology of infection and corruption, and sometimes the very same passages from canon law (such, for example, as Gratian's warning that 'often the fellowship of evil persons corrupts even the good') appear in conciliar injunctions for the control of lepers.[21] Sufferers might actually be branded along with Jews as scapegoats: the most notorious instance of such victimisation occurred in France, in 1321, when a number of lepers in the Languedoc were burnt at the stake for their reputed complicity in a Jewish plot to poison the water supply. Once news of their machinations reached Philip V, reprisals followed throughout France, with lepers being either condemned to death or incarcerated for life. Besides predictable claims that they had desecrated the Host *(et in dictis pestiferis potionibus, quod terribile est audire, corpore Christi cribrato et apposito)* as Jews were frequently alleged to do, they also faced charges of international conspiracy. They had, it was said, held four separate councils in different places, so that representatives from all the *leprosaria* in the world (except, curiously, two in England) could pool their resources.[22] Similar assertions about a global network of councils and conspirators had been made previously in the mid-twelfth century by Thomas of Monmouth in his *Life and Passion of St William the Martyr of Norwich*, on this occasion with regard to the

Jews and their supposed involvement in the ritual murder of Christians.[23]

Significantly in this context, the heretic, another enemy of medieval society, was often described in medical terms as a spiritual leper, infected by a poisonous contagion from which his soul was unlikely to recover, expelled from the community of the faithful and driven byn uncontrollable sexual urges to contaminate those who fell into his clutches.[24] The horrific effects of *lepromatous* leprosy and the fear it inspired made it seem an especially appropriate punishment for the two sins of concupiscence and pride, which, in turn, were invariably represented as leprosy or cancer of the soul. 'For just as leprosy makes the body ugly, loathsome and monstrous', ran one medieval homily, 'so the filth of lechery makes the soul very loathsome spiritually, and the swelling of secret pride is leprosy, that no man may hide'.[25] The widespread rumour, put about by his many enemies, that Henry IV had turned leprous after ordering the execution of Archbishop Scrope, in 1405, served to reinforce the image of an arrogant usurper, brought low by the wrath of God. Whatever his real, physical symptoms (which suggest heart disease) Henry's conduct marked him out as morally leprous. Medieval congregations were familiar with the biblical story of King Uzziah, who had contracted leprosy after merely presuming to serve as a priest in the Temple (Chronicles II, XXVI vv. 18–21); and most collections of improving literature contained at least one cautionary tale about the dreadful diseases likely to befall vain and frivolous women. Another type of homily, concerning the priest or visionary permitted by God to see and diagnose the spiritual ailments of people taking communion, was likewise intended to shock by invoking an image of decay and corruption.[26]

The impact of these ideas upon the medieval laity is hard to judge. Christ's recourse to the home of Simon the Leper, his miracles of healing and manifest desire to comfort all sinners, however deformed or disturbed they might be, provided a powerful inducement to greater clemency. So too did the Church's teaching about almsgiving as a means to salvation: although the relative merits of the recipient and the effectiveness of his or her intercessionary prayers were important factors in determining the outcome of charitable effort, the connection between leprosy and sin seems to have weighed less powerfully with donors than the belief that they could benefit their immortal souls by helping the sick. Yet the leper continued to inspire unease as well as sympathy.

The Norfolk mystic, Margery Kempe (whose religious sensibilities aroused grave misgivings among many of her contemporaries), records, with remarkable candour, how she begged God to punish her own son after he 'fel in-to the synne of letchery'. Soon afterwards 'hys colowr chawngyd' and 'hys face wex ful of whelys and bloberys as it had ben a lepyr'. To compound his suffering, the merchant for whom he had previously worked 'put hym owt of hys seruyse for no defawte he found wyth hym, but perauentur supposyng he had ben a lazer as it schewyd be hys visage'. Ignoring the appeals of friends and neighbours, Margery refused to pray for the young man until he came in person to beg her forgiveness, confess his sins and promise that he would never misbehave again. Not surprisingly, in view of the fate hanging over him, he soon complied and was cured at once of 'that gret sekenes for whech men fleddyn hys company and hys felaschep as for a lepyr'.[27] The case of Margery's son is particularly interesting in light of the modern debate over the existence of syphilis in Europe before the discovery of America, and the possibility that many presumed lepers were in fact the victims of an early, pre-Columbian strain of *Treponema*. Since 1985, when Luke Demaitre dismissed the palaeopathological findings from excavated skeletons as too 'controversial' to clinch the argument, further evidence of cranial lesions produced by treponemes (which cause other diseases besides syphilis) has been found in pre–1493 burials.[28]

From the same Norwich cemetery, which lay in a poor area of the city near the Fye Bridge *leposarium*, and was closed in the 1460's, also come human remains bearing clear signs of *lepromatous* leprosy. If, as seems increasingly likely, confusion between leprosy and sexually transmitted disease occurred in the Middle Ages, the assumption that lepers were promiscuous might have had some limited justification in fact. One thing is beyond doubt: all the protagonists in Margery's tale of her son's misdemeanours believed that leprosy, or in this case its simulacrum, could be used by God to chastise wastrels and profligates. As we shall see, she was not always so inflexible in her view of the disease, which reminded her of Christ's passion on the cross, but even here its moral dimension still ranked uppermost.

It was, moreover, deemed appropriate that the parish priest, who assumed responsibility for the cure of souls and the spiritual health of his flock, should also be charged with the task of diagnosing lepers. Some authorities, such as Bishop Bronescombe of Exeter (d.1280), maintained that this was a sacerdotal function (as established in Leviticus chapters 13 and 14), although the local clergyman must often have been approached for more pragmatic reasons.[29] Those with a decent level of education almost certainly possessed a working knowledge of medical theory (references to which abound in medieval sermons), and a few might actually have studied the subject in depth at university. Even during the later Middle Ages, when the emergent medical profession began to assert its claims to a monopoly of practice in towns, an expert opinion was not always readily available. Quite possibly the guild of barbers, which was active in Norwich from at least the late-fourteenth century onwards, maintained a regular check at the city gates for suspect lepers (as was the case in London), but we know nothing about the procedures involved, and no local evidence survives of any formal machinery for sequestration. In Scotland, powers of search devolved by an act of parliament of 1427 upon senior clergy, who were expected to enquire about lepers when visiting the parish churches under their jurisdiction. Laymen 'swa smyttit' were to be 'denuncit to the king', while clergy remained under the authority of the bishop.[30]

In small towns and rural areas the priest would, of necessity, take it upon himself to offer advice. As late as the 1430s a dispute arose at Sparham, a few miles to the north west of Norwich, over the vicar's apparent misdiagnosis of a parishioner. Having determined that one John Feltard was 'gretely infect with the seknes of lepre', and vainly lectured him in the confessional about the serious risk of contagion, the vicar felt he had no choice but to issue a general warning to the rest of his congregation. Far from agreeing to live as a recluse, Feltard filed an action for trespass against him at the Norwich assizes, and also embarked on litigation for the recovery of lost earnings. Clearly, even the suspicion of leprosy still had serious repercussions, as 'the meniall servauntes of the seid John, undrestandyng that he was infect with the seid sekenes, wold no legger abyde with hym, but they and all other men seyng the seid seknes upon hym so evydently wold not be accompanyed with hym, but eschewed to come nygh hym'.[31]

Although they might be shunned and victimised by neighbours or cruelly exploited by quacks and charlatans, many lepers contrived to remain at large in their communities. Accounts of the French 'conspiracy' of 1321 record that, whereas any Jew approaching the wells or fountains where Christians lived would immediately have fallen under suspicion, the presence of lepers was more or less taken for granted. Indeed, far from staying behind closed doors, some had the temerity to go about their daily business, regardless of the consequences. This was particularly the case in the later Middle Ages, when repeated (and clearly ineffectual) attempts were made to clear them off the streets of European towns and cities.[32] The leper, with his or her begging bowl and warning bell, had long been a feature of urban life, but local authorities, including those of Norwich, appear to have grown lax with regard to the enforcement of regulations restricting freedom of movement, dress and association. Despite individual cases to the contrary, from the mid-fourteenth century onwards the disease seemed far less threatening: some *leprosaria* were closed down or converted to other uses, while those which continued to receive lepers experienced a sharp decline in admissions.

A number of theories have been advanced to explain this phenomenon, which was in part due to a gradual rise in collective levels of resistance first to *lepromatous* leprosy and then to the *tuberculoid* strain. The development of relatively accurate diagnostic techniques by the medical profession (at least in the main centres of population) removed sufferers who might otherwise have posed a long-term problem. Improved standards of living among those who were fortunate enough to survive successive outbreaks of plague from 1348 onwards clearly helped to ameliorate the overcrowded, unhealthy conditions in which the disease can spread. This factor is likely to have proved especially important in Norwich, where the population fell by perhaps as many as 19,000 over four decades. Changes in the cereal-based peasant diet after the Black Death also played a significant part in building up resistance, not least because more people could afford to eat animal protein on a regular basis. It has been argued, too, that the widespread consumption of adulterated flour containing bark, acorns and straw during periods of hardship may have broken down the body's natural defences against leprosy by causing changes in cell structure favourable to the *Mycobacterium leprae*. Once higher quality cereals and purer wheat flour became readily available, the poor ceased to be so vulnerable.[33]

Another thesis, developed by Keith Manchester, maintains that childhood exposure to pulmonary (human type) tuberculosis, which is spread by bacteria of the same genus (*Mycobacterium*) as leprosy, would enable an individual to build up cross-immunity. Pulmonary tuberculosis is a highly contagious 'human density-dependent' disease, said by Manchester to have become endemic in England as a result of the growth of towns during the later Middle Ages and to have bestowed a degree of protection against leprosy, especially among the young. Some of the historical evidence produced in support of this theory is, however, unconvincing, since it presupposes an unrealistically low level of urban population before the Black Death. His second suggestion, that bovine tuberculosis (which is closely related to the human strain) may have infected the population as dairy farming became widespread, seems more plausible when the above-mentioned dietary changes are taken into account.[34] Increased levels of meat and milk consumption after 1350 would certainly have exposed a substantial number of people to the risk of consuming contaminated food. Yet it looks as if the decline of leprosy may be more closely linked to climatic changes, following a fall of about half a degree centigrade in the average yearly temperature in Britain after 1300. During the earlier 'Warm Epoch', conditions were ideal, not only for the incubation of the disease, but also for the proliferation of the insects and parasites which help to transmit it. Leprosy bacilli cannot survive for long outside the body in temperatures below twenty degrees centigrade, but in warmer, humid conditions they thrive for well over a week. The onset of the 'Little Ice Age' in 1500 marked a further fall in average temperature and thus prevented a recurrence of the disease.[35]

The Hospital of St Mary Magdalen

This, the oldest and largest of Norwich's six *leprosaria*, lay at a suitable distance from the city on the Sprowston side of Thorpe Wood, and was reputedly founded as a work of Christian charity by Herbert de Losinga (d.1119), the first bishop of Norwich, on land granted to him and his new cathedral by Henry I.[36] It had certainly opened its doors by the middle of the twelfth century, as a contemporary account of miraculous happenings associated with the death of William, the boy martyr, at Easter 1144, provides an incidental glimpse of the monastic regime then in force there. On the evening of Good Friday a shooting star had appeared over the spot in Thorpe Wood where the body lay, and had been observed by many people:

> ... the lady Legarda, formerly wife of William of Apulia, with her attendants saw it too, she who for the love of God has her dwelling hard

by St. Mary Magdalen's attending upon the sick, and, engaged in such services, lives as a beggar for the salvation of her soul. But the sick people of that place in the same night as they were getting up for the midnight office in the silence of the night, when Legarda showed it them, saw the brightness of that same light.[37]

Most of the surviving foundation charters or statutes of medieval hospitals contain quite elaborate rules about the liturgical practices to be followed by personnel and patients alike. Those for St Mary's have been lost, but may be presumed to have required the lepers to observe the eight daily offices of the *Opus Dei*, of which the first, Vigils or Nocturns (later Matins), took place at two or three in the morning. Regulations for the *leprosarium* at Dudston, near Gloucester, drawn up shortly before 1115, for example, insisted that all but the completely bedridden should rise for Matins and attend the other services, although laymen were allowed to say a specific number of prayers instead of repeating the offices themselves. The ability to recite the Creed, the *Ave Maria* and the *Pater Noster* was, in fact, a condition of entry, although the daily ritual was so onerous and repetitive that even the most ignorant must soon have become word-perfect.[38] A constant round of religious observance, dedicated to the welfare of the souls of patrons and founders, was the price usually paid by the sick poor of medieval England in return for shelter, food and basic nursing in a hospital. But rather more seems to have been expected of lepers, whose disease was, as we have seen, commonly associated with sexual depravity, and who were believed, in one way or another, to be suffering the consequences of their own or their parents' wrongdoing.

The choice of Mary Magdalen as patron saint was singularly appropriate in view of current assumptions about leprosy, although her popularity as the dedicatee of *leprosaria*, hospices and, at a later date, refuges for reformed prostitutes, sprang from a series of misunderstandings about the identity of at least four and possibly seven different New Testament characters. The penitent saint of medieval legend was, in fact, held to possess a variety of attributes, whose ambivalent, sometimes contradictory nature reflected contemporary attitudes to the female sex in general and the sick or mentally disturbed in particular. She was a conflation of the Mary Magdalen who had been freed of 'seven devils' by Christ and had witnessed both the crucifixion and the resurrection; of the unnamed sinner who had anointed his feet with precious ointment in the house of Simon the Pharisee; of at least one other female who had done likewise while he was visiting Simon the Leper; and of the pious Mary of Bethany, whom Origen (d.254) had hailed as a model of the contemplative life. Further misidentification with women of dubious moral character known to Christ encouraged the idea that she had once herself been a prostitute; and this, in turn, helped to strengthen her already close association with leprosy, the disease of profligates and lechers.[39]

Similar myths and legends attached themselves to the Magdalen's companion,

Lazarus. But here, too, there had been a mistake, again resulting from confusion about biblical sources. Despite the frequent use of his name in the context of 'lazars' and 'lazar houses', Mary of Bethany's brother, Lazarus, whom Christ raised from the tomb, had died suddenly of an unidentified sickness which was certainly not leprosy (John XI vv. 2–44); and it was Mary's presumed link with Simon, together with St Luke's story of another Lazarus, the beggar 'full of sores' (XVI vv. 19–31), which led to his subsequent personification as the archetypical leper. To medieval men and women, however, Mary's connexion with and sympathy for social outcasts went unquestioned. Indeed, the guild of St Mary Magdalen at Launceston in Cornwall actually admitted lepers and staff from the local *leprosarium* as full members and beneficiaries of the fraternity's religious and charitable work.[40]

Although Mary of Bethany's sister, Martha, was generally regarded as the exemplar of the active Christian life pursued by medieval hospital nurses, St Mary Magdalen's devotion to the body of Christ also offered an ideal of selfless womanhood. Commonly represented carrying a jar of ointment, she became the patron saint of apothecaries, and the sister order to the Knights Hospitallers of St John bore her name. Her association with healing – of the soul as well as the body – was reiterated in medieval verse, which also depicted her as the repentant patient cured 'from many ailments by the Doctor's word.' Nursing in the earlier, quasi-monastic leper houses appears often to have been undertaken by healthy volunteers, who dedicated themselves to the care of the sick out of Christian piety. Having usually taken vows of chastity and obedience, they accepted the same strict code of discipline as their patients, who might be beaten or deprived of food if they proved recalcitrant. Since all goods were held in common, the nurses must also have relinquished their personal property, choosing instead to live in apostolic poverty as the lady Legarda did in Norwich. An unusual degree of self-sacrifice was required of those who dedicated their lives to the service of lepers, not least because they themselves encountered considerable prejudice. The book of miracles of St Gilbert of Sempringham (d.1198) records how he received a leprous novice into his new order. She was tended with great devotion for twelve years in the infirmary by the novice mistress, until the time of her miraculous cure. 'Because she used to massage her with ointment', the nurse reported, 'she herself was avoided by the other nuns, who were afraid they would catch the infection from her.'[41]

Remarkable as it was, Gilbert's readiness to accept a (presumed) leper into the monastic community serves as a reminder that many *leprosaria*, including one dedicated to St Mary Magdalen on the Gaywood Causeway outside Bishop's Lynn, accommodated other sick men and women as well.[42] Paradoxically, in view of the hostility often directed against lepers during this period, there was, at the other extreme, a powerful conviction that spiritual merit might be gained by associating with and tending the most deformed and rejected members of society. For although the leper bore the marks of divine displeasure because of his transgressions, he also seemed to have been granted the promise of eternal life in return for temporal suffering. Both Henry I's queen, Matilda (d.1118), and St Hugh of Lincoln (d.1200) had, for instance, welcomed lepers into their private apartments, washing their ulcerated sores and even kissing them, despite the current belief that contagion could spread on the breath or even the gaze of victims. To St Hugh, 'swollen. livid, diseased and deformed faces, with the eyes either distorted or hollowed out and the lips eaten away' were an external sign of 'internal spleandour', a physical manifestation of 'the flowers of Paradise and the lucent pearls in the crown of the eternal king'.[43]

St Francis of Assisi (d.1226) took a similar view of the disease, which, it is now believed, he may well have contracted himself as a result of continuous exposure to infection while he was sick and malnourished. He certainly impressed upon his followers through his own teaching and example that they should 'rejoice when they are living among common and despised people, among the poor and the weak, the sick and the lepers, and those who beg by the wayside'. But although he made a point of addressing lepers as his 'Christian brothers', and even once (as a penance) shared the same dish of food with one who was badly ulcerated and bleeding, this aspect of his mission did not appeal to senior figures in the ecclesiastical hierarchy. With the relaxation of the rules of the Franciscan order, the ideals of poverty and service were changed in ways never envisaged by the founder.[44] As Geoffrey Chaucer noted with some asperity when describing his 'wanton and merry' Friar:

> He knew the tavernes wel in every toun
> And everich hostiler and tappestere
> Bet than a lazar or a beggestere;
> For unto swich a worthy man as he
> Acorded nat, as by his facultee,
> To have with sike lazars aqueyntaunce.
> It is nat honest, it may nat avaunce,
> For to delen with no swich poraille [rabble],
> But al with riche and selleres of vitaille.[45]

Yet even in the fifteenth century, when leprosy was in retreat and many isolation hospitals had been given over to other uses, a few devout men and women still tried to follow St Hugh's example. Notwithstanding her inflexible conduct towards her own son, Margery Kempe expressed a keen desire to visit the local lazar house (probably at Bishop's Lynn, where she lived, but just possibly in Norwich), and kiss the inmates. Having obtained the reluctant consent of her confessor, who forbade her to go near the men,

> than was sche glad, for sche had leue to kyssyn the seke women, and
> went to a place wher seke women dwellyd whech wer ryth ful of the
> sekenes, and fel down on hir kneys be-forn hem, preyng hem that sche

myth kyssyn her mowth for the lofe of Ihesu. And so sche kyssyd ther ij
[two] seke women with many an holy thowt and many a deuowt teer,
and, whan sche had kyssyd hem and telde hem ful many good wordys
and steryd hem to mekenes and pacyens that thei xulde not grutchyn
wyth her sekenes, but hyly thankyn God therfor, and thei xulde han gret
blysse in Heuyn thorow the mercy of owr Lord Ihesu Crist.[46]

Unfortunately, we are not told how the lepers responded to this advice.

St Mary's hospital, Sprowston, accommodated both men and women, who
would have been strictly segregated, as was invariably the case in such institutions.
Here again, the widespread assumption that leprosy was not only retribution for sin,
but actually exacerbated its victims' moral predicament by making them even more
libidinous, is perhaps reflected in the arrangements devised for communal living. At
both Dudston and the leper hospital of St Nicholas, founded slightly earlier by
Archbishop Lanfranc at Harbledown, near Canterbury, male and female lepers
dwelt in separate houses and were forbidden under the threat of draconian
punishment from fraternising in any way with members of the opposite sex. At
Harbledown these lodgings were built of wood, and clustered around a detached
stone chapel where the community assembled for worship.[47]

The large (and now heavily restored) infirmary hall of the Norman chapel used
by the lepers at Sprowston still stands, although all signs of any surrounding huts

*2. The stone chapel of the leper hospital at Sprowston, founded by Herbert de Losinga in the
early-twelfth century, and now a public library. The chapel is heavily restored, but the west door
(to the right of the picture), is believed to be original.*

have long since disappeared. For part of its length, along the western half, the chapel contained an upper storey or gallery which served as a ward for the most advanced, bedridden cases. Perhaps the two levels were used to segregate male and female patients: both sexes would have been able to lie in full view of the high altar, deriving spiritual consolation from the daily round of prayer, and, most notably, from the elevation of the host, with its promise of healing through the medicine of Christ's blood. An inventory of church goods made there in 1368 records a more than adequate provision of service books, vestments and ornaments for daily use, as well as two bells, one to be rung during mass and a 'kynkebelle', or clapper, which alerted passers-by that there were lepers in the vicinity. In accordance with directives from Rome, the hospital possessed its own cemetery, where the sick might be interred separately, away from healthy men and women. When Gilman Road, which runs over the site, was constructed, archaeologists had the opportunity to examine skeletal remains, and found evidence of several cases of *lepromatous* leprosy.[48]

Like most of the smaller hospitals of medieval England, St Mary's derived its income from two sources: land settled upon it by the founder and other pious benefactors, and gifts of money or food proffered on an ad hoc basis by local people. As a rule, *leprosaria* were heavily dependent on public charity, but a steady flow of modest grants of land and rents made during the thirteenth century provided a regular income assessed at £10 a year in 1535 (the annual wage of a skilled master mason then stood at about half this sum). In addition, the hospital enjoyed the right to hold an annual fair for three days in July, around the feast day of the patron saint, from at least 1286 onwards.[49] Although the lepers at Sprowston did not, apparently, see fit to criticise the master in any way when official enquiries were being held in 1368, his fifteenth-century successors seem to have been less scrupulous in the matter of finances, at least to the extent of creaming off the regular profits to pay their salaries. Most of them were absentee pluralists, who customarily owed their advancement to patronage from the bishop rather than the assiduous discharge of pastoral responsibilities. To take just one example, Simon Thornham, an Oxford graduate presented to the mastership in 1444, occupied during his career a total of nine East Anglian rectories, two deaneries and a canonry at the prestigious college of St Mary in the Fields, Norwich. His appointment as master of St Giles's (Bishopgate), the richest and most important of the city's medieval hospitals, in 1451, can have left him even less time for the lepers and other sick patients at Sprowston, who had become increasingly dependent on alms for survival.[50]

There is now no means of telling how much money could be raised from this source, which must have fluctuated from month to month and year to year. In 1245 and 1334 the brethren of St Mary's and their accredited agents had been granted royal letters of protection enabling them to beg in churches (presumably throughout England), but thereafter they seem to have relied on local charity.[51] If the evidence from wills left by Norwich residents between 1370 and 1532 is any guide, help from this quarter was extremely limited, with an average of less than three per cent of testators making any provision at all for the inmates. Given their comparative generosity to the five other leper hospitals then situated just outside the city gates, which were remembered by at least a third of those who made wills, it looks very much as if St Mary's had already entered a period of decline, becoming hardly more than a wayside chapel.[52]

There may, however, have been other reasons for the citizens' apparent reluctance to assist this particular institution. Whereas successive bishops of Norwich, from de Losinga onwards, had retained the uncontested right of presentation to St Mary's, the ownership of its various properties was less straightforward. Among the many disputes over contested franchises which brought them into conflict with the prior of Norwich during the second quarter of the fifteenth century was a claim by the mayor and corporation to exercise jurisdiction over the Magdalen hospital, its estates and annual fair. In July 1441, while the fair was actually in progress, the mayor became involved in a violent affray at the hospital leading to the arrest and imprisonment of a clerk. This direct challenge to the prior's legal authority was one of many incidents culminating in the dramatic events of Gladman's Insurrection, in February 1443, when an angry mob threatened to burn down the priory and kill all the monks. Not surprisingly, any hope of compromise now vanished, and it was not until 1532, when the prior could no longer wield any political influence, that the civic authorities once again established an official presence at the fair.[53]

Allegations investigated by the government, in 1507, that the bishop of Norwich had actually given the patronage of the house, together with all its lands, rents and profits, to St Giles's hospital without first seeking royal approval, proved groundless, although it is easy to see why the mistake occurred.[54] During his time as bishop, James Goldwell (d.1499) had installed his ambitious younger brother, Nicholas, as master of St Mary's for life, and then presented him to the mastership of the other hospital as well. Thus, for the second time in less than half a century, the two institutions shared the same master, an arrangement beneficial to neither.[55] If they were ever seriously considered, plans to absorb St Mary's permanently into the complex administrative network of what was now a grand college for secular priests must have constituted a further irritant to the civic authorities, as St Giles's had gradually abandoned many of its responsibilities towards the sick poor (see Chapter III). Dissatisfaction with the ecclesiastical establishment may well have led potential donors to look elsewhere, seeking ways in which their largesse could be more effectively deployed, not least for the salvation of their own immortal souls.

The Five City Leper Hospitals

An edict of the third Lateran Council of 1179, ordering the confinement of lepers, who not only lost all their legal rights (and thus any claim to own property), but were sometimes (theoretically) obliged to undergo a ceremony modelled upon the offices of the dead, provides an eloquent testimony to the fear of contagion then sweeping Europe. Because the leper occupied a world halfway between life and death, and was, indeed, commonly believed to be suffering the pains of purgatory on earth, it seemed appropriate that leprosaria should stand on the boundaries of towns and cities, at bridges, gates and fords.[56] The *Leges Quatuor Burgorum* of David I of Scotland stipulated that, once confined in 'the spytaile of the burgh', if necessary at public expense, 'mysal men' [lepers] should not be allowed to wander begging about the streets from door to door. Instead, they were to 'site at the toune end and their ask almous at furth passand men and ingangand'. The presence of lepers soliciting alms in urban churches and churchyards led the Scottish parliament of 1427 to reiterate this order. They were, henceforward, ordered to stay 'at thare awin hospitale ande at the porte of the toune et vthir places outewith the borowis'.[57] Like the medieval anchorite or anchoress, another figure dwelling on the spiritual as well as the topographical margins of society, in some parts of Europe the leper was pronounced dead to the world: whereas the former might share his or her cell (called a sepulchre) with an open grave, the latter had to endure an even more painful reminder of mortality.[58]

Far from being truly isolated in the depths of the country, leper houses served as a constant reproach to sinners, as well as a memorial to the generosity of devout benefactors. By the close of the Middle Ages, London had ten such hospitals, half of which had been founded by the citizens themselves, scattered in a ring on the major roads leading to the capital. York meanwhile acquired five suburban *leprosaria*, and Bishop's Lynn no less than six, albeit of quite modest size.[59] Visitors approaching Norwich from the south, west or north, through St Stephen's (Needham), St Giles's, St Benedict's, St Augustine's or the Magadalen (Fye Bridge) gates were likewise brought face to face with the grim reality of the disease, and the need to assist its victims. Because the prevailing wind came from the east, especially in summer, and it was believed that contagion spread on the air, no leper hospitals were built on that side of the city, even though the river Wensum placed such an effective barrier between town and country.

Comparatively little is known about the early history of these five *leprosaria*, whose origins remain obscure. In his will of 1256, Bishop Walter Suffield of Norwich left the substantial sum of £5 to be shared among local lepers, whether they were living in isolation as recluses or together in special communities, but he did not describe any of the latter. Since he bequeathed a further 20s to the lazar house at Sprowston, we may reasonably assume that the city already possessed at least two or three leper hospitals, but, as is so often the case, the surviving documentary evidence is much later in date. Significantly, the bishop promised 2d to every leper present at his funeral, on the clear assumption that they would be allowed to congregate together in public, albeit at a safe distance from the other mourners.[60] St Stephen's, which occupied a site near the present Norfolk and Norwich Hospital, stood on land belonging to the priory of Horsham St Faith, a Benedictine house situated a few miles north of Norwich. The hospital is said to have had its own chapel, where mass could be celebrated daily for the spiritual health of the inmates. As at Sprowston, those near to death probably lay in the nave; but we know that from 1315 onwards, if not before, the hospital complex contained four 'leper cottages' as well. Although the mastership resided in the prior's gift, new incumbents had to be approved by both the bishop *and* the mayor, who probably exercised some control over day to day administrative matters. It would be interesting to know if Matilda Breton, a suspect leper who was temporarily removed from the lands of the prior of Horsham St Faith, in 1288, until the manor court could decide her fate, ever found refuge here.[61]

St Giles's (not to be confused with its namesake in Bishopgate) appears to have been a rather less regulated institution, which in 1308 comprised a small settlement of lepers on the western approach to the city. It was then that Walter Knot made a conveyance of 'seven cottages in which leprous people dwell, lying together without St Giles's gate, on the north side of the King's highway'. Quite possibly other accommodation had been set aside for their use, but the records are silent on this point.[62] The order of service allegedly observed in parts of France on the removal of a leper from society assumed that, after the last rites had been intoned and a symbolic shovel of earth had been cast over their feet, he or she would be escorted by the priest to a small house or cottage in the open fields rather than a hospital as such, and provided with the basic necessities for survival by begging.[63] That many sufferers in Norwich preferred to congregate informally, in modest extra mural lodgings provided by friends, family or benefactors rather than seeking admission to a more regimented, quasi-religious community seems quite likely. However parlous their financial situation may have been, such small groups enjoyed a remarkable degree of autonomy and even freedom of movement. Although the wandering bands of lepers which feature so prominently in French and German literature do not appear in medieval English sources, some evidence of mobility does come to light. In 1348, for example, a tenement in Kingston-on-Thames, 'where a house of lepers was', reverted to the Crown because the lepers themselves 'had abandoned the same and thrown down and carried away the houses then and there' during a period of political upheaval twenty-four years earlier.[64]

Dependence upon the begging bowl alone posed a bleak alternative to rigidly institutionalised philanthropy of the kind on offer at Sprowston, but groups of lepers could at least pool their resources. The better organised managed to appoint agents or proctors to solicit for alms on their behalf: as late as 1529, the residents of the hospital of SS Mary and Clement, outside St Augustine's gate, chose one Thomas Parys to act for them throughout England, on the condition that he rendered four accounts each year and took immediate action against any imposters. Such requirements suggest that quite large sums were at stake; yet although it possessed a common seal and was the only one of Norwich's nineteen medieval hospitals to be founded by a member of the nobility (either the countess of Lincoln who died shortly before 1266, or her namesake, another Margaret, active at the turn of the century), this particular house was certainly not rich.[65]

Like St Benedict's, a *leprosarium* of similar age and size outside the walls at Upper Westwick, it could not afford to maintain a private cemetery, but had to defy canon law by burying its dead in the nearest churchyard. In ruling that lepers should

3. A sufferer from lepromatous leprosy seeks alms with the cry 'sum good my gentyll mayster for God sake'. The bell serves to attract gifts, while also warning the public to keep at a safe distance. Figures such as this would have been a familiar sight at the gates of medieval Norwich.

be forced to live and die in strict segregation, even to the extent of being buried separately, the synod of Westminster of 1200 had reinforced earlier decrees from Rome. Lepers were allowed, even encouraged, to support their own priests and cemeteries so that they might benefit from the solace of the Christian religion; but, in theory at least, they could not expect to share churches or burial facilities with the healthy.[66] As we have already seen, provision of a decent funeral, with lights, prayers and masses, was one of the major responsibilities of the medieval hospital: it could promise the sick poor that however protracted or acute their suffering might have been on earth, they would at least be assured a fitting passage into the next world, and an appropriate remission of the pains of purgatory. Although they already seemed to be serving out their alloted term of purgation, lepers were still anxious to secure for themselves the spiritual merits of an interment performed according to Christian rites, as well as due commemoration through obits and offerings. But it was one thing for a pious donor to provide food and housing for a small community of lepers, and quite another to find the resources necessary to maintain a church or chapel, which, in any event, required episcopal approval and supervision.[67]

By the fifteenth century, if not earlier, however, the ecclesiastical authorities appear to have relented sufficiently to permit the occasional burial of patients from leper hospitals without cemeteries in Norwich churchyards. It might be argued that the individuals involved were not leprous at all, but came instead from the ranks of the sick poor who increasingly took over places originally intended for lepers. Skeletal evidence from the churchyard of St Margaret in Combusto, Magdalen Street, suggests otherwise. So too does the survival of wills drawn up by two members of the Wellys family, both of whom specifically describe themselves as victims of the disease while still requesting burial in the cemetery of All Saints Church, Fye Bridge (with which their local parish church of St Margaret had recently been amalgamated). These documents, dated 1448 and 1468 respectively, also reveal an important change in the legal status of lepers having taken place since the mid-thirteenth century, when they had been ranked, along with madmen and imbeciles, as persons incapable of giving or receiving property.[68]

Henry Wellys, who drew up his last testament in 1448, 'struck down by the disease of leprosy and staying outside the Fye Bridge gate of the city of Norwich', was an inmate of St Leonard's hospital, the largest of the five civic *leprosaria*. Here it was not only possible for a segregated leper to retain his personal possessions, but also for him to make and seal a will like anybody else, and rest assured that it would be proved in exactly the same way. At all events, Wellys seems to have been free to bequeath all his modest possessions (including 6s 8d towards the building of 'a new chapel for lepers outside the said gates'), and to appoint two fellow-sufferers as his executors.[69] We know from a royal grant of four oak trees from Sherwood Forest made to Robert Stanford, the keeper of the hospital, in 1335, that some of the inmates lived, as was so often the case, in wooden houses or huts then badly in need of repair. The dedication to St Leonard, the patron saint of prisoners, whose cult had a predictable appeal to lepers as well, may perhaps indicate a fairly early date of foundation by the civic or ecclesiastical authorities, once it became evident that Norwich would need more than one lazar house. Quite possibly standards of living improved towards the close of the Middle Ages: Richard Wellys, who had followed his kinsman into the Fye Bridge hospital by 1466, remained a man of means, with over £9 in cash and uncollected debts of £3 11s at his disposal when he died.[70] Yet the impression that most lepers led a hand to mouth existence remains strong.

None of Norwich's *leprosaria* possessed either the land or the resources to fund themselves without public assistance, and were obviously incapable of producing all their own food. Some of the fitter, more mobile inmates may have cultivated gardens and tended cattle (which was another reason for siting leper houses in the open fields). In 1312–13, William the Watchman, who presided over one of the city gates, was fined by the leet of Wymer and Westwick for confiscating two beasts from a leper named Beatrice de Cringlethorpe. The animals had, in fact, been distrained by a local linen draper, against whom Beatrice had successfully raised the hue and cry: clearly, she and the other members of her community (probably St Benedict's) could rely upon the protection of customary law when their property was at risk. They needed tangible help as well. A significant proportion of alms would have been given in kind, both informally by friends and relatives and as part of the regular distribution of loaves and cash doles undertaken by the almoner of Norwich Cathedral Priory on the anniversaries of former bishops. His account for 1279–80 lists lepers, prisoners and 'other paupers' as the recipients of such charity; in 1311–12 over £7 was shared out between the three groups; and in the consecutive accounts for 1395–96 and 1396–97 reference is made to annual payments of 20s 'to the lepers at the gates of the city in alms by equal portions'. In other years the lepers of Norwich were probably subsumed in the general category of 'the poor' to whom relief was given.[71] Yet support from this quarter (which was, in any event, subject to harsh cuts during the fifteenth century) did not alone suffice, and it was understood that the active lepers or their nurses would sometimes have to venture into the market place, either to buy or beg for supplies. In accordance with contemporary ideas about contagion, the civic authorities evolved an elaborate set of rules regarding dress and demeanour, designed to protect healthy people from the touch, gaze or polluted breath of anyone coming from a lazar house. A civic ordinance of 1473 reiterated one of these restrictions, insisting that 'the buyers of victuals for the lepers near the city for the future shall not touch any victuals with their hands, but with a wand', and imposing penalties on the butchers and fishmongers who had hitherto grown careless about the possible spread of contagion.[72]

Repeated attempts in London and other leading towns and cities of England to clear lepers off the streets during the late-fourteenth and fifteenth centuries suggest that the populace as a whole had grown more tolerant – or at least less fearful – of those they believed to have been stricken by the disease. In 1346, for example, orders were issued from Chancery for the immediate expulsion of suspects from Bishop's

Lynn, where at least one lazar house had recently been demolished. 'All having the taint of leprosy shall leave the town and suburb within fourteen days,' ran the royal decree, 'and go to solitary field places at a notable distance therefrom and stay there, seeking the food they need by those who will attend thereto'.[73]

Not everyone in Norwich was over-scrupulous about avoiding contact with such outcasts: in 1312, for example, one Richard de Catton was presented in a local court for acquiring twenty combs of wheat and other goods from a leper living in the hospital outside St Augustine's gate, who evidently turned a handy profit for the house by helping local traders to evade the tariff on corn imposed within the city walls by the bailiffs. In this context it is worth noting that Catton's offence was specifically commercial and had nothing to do with the health of his business partner. From time to time, the leets of medieval Norwich drew attention to lepers who remained illicitly in the community, although measures against them were at best half-hearted. Whereas in 1374–75 a webster named Thomas Tytel was ordered to leave the city because of his condition, another suspect 'lodging in a house in Normanspital' did not apparently face expulsion. St Paul's or Norman's hospital (considered in the next chapter) may perhaps have found room in a remote corner of the precincts for men and women suffering from what were perceived to be infectious diseases, as also, on at least one occasion, did St Giles's in Bishopgate; but not all these people sought anonymity or protection. The experience of Isabel Lucas, a known leper charged repeatedly in the 1390s with nuisance for failing to clean out her drains and also, with astonishing effrontery, of selling home-brewed ale without a licence, provides a case in point.[74]

By the early sixteenth century, most of the city's *leprosaria* had opened their doors to the sick and infirm poor, who soon constituted the majority of inmates. Once the desire for strict segregation became less pressing, and leprosy itself began gradually to disappear, facilities could be made available for other unfortunates. These newcomers possibly lived for a while alongside the dwindling number of lepers and may themselves have been suffering from disfiguring or contagious diseases. By 1469 the hospital at St Stephen's gate had become a home for 'the poor' rather than the leprous; and it continued to function as an almshouse until well after the Reformation. In 1541 the master, William Rye, stood charged by the civic authorities with breaking statute law by hiring perfectly healthy agents to solicit alms on his behalf, and of supplying them with the necessary credentials authenticated 'under the place seall'. Nor was he the only offender: 'oon Creyforth', the proctor of the former leper house at St Giles's gate, had apparently been selling similar licenses for 8s 6d a year, while also exploiting the paupers in his care. The testimony against him further alleged that he 'usith to gett pour lame and diseased personz, promysyng them to fynd them; and when he hath them he compellith them to begge for thir lyuyng or elles they shall haue nothyng of hym'. Since he, too, was 'an heile and clene man', the keeper of 'the sikehouse' at the Westwick gate (previously St Benedict's) and his four able-bodied servants likewise came under suspicion, although in the event only Rye and Creyforth were bound over in substantial sums to surrender all the licenses they had issued.[75]

Norwich's five extra mural hospitals may still occasionally have received lepers, for in 1548 their keepers were summoned before the mayor to report how many 'lazars' remained. Official anxiety about the number, condition and status of the individuals admitted to these institutions was clearly intensified by the growing problem of vagrancy and the corresponding severity of poor law enactments, which drew a sharp distinction between the 'sturdy beggar' and those who were manifestly incapable of supporting themselves. The responsibilty for feeding and housing such people now fell, by law, upon the parish where they had been born, so it is easy to see why the corporation wished to ensure that the maximum number of places would be available for genuinely deserving cases. Henceforward, the mayor alone enjoyed the right to decide who might be given bed and board, reserving for the impotent poor a place once occupied by the leper.[76]

Evidence from Cambridge, which shows that the erstwhile leper hospital of St Anthony and St Eligius received the mad as well as infirm paupers during the sixteenth century, would appear to support Michel Foucault's contention that the empty lazar houses of Europe became places for the incarceration of dangerous lunatics. The 'insistent and fearful figure which was not driven off without first being inscribed within a sacred circle' was, he argued, now the madman rather than the leper.[77] Quite possibly Norwich's new 'sikehouses' were sometimes used as places where the deranged could be securely kept, but no formal arrangements for the institutional custody of the insane seem to have been made in the city at this time. Only one medieval English hospital – that of St Mary Bethlehem (Bedlam) in London – actually specialised in caring for, or at least housing, the mentally ill; and many establishments refused to admit them under any circumstances. This was in part for purely practical reasons to do with safety and noise, although the lunatic, like the leper, might be stigmatised as a sinner to be kept at arm's length. Loss of reason (which represented the divine in man) seemed an even worse punishment than the physical torments of *lepromatous* leprosy. A widespread belief in demonic possession meant, moreover, that the seriously disturbed were liable to suffer extremes of physical violence as well as being forcibly restrained with chains and shackles.

Whereas the law offered protection to those who owned or were likely to inherit property, poor lunatics, without families or friends, faced expulsion from the community. Margery Kempe describes how she herself was shut away under lock and key during a bout of puerperal psychosis, and how, at a later date, she faced constant abuse because of her disconcerting behaviour *(sum scornyd her and seyd that sche howlyd as it had ben a dogge, and bannyd hir and cursyd hir)*. A few people believed that Margery's conduct betokened unusual holiness and spoke up on her behalf: other eccentric or dangerous characters were less fortunate. In 1541, for example, the mayor and aldermen of Norwich issued orders for the removal of one

Ralph Chamberlain, 'beyng vexed wyth a devyll and beyng lunytick', and threatened him with imprisonment should he return.[78] Although members of the medical profession applied humoral theory to the diagnosis and treatment of madness (as they did to leprosy), most ordinary men and women felt that it could only be cured through divine intervention. The shrines and pilgrimage centres of medieval Norfolk attracted the friends, relatives and keepers of the insane, who dragged their charges along, often in chains or bound with ropes, in the hope of a miracle.[79] But none of the cases so carefully recorded by the local clergy, suggest that these unfortunates had been living in hospitals.

END NOTES

1   For a discussion of modern responses to leprosy, see N.E. Waxler,'Learning to be a Leper: a Case Study in the Social Construction of Illness', in *Social Contexts of Health, Illness and Patient Care*, ed. E.G. Mishler (Cambridge, 1981), pp. 169–94; and for general background P. Richards, *The Medieval Leper and his Northern Heirs* (Cambridge, 1977), passim.

2   C. Wells, *Bones, Bodies and Disease* (London, 1964), p. 94.

3   *Account of the Executors of Richard, Bishop of London 1303, and of Thomas, Bishop of Exeter 1310*, ed. W.H. Hale and H.T. Ellacombe (Camden Society, new series, X, 1874), pp. ix, 28–29. M.I. Somerscales, 'Lazar Houses in Cornwall', *Journal of the Royal Institution of Cornwall*, new series, V (1965), pp. 61–99, provides a general survey of Cornish leper hospitals, but is not entirely reliable.

4   *The Register of Walter de Stapledon, Bishop of Exeter*, ed. F.C. Hingeston-Randolph (London, 1892), p. 342. These steps were taken *'quod quia sine periculo idem Vicarius non potuit inter sanos ita communiter prout consuevit conversari'*: he was deemed a threat to the healthy.

5   E. King, *Peterborough Abbey 1086–1310* (Cambridge, 1973), pp. 27–28, 38.

6   R.I. Moore, *The Formation of a Persecuting Society* (Oxford, 1987), p. 52; P.H. Cullum, 'Leperhouses and Borough Status in the Thirteenth Century', in *Thirteenth Century England III*, ed. P.R. Coss and S.D. Lloyd (Woodbridge, 1991), pp. 37–46.

7   D. Knowles and R.N. Hadcock, *Medieval Religious Houses, England and Wales* (London, 2nd edn, 1971), pp. 310–410.

8   A lucid description of the disease may be found in S.N. Brody, *The Disease of the Soul: Leprosy in Medieval Literature* (Cornell, 1974), pp. 21–32. See also, K. Manchester, 'Tuberculosis and Leprosy in Antiquity: An Interpretation', *Medical History*, XXVIII, pp. 162–73, especially pp. 167–68.

9   As, for example, in Robert Henryson's 'Testament of Cresseid', in *Chaucerian and Other Pieces*, ed. W.W. Skeat (Oxford, 1959), pp. 338–46.

10   C. Wells, 'A Leper Cemetery at South Acre, Norfolk', *Medieval Archaeology*, XI (1967), pp. 242–48.

11   Cullum, 'Leperhouses and Borough Status', pp. 39–40; J. Magilton and F. Lee, 'The Leper Hospital of St James and St Mary Magdalene, Chichester', in *Burial Archaeology: Current Research, Methods and Documents*, ed. C.A. Roberts, F. Lee and J. Bintliff (British Archaeological Report, British Series, CCXI, 1989), pp. 249–65.

12   Jacquart, *Le Milieu Medical en France*, p. 128; A. Bourgeois, *Lepreux et Maladreries du Pas-de-Calais* (Arras, 1972), pp. 28–31.

13   L. Demaitre, 'The Description and Diagnosis of Leprosy by Fourteenth-Century Physicians', *Bulletin of the History of Medicine*, LIX (1985), p. 334.

14   *The Cyrurgie of Guy de Chauliac*, ed. M.S. Ogden (Early English Text Society, CCLXV, 1971), p. 381.

15   *Calendar of Close Rolls*, 1468–76 (London, 1953), pp. 30–31. In 1312 the mayor and bailiffs of Winchester and sheriff of Hampshire were ordered to allow Peter de Nutleigh to return to the city after an examination before the royal council by 'physicians experienced in the knowledge of the disease' had confirmed that he was not a leper (ibid., *1307–13* (London, 1892), p. 559).

16   Demaitre, 'Description and Diagnosis of Leprosy', pp. 329–39.

17   *The Cyrurgie of Guy de Chauliac*, p. 381. His criteria for establishing a clear-cut case of leprosy are summarised in Bourgeois, *Lepreux et Maladreries*, pp. 17–19.

18   Notably Moore, *Persecuting Society*, pp. 11, 47–65, 75–80.

19   V.D. Lipman, *The Jews of Medieval Norwich* (London, 1967), pp. 50–64.

20   *Councils and Synods II, 1205–1313*, ed. F.M. Powicke and C.R. Cheney (2 parts, Oxford, 1964), part I, *1205–65*, pp. 120–21.

21   J.A. Watt, 'The English Episcopate, the State and the Jews: the Evidence of the Thirteenth-Century Conciliar Decrees', in *Thirteenth Century England II*, ed. P.R. Coss and S.D. Lloyd (Woodbridge, 1987), pp. 138–41.

22   *Chronique Latine de Guillaume de Nangis*, ed. H. Geraud (2 vols, Paris, 1843), vol. II, pp. 31–34; *Les Grandes Chroniques de France*, ed. J. Viard (10 vols, Paris, 1920–53), vol. VIII, pp. 357–59.

23   For this specific allegation, see G.I. Langmuir, 'Thomas of Monmouth: Detector of Ritual Murder', *Speculum*, LIX (1984), pp. 835–36.

24   R.I. Moore, 'Heresy as a Disease', in *The Concept of Heresy in the Middle Ages*, ed. W. Lourdaux and V. Verhelst (Mediaevalia Louaniensia, series 1, IV, 1976), pp. 1–11.

25   *English Metrical Homilies*, ed. J. Small (Edinburgh, 1862), pp. 129–30.

26   Rawcliffe, *Medicine and Society*, p. 15.

27   *The Book of Margery Kempe*, ed. S.B. Meech (Early English Text Society, CCXII, 1940), pp. 221–23.

28   Demaitre, 'Description and Diagnosis of Leprosy', pp. 328–32, summarises the debate. I am grateful to Dr Ann Stirland for discussing her own findings with me: these are shortly to be published in a report produced jointly by her and Jayne Bown, *Criminals and Paupers: Excavations at the Site and Churchyard of St Margaret Fyebridgegate, Magdalen Street, Norwich* (East Anglian Archaeology, forthcoming, 1996).

29   Cullum, 'Leperhouses and Borough Status', p. 39 note 7.

30   Rawcliffe, *Medicine and Society*, pp. 135–36; *The Acts of the Parliament of Scotland* (12 vols, Edinburgh, 1844–75), vol. II, p. 16, cap. VIII.

31   Public Record Office, C1/46/158.

32   *Chronique Latine de Guillaume de Nangis*, vol. II, p.33; Geremek, *Margins of Society*, p. 175; M.B. Honeybourne, 'The Leper Hospitals of the London Area', *Transactions of the London and Middlesex Archaeological Society*, XXI (1967), pp. 5–8.

33   *Histoire des Hopitaux en France*, p. 47. For changes in the peasant diet, see Dyer, *Standards of Living*, pp. 151–60.

34   Manchester, 'Tuberculosis and Leprosy', pp. 162–73; C.A. Roberts, 'Leprosy and Leprosaria in Medieval Britain', *Museum of Applied Science Centre for Archaeology*, 1 (1986), pp. 18–19.

35   K. Duncan, 'Climate and the Decline of Leprosy in Britain', *Proceedings of the Royal College of Physicians of Edinburgh*, XXIV (1994), pp. 114–20.

36   T. Tanner, *Notitia Monastica* (London, 1744), p. 346. The Norfolk County Council has produced an excellent booklet about the history of this building by T. Nuthall, *Lazar House: From Hospital to Library* (Norwich, 1993).

37   Thomas of Monmouth, *The Life and Miracles of St William of Norwich*, ed. A. Jessopp and M.R. James (Cambridge, 1896), p. 31.

38   E.J. Kealey, *Medieval Medicus: A Social History of Anglo-Norman Medicine* (Johns Hopkins, 1981), pp. 107–16.

39   S. Haskins, *Mary Magdalen: Myth and Metaphor* (London, 1994), chapter I, passim.

40   Somerscales, 'Lazar Houses in Cornwall', pp. 71–72.

41   Haskins, *Mary Magdalen*, pp. 217, 449 note 52; *The Book of St Gilbert*, ed. R. Foreville and G. Keir (Oxford, 1987), pp. 282–85.

42   *The Victoria History of the County of Norfolk, II*, ed. H.A. Doubleday and W. Page (London, 1906), pp. 441–42.

43   Matthew Paris, *Chronica Majora*, ed. H.R. Luard (7 vols, Rolls Series, 1872–84), vol. II, p. 130; *The Life of St Hugh of Lincoln*, ed. D.L. Douie and H. Farmer (2 vols, London, 1961–62), vol. II, pp. 12–14.

44   J.R.H. Moorman, *The Sources for the Life of S. Francis of Assisi* (Manchester, 1940), pp. 45, 47, 136–45; idem, *A History of the Franciscan Order* (Oxford, 1968), pp. 5–6, 8; Thomas de Celano, *Vitae I et II* (First and Second Lives of St Francis of Assisi, *Analecta Franciscana*, X, 1926–41), pp. 16, 136; *Scripta Leonis, Rufini et Angeli Sociorum S. Francisci*, ed. R.B. Brooke (Oxford, 1990), pp. 125–27, 268–70.

45   *The Works of Geoffrey Chaucer*, ed. F.N. Robinson (Oxford, 1970), p. 19.

46   *The Book of Margery Kempe*, p. 177. Although disconcerting to many of Margery's contemporaries, such behaviour was entirely characteristic of certain later medieval (usually female) mystics. See, for example, Bynum, *Holy Feast and Holy Fast*, pp. 145, 171–74, 182, 363–64 n.200.

47   Eadmer, *Historia Novorum in Anglia*, ed. M. Rule (Rolls Series, 1884), pp. 15–16; Kealey, *Medieval Medicus*, pp. 86–87.

48   R. Gilchrist, 'Christian Bodies and Souls: the Archaeology of Life and Death in Later Medieval Hospitals', in *Death in Towns: Urban Responses to the Dying and the Dead, 100–1600*, ed. S. Bassett (Leicester, 1992), pp. 80–82; *Inventory of Church Goods Temp. Edward III*, ed. A. Watkin (Norfolk Record Society, XIX, 1947–48), part I, pp. 33–34; B. Ayers, *The English Heritage Book of Norwich* (London, 1994), p. 57.

49   *Valor Ecclesiasticus* (6 vols, London, 1810–34), vol. III, p. 368; J. Kirkpatrick, *History of the Religious Orders and Communities of the Hospitals and Castle of Norwich Written about the Year 1725* (London, 1845), pp. 72–73. The hospital was endowed with property in Cringleford, Catton and Westfield (Norfolk County Record Office, Phi/95; DCN 44/22/5–8, 45/40/42; British Library, Department of Manuscripts, Add. Ch. 26726).

50   A.B. Emden, *Biographical Register of the University of Cambridge* (Cambridge, 1963), pp. 584–85.

51   *Calendar of Patent Rolls*, 1232–47 (London, 1906), p. 450; 1330–34 (London, 1894) p. 550.

52   N. Tanner, *The Church in Late Medieval Norwich*, p. 135.

53   *Records of the City of Norwich*, vol. I, pp. 327, 340–41; vol. II, pp. 120–21.

54   Public Record Office, E368/280, Easter 22 Hen. VII, rot. 26–26v.

55   Nicholas Goldwell's numerous appointments are listed by A.B. Emden in his *Biographical Register of the University of Cambridge*, pp. 262–63; and *Biographical Register of the University of Oxford to 1500* (3 vols, Oxford, 1957–59), vol. II, p. 786.

56   Gilchrist, 'Christian Bodies', pp. 113–15. Some female mystics, such as Alice of Schaerbeke, believed that the torments of leprosy would not only purge their own souls of sin but would help to release other souls from purgatory (Bynum, *Holy Feast and Holy Fast*, pp. 234, 248–49).

57   *Acts of the Parliament of Scotland*, vol. I, p. 344, cap. LVIII; vol. II, p. 16, cap. VIII. Evidence of controlled access to towns and cities may be seen in a popular German print of 1493 depicting the lepers' banquet in Nuremberg (*Medicine: An Illustrated History*, ed. A.S. Lyons and R.J. Petrucelli (New York, 1978), p. 349 and plate no. 528.

58   Moore, *Persecuting Society*, p. 61. The female recluse was advised to 'scrape up earth every day out of the grave in which [she] shall rot. God knows, the sight of her grave near her does many an anchoress much good ... She who keeps her death as it were before her eyes, her open grave reminding her of it ... will not lightly pursue the delight of the flesh': *The Ancrene Riwle*, ed. and trans. M.B. Salu (Exeter Medieval English Texts and Studies, 1990), pp. 51–52. I am grateful to Dr Roberta Gilchrist for drawing my attention to this reference.

59   Honeybourne, 'The Leper Hospitals of the London Area', pp. 5–7; Cullum, 'Hospitals and Charitable Provision in Medieval Yorkshire', pp. 35–37 and Appendix; F.B. Blomefield, *An Essay towards a Topographical History of the County of Norfolk* (11 vols, London, 1805–10), vol. III, p. 528. Continental leper hospitals were similarly situated: see, for example, J.H. Mundy, 'Hospitals and Leprosaries in Twelfth and Early Thirteenth-Century Toulouse', in *Essays in Medieval Life and Thought*, ed. J.H. Mundy, R.W. Emery and B.N. Nelson (Columbia, New York, 1955), pp. 182–88; and Bourgeois, *Lepreux et Maladreries*, p. 39.

60   Norfolk Record Office, case 24, shelf B, no. 2.

61   *Calendar of Norwich Deeds*, 1307–1341, ed. W. Rye (Norwich, 1915), p. 59; *Victoria History of the County of Norfolk*, II, p. 449; Clark, 'Social Welfare', p. 397.

62   T. Tanner, *Notitia Monastica*, p. 368.

63   Richards, *The Medieval Leper*, p. 124, assumes that the service was widely used in England, but there is no evidence of its inclusion in medieval manuals (*Manuale ad Usum Percelebris Ecclesie Sarisburiensis*, ed. A. Jefferies Collins (Henry Bradshaw Society, XCI, 1960), pp. 182–85). Some French ecclesiastical authorities objected to this ritual as a misuse of the liturgy: R.C. Finucane, 'Sacred Corpse, Profane Carrion: Social Ideas and Death Rituals in the Later Middle Ages', in *Mirrors of Mortality: Studies in the Social History of Death*, ed. J. Whaley (London, 1981), p. 55.

64   *Calendar of Fine Rolls, 1347–56* (London, 1922), pp. 99–100. For a good example of the leper in French literature, see *The Romance of Tristan*, ed. R.L. Curtis (Oxford, 1994), pp. 156–62.

65   Norfolk Record Office, Misc 1/5. Margaret de Lungespee (d. by 1310), first wife of Henry de Lacy, earl of Lincoln, seems the more likely candidate of the two. Her husband was himself a generous patron of the Church in Suffolk, and since both their sons died young in accidents they had every motive to commemorate their souls (G.E. Cockayne, *The Complete Peerage*, ed. V. Gibbs and others (12 vols, London, 1910–59), vol. VII, pp. 677–80, 682–87).

66   *Victoria History of the County of Norfolk*, II, p. 449; *Councils and Synods, 1066–1204*, ed. D. Whitelock, M. Brett and C.N.L. Brooke (Oxford, 1981), p. 1068; Richards, *The Medieval Leper*, p. 124.

67   Rubin, *Charity and Community*, pp. 103–4.

68   Henry Bracton, *De Legibus et Consuetudinibus Angliae*, ed. T. Twiss (6 vols, Rolls Series, 1878–83), vol. I, pp. 94–95; *The Mirror of Justices*, ed. W.J. Whittaker (Selden Society, VII, 1985), pp. 39, 44–45, 47. The legal status of the leper is discussed in Brody, *Disease of the Soul*, chapter II, passim. From 1344 the inmates of St Julian's leper house in St Albans were allowed to dispose freely of one third of the possessions they had brought with them when joining the community, but the master's consent had to be obtained first. The rest of their goods went to the hospital (Thomas Walsingham, *Gesta Abbatum Monasterii Sancti Albani*, ed. H.T. Riley (3 vols, Rolls Series, 1867–69), vol. II, pp. 503–10).

69   Norfolk County Record Office, Norwich Consistory Court Wills, Reg. Aleyn, f. 9.

70   *Calendar of Close Rolls, 1333–37* (London, 1898), p. 440; Norfolk Record Office, Norwich Consistory Court Wills, Reg. Jekkys, f. 43.

71   *Leet Jurisdiction in the City of Norwich*, p. 58; Norfolk Record Office, DCN 1/6/4, 9, 26, 27.

72   Richards, *The Medieval Leper*, p. 124; *Records of the City of Norwich*, vol. II, p. 101. At York and in other northern towns lepers were allocated supplies of food, see Cullum, 'Hospitals and Charitable Provision in Medieval Yorkshire', pp. 31–32.

73   *The Making of King's Lynn*, p. 213; *Calendar of Close Rolls, 1346–49* (London, 1905), pp. 61–62.

74   *Leet Jurisdiction in the City of Norwich*, pp. 59, 71–72; Norfolk County Record Office, DCN 79/3. In 1429 William Setman, a notable benefactor of the sick poor, left 6s 8d a year for life to Alice Colman, *leprosa*, but is is unclear if she was living in the community (N. Tanner, *The Church in Late Medieval Norwich*, p. 243). It is interesting to compare these cases with one of 1310, heard before a manorial court at Heacham, Norfolk. This reveals the existence of a sophisticated legal machinery for securing the protection of a leper's goods and ensuring that he or she left the community when positively diagnosed (Clark, 'Social Welfare', p. 396).

75   Norfolk Record Office, Norwich Consistory Court Wills, Reg. Jekkys, f. 169; *Records of the City of Norwich*, vol. II, pp. 169–70.

76   *Records of the City of Norwich*, vol. II, pp. xcvi-c.

77   Rubin, *Charity and Community*, p. 126; M. Foucault, *Madness and Civilisation*, trans. R. Howard (London, 1971), p.6.

78   Rawcliffe, *Medicine and Society*, chapter I. For recent specialist literature on the subject see also, Horden 'A Discipline of Relevance', p. 361.

79   As, for example, *The Life and Miracles of St William of Norwich*, pp. 203–5.

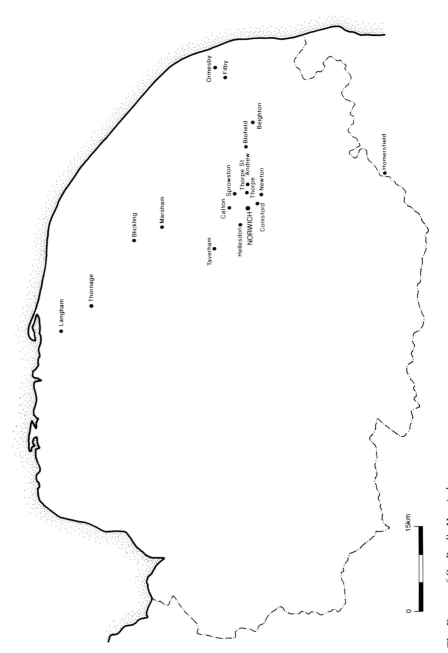

Ormesby

Filby

Beighton

Blofield

Thorpe St.
Andrew

Catton

Sprowston

Thorpe

Newton

Marsham

Hellesdon

NORWICH

Consford

Blickling

Taverham

Thornage

Homersfield

Langham

The Estates of St. Paul's Hospital

15km

0

CHAPTER II

St Paul's or Norman's Hospital

The arrival of the Normans in England was marked by an enthusiasm for the construction of new hospitals, which tends, in retrospect, to be overshadowed literally as well as figuratively by their achievements as military and ecclesiastical architects. Having established their presence in Norwich through the erection of two impressive stone-built monuments to colonial power – the castle and the cathedral – the city's new rulers soon turned their attention to charitable relief. The problem of caring for a growing number of sick or elderly individuals who lacked the means to support themselves may well have grown almost as pressing as that posed by the spread of leprosy, for Norwich was expanding rapidly during a period when recurrent years of famine, cattle plagues and low crop yields took a heavy toll of the most vulnerable members of society. Much of the initial impetus for the setting up of hospitals throughout England came from prominent churchmen, mindful of their responsibilities in this quarter, but the laity, most conspicuously in the persons of Henry I (d.1135) and his saintly first queen, Matilda (d.1118), followed (and sometimes outshone) their example. Royal involvement had the further advantage of attracting other powerful and wealthy benefactors, while also offering protection from predatory or litigious neighbours.[1]

With the exception of the Cathedral almonry, considered above, the first institution specifically established in Norwich for the relief of the sick poor was St Paul's hospital, which may in practice have been intended to ease the almoner's burden. Bishop Herbert de Losinga (d.1119) clearly played an important part at the planning stage, but, like so many hospitals of the period, it was a monastic rather than an episcopal foundation, set up in the early-twelfth century by Ingulf, the first prior of Norwich, and commonly known as 'Normanspital' after the monk whom he reputedly chose to be master.[2] Liberal gifts of property in Norfolk came from such influential benefactors as Everard, the city's second bishop (res. 1145), and Richard Beaufo, who served as archdeacon of Norwich (to 1115) before becoming bishop of Avranches. They, in turn, could rely upon the active support of King Henry, who was named, along with his successor, King Stephen (d.1154), the latter's wife, Matilda of Boulogne (d.1152), and Henry II (d.1189) on the list of patrons for whose souls prayers were to be said in perpetuity.[3]

The hospital of St Paul stood on land to the north of the river Wensum previously acquired from a pious donor by the Cathedral priory, in what was later to become the sub-leet of St Clement Fyebridge.[4] Because of successive nineteenth and twentieth-century road building and housing schemes in the area between Fishergate and Cowgate, no trace of either the medieval fabric or the adjacent parish church of St Paul (built at the same time on the other side of a narrow lane on the northern boundary of the precincts and bombed in the Second World War) now survives. At first, however, the hospital and its church constituted 'an island of urban development' in the open fields; and although they both lay some distance within the fourteenth-century city walls, the area immediately to the north and north-west was still uninhabited three hundred years later.[5] It was, indeed, a common practice to place hospitals for the sick poor as well as *leprosaria* on the outskirts of towns: a house of even moderate size, especially when served by its own church or chapel, would require a substantial amount of vacant land; and since most institutions provided hospitality for indigent wayfarers such a location gave easy access to travellers. Many patients might, moreover, be near to death, and thus, like lepers, occupy a position which was both symbolically and geographically on the edges of society.[6]

Although conceived on a relatively modest scale in comparison with Archbishop Lanfranc's three foundations for the sick and aged in Canterbury (which together housed nearly one hundred paupers, sixty lepers and an unspecified number of elderly priests), or St Leonard's hospital, York, with facilities for over 200 patients, St Paul's did far more than simply provide reserved accommodation for twenty or so 'poor and feeble people'.[7] The one surviving copy of the regulations, which are listed on a torn and undated roll, apparently compiled before the end of the thirteenth century, suggests that food and shelter had long been made available to any traveller in need of alms, while 'the sick, infirm and child-bearing poor of the city' could traditionally find succour there when they were ill.[8] As we have already seen, the demands of feeding, lodging and clothing a constant stream of pilgrims, beggars and local poor placed a greater strain on the resources of many English hospitals than the cost of supporting resident inmates. Philanthropists, such as Henry of Blois (d.1171), bishop of Winchester, who planned to house just thirteen paupers at the hospital of St Cross, but arranged for a hundred 'men of good conduct' to be given a square meal in the refectory every day, had therefore to ensure that a regular income would be forthcoming to meet this additional charge.[9]

The Endowment

Local historians have often associated Herbert de Losinga with the foundation of St Paul's hospital, but although the original idea was quite probably his most of the formal arrangements took shape a few years after his death.[10] According to an entry in the first register of Norwich Cathedral Priory, the hospital was officially established in the time of Bishop Everard with a grant from the prior and monks of Holy Trinity comprising the actual site of St Paul's, a share of tithes from the Norfolk parish churches of Blickling and Marsham, and, significantly, land in Sprowston, together with a stretch of property between what is now Mousehold Heath and the river Wensum, to the north-east of the city. The last two endowments were part of the manor of Thorpe, which Bishop Herbert had been given by Henry I for the support of his new cathedral, and where he had recently been instrumental in setting up Norwich's first leper house. A note that the monks made their gift 'for the upkeep of the poor for the soul of Herbert the Bishop and for the health of Bishop Everard' suggests that the latter probably inherited his predecessor's supervisory mantle, helping to bring an existing project to fruition.[11] Two years before Everard's consecration (which did not take place until 1121), the hospital had secured a title to one half of the tithes of the monastic church of Taverham in Norfolk, likewise for the benefit of the poor; and there is good reason to suppose that Richard Beaufo, sometime archdeacon of Norwich, had long been contemplating a role as one of the institution's leading patrons. It was, however, during Everard's time that he finally made over to St Paul's all the buildings, glebes, tithes and advowsons of his four parish churches in Ormesby, and that his kinsman, Adam de Beaufo, fully released any reversionary interest he might have in them. This grant was then consolidated by a personal gift from King Henry of the tithes and lands belonging to the royal hall there (*aula mea de Ormesby*) for the use of the new hospital; and the appropriation of the churches of St Margaret, St Michael, St Paul and St Andrew, Ormesby, *'ad opus hospitalis sancti Paulo in Norwico ac sustentationem pauperum in eodem hospitalis languentium'* was ratified by successive episcopal charters.[12] During the mid-fifteenth century, this joint endowment by the King and the archdeacon produced a net return of between £25 and £33 a year, and thus accounted for at least half of the 'hospital's regular annual income from property and franchises, which averaged about £55. A useful sum of £4 11s 3d a year was also being collected from the sheriff of Norfolk at Norwich Castle, the original grant having been made before 1127 by King Henry, in the form of a daily pension of 3d to be enjoyed by the hospital 'of the poor men of St Paul' for the health of his and his parents' souls.[13]

Additional help was forthcoming from Theobald of Bec, the archbishop of Canterbury, who at some point between 1139 and 1145 not only confirmed the hospital in all its possessions, but also dedicated the church and promised a perpetual indulgence of eight days' remission of penance to visitors arriving with charitable donations during the octave of the festival of the patron saint.[14] The feast of the decollation of St Paul fell on 30 June, but it was, in fact, the miracle of his conversion (25 January) which made him a popular choice as the dedicatee of hospitals. After his blinding vision on the road to Damascus, Paul (then Saul) of Tarsus, a sworn enemy of the Christian faith, had experienced physical and spiritual healing at the hands of the disciple, Ananias ('immediately there fell from his eye as it had been scales; and he received sight forthwith, and arose and was baptized': Acts

IX, v. 18), just as the bedridden sick hoped to do through the mediation of the Church. He had gone on, moreover, to perform a variety of miraculous cures himself, while preaching the need for compassion towards the suffering poor. It was thus particularly appropriate that Bishop Everard should offer an even more generous remission of forty days' penance to those who made the annual pilgrimage to the hospital church 'with oblation of alms or pious disposition of heart'. The freedom of the hospital and its residents from economic or legal interference by the civic authorities was also stressed, although Everard understandably placed great importance upon the obligation, incumbent upon staff and patients alike, to pray for the souls of their benefactors – among whom his own name occupied a prominent place.[15]

Another of these early deeds actually lists the eighteen tenants (including a cook, a carpenter and a baker) whose 'honest calling' made them eligible as residents of the area in and around the hospital precincts. 'Spiteland', 'Cow's Croft' or 'the Parish of St Paul', as this enclave was variously described, ranked as one of the four exempt jurisdictions claimed, much to the irritation of the citizens, by successive priors of Norwich.[16] The impressive series of royal charters confirming these liberties in the face of opposition, if not outright harassment, from the mayor and bailiffs cannot have come cheaply, and represented a considered investment on the part of the Cathedral Priory. Henry I, Henry II, John, Henry III, Edward I and Henry VIII in turn upheld the rights and privileges of St Paul's, most notably with regard to its exemption from outside tolls, customs and legal actions brought in the city courts.[17] So too did letters from the papal legate, the above-mentioned Henry of Blois, placing the hospital under the direct protection of the Holy See, and threatening sentence of anathema upon anyone who 'rashly disturbed' the people living there. Bulls of 1176, 1273 and 1274 included St Paul's and its possessions on the general list of monastic properties to enjoy this privilege; and in February 1273 (shortly after part of the Cathedral had been burnt down by the rioting citizenry) Gregory X issued a specific confirmation of liberties to the master and brethren, who must, understandably, have felt vulnerable to attack.[18]

An exact chronology of other twelfth– and thirteenth-century acquisitions is difficult to establish. When, in August 1198, John of Oxford, the then bishop, appropriated the neighbouring parish church of St Paul to the hospital, its revenues had been further augmented by one third of all tithes from the episcopal demesnes at Blofield, Thorpe St Andrew, Thornage and Langham, as well as half those from monastic properties in Newton.[19] The date of Walter Suffield's grant of further tithes from Thornham, Homersfield and Beighton may safely be ascribed to the early years of his episcopacy (he was consecrated in February 1245), since from 1248 or so onwards the establishment of his own hospital of St Giles, Bishopgate, took priority over other charitable ventures.[20] Suffield seems to have been the last of the house's ecclesiastical benefactors, and by then the modest but steady flow of lay gifts had also begun to decline, probably because his new foundation proved more attractive to local philanthropists.

Unlike St Giles's hospital, which would have been a far less impressive institution without the active support and involvement of some of Norwich's leading citizens, St Paul's derived most of its property from the Church. Yet if individual endowments were rarely made on anything approaching the scale of benefactions from senior clergy, the collective contribution of the laity should not be underestimated. It is, for example, important to remember that the original site of the hospital was given to the Cathedral monks by a landowner named Thurstan, and that Richard Beaufo's grant of land and tithes in Ormesby inspired a number of piecemeal gifts intended to consolidate this part of the estates.[21] Smallholdings worth a few shillings in Catton, Hellesdon and 'le Galetrehil' on the outskirts of Norwich likewise came from pious donors; by 1437 twenty-six separate rents in St Paul's parish were producing an annual income of 24s 9d; and between them tenements in six other city parishes then contributed at least 10s a year to the hospital's coffers.[22]

Although some of these properties had been purchased as an investment, the majority came from pious donors, anxious about the welfare of their immortal souls. An undertaking by Bishop John Gray, made in March 1201, that anyone helping the hospital in its financially demanding work for pilgrims, the sick and the infirm would be allowed to share in the spiritual merits accumulated through the prayers of the Cathedral monks may have prompted at least one major endowment: Morell de Morley and Emma, his wife, who had previously been at odds with the monastic community over the ownership of land in Filby, agreed to settle their interest upon the hospital, together with certain tithes, in return for full admission into the fraternity of Holy Trinity.[23] Similarly, in about 1263, John Knott of Norwich made over 'to God, the Blessed Virgin Mary and the hospital of St Paul' rents worth 8s 6d in Conisford for the health of his soul and the salvation of the souls of his ancestors; and at the end of the century Alice Bertram conveyed a plot in Blickling to St Paul's on behalf of her late husband and the recently deceased Queen Eleanor.[24] Alice's gift appears to have been made in contravention of the Statute of Mortmain of 1279, which prohibited the alienation of property to the Church without royal licence. This measure, intended to halt the steady erosion of crown revenues because so much land was being settled in perpetuity upon religious bodies, probably came too late to restrict the hospital's territorial expansion. At all events, neither the bishop nor the prior of Norwich ever sought permission at Westminster for any subsequent acquisitions to its holdings.

Along with a constant need to attract additional funding for the support of the sick poor, went the pressure of defending the property and franchises which the hopital already owned. Squabbles over legal titles were a commonplace of medieval life, whether lay or ecclesiastical, and disputes with neighbouring clergy, such as the vicar of Marsham, who in 1245 objected to paying tithes to the hospital, could hardly be avoided. In this instance, as in others, the quarrel was successfully settled through the arbitration of the bishop (Walter Suffield), who upheld the house's title to a share of the incumbent's annual receipts.[25] But what was to be done when the bishop himself proved intransigent? At the close of the fourteenth-century, the hospital was drawn into a serious conflict of interests between the bishop, in the intimidating person of Henry Despenser, probably the most colourful character to hold the see of Norwich, and the prior of Holy Trinity regarding the former's authority over the Cathedral monks. The prior's insistence upon a traditional right to nominate, inspect and if necessary remove the master of the hospital was referred, along with other contentious issues, to the mediation of the archbishop of Canterbury and the bishop of Hereford by papal mandate, in 1395, but the case had still to be settled seven years later. Ultimately, a compromise solution left the monks in control of the day to day management of St Paul's, which remained safely in the hands of an obedientiary appointed by the prior, while the bishop exercised the right of visitation.[26]

One of his principal concerns on such occasions was to ensure that the hospital statutes were being properly observed, and we are fortunate that some of the early (if not original) rules still survive. They reveal an obvious compassion for the plight of the sick and destitute, who were, however, to be carefully distinguished from the less deserving poor capable of supporting themselves. Discrimination in the matter of charitable effort by English monastic houses and a general move towards institutionalised, formal almsgiving may be clearly discerned from the twelfth century onwards, so it is hardly surprising that a degree of selectivity was maintained in this respect.[27] Yet, in theory at least, St Paul's still cast its net widely, offering help to a variety of needy cases.

The Hospital Statutes

As noted above, the founders, or their immediate successors, aimed to support up to twenty frail and impoverished people at any given time, never upon payment and only until they were well enough to make way for others. In addition, genuinely poor wayfarers seeking overnight accommodation were to be welcomed with bread and a dish of food, and sent off in the morning with more bread, according to their needs. Theoretically, at least, the portions appear to have been generous, being about half the size of the daily ration allocated to each of the hospital brethren. Since the latter were warned never to sell off what they could not eat, but to distribute any surplus as alms under the supervision of the master, it looks as if the monastic custom of sharing meals – or at least substantial quantities of leftovers – with the poor was observed. Evidently on the assumption that he would continue to be fed and clothed at the expense of the Cathedral priory, to which he belonged, the master was himself urged to apportion the standard allowance of food made to him from the hospital kitchens between two beggars every day at the gates. Christ had exhorted his followers to provide the destitute with clothing as well as food and drink, and the statutes also made provision for an annual expenditure of at least one mark (13s 4d) on shoes and two marks on cloth at Christmas. A minimum of about seventy-five yards of cheap blanket could thus have been divided up to make cloaks and jackets during the bitter East Anglian winter.[28]

The requirement that board and lodging should neither be offered for money or goods, nor made available to the healthy had a practical as well as a moral dimension. As direct heirs to a longstanding monastic tradition, hospitals customarily opened their doors to travellers of all types and social classes. The Latin word *xenodochium* was used interchangeably to describe a guest-house, institution for the sick or home for the elderly; and in some cases, especially on pilgrim routes or the outskirts of large cities, the provision of *hospitality* might well take precedence over everything else.[29] Yet whereas hospitals were supposed to give priority to poor pilgrims, along with other needy travellers, the temptation to provide well-heeled visitors with lodgings in return for cash or other, less tangible benefits was obviously great. But influential guests were far less amenable to discipline than grateful paupers, and sometimes behaved very badly indeed.

As the prior of the London hospital of St Mary's, Bishopsgate, learned to his cost, in 1378, not all boarders, however affluent, were prepared to settle their accounts. While living on the premises that summer, Sir Robert Aleyn's wife and her attendants had allegedly run up an enormous bill of £19 for 'dishes of cookery' and other comestibles, which they then refused to pay. After a delay of five years, the hospital authorities decided to incur the further expense of a lawsuit, although this was at best an uncertain gamble.[30] Over-indulgence apart, Lady Aleyn's conduct during her sojourn at St Mary's seems to have been unimpeachable, but some visitors posed far more than just a financial threat to their hosts. The probability that outsiders would disturb the quiet atmosphere essential for physical and spiritual regeneration prompted many benefactors (including Bishop Suffield, the founder of St Giles' hospital, discussed in Chapter IV) to insist that certain categories of people, such as female visitors, youths and henchmen, should be kept at arm's length.

A fundamental aspect of the *regimen sanitatis*, through which medieval physicians sought to safeguard their patients' health by preventative means, concentrated upon the need to avoid noise and stress; and these recommendations were redoubled in the case of illness.[31] Even more important, in the context of the medieval hospital, was the obligation to perform the daily offices and say the intercessionary prayers dedicated to the salvation of the souls of patrons and patients alike. From both a medical and theological point of view, therefore, it was essential to avoid unpleasant distractions, which could also undermine discipline. In 1470, for example, the master of St Germanus' hospital in Tranent, East Lothian, was upbraided for failing to admit the sick poor, while allowing laymen to take up residence with their wives and children 'as it were a private house, with occasional bloodshed'.[32] Probably the most outrageous of many cases of misbehaviour in hospital precincts occurred during the early-sixteenth century at St Mary's in the Newarke, Leicester, where the patron, Lady Hungerford, and her second husband came to stay with a large retinue of servants. Among the eighteen charges of riotous behaviour, drunkenness and affray levelled against this ill-disciplined crew were allegations that bear-baiting, 'May games', 'common spectacles' and pageants about Robin Hood had been staged in the hospital, while 'dogs, hawks and hounds came daily to the church ... defiling it shamefully, and barking and crying out when men be at divine service'. The accused countered by claiming that the canons and vicars kept dogs, too, which were 'indifferently whipped out from the choir'.[33]

It is to be hoped, then, that St Paul's remained a tranquil haven for the infirm, sick and child-bearing poor of Norwich, who had initially been promised food, rest and nursing appropriate to their requirements. The statutes suggest (but do not make absolutely clear) that these men and women constituted a separate category from the twenty 'feeble paupers', who might more accurately be described as almsmen. In this case, the average number of patients at any given time may well have been twice or even three times as large. Bishop Gray's attempt to encourage donations, in 1201, noted that the hospital's existing resources were insufficient to support the flood of pilgrims and sick paupers then seeking help: clearly, at this point, if not later, an attempt was being made to accommodate as many people as possible.[34]

Pregnant women and nursing mothers, who not only threatened to disrupt the highly regimented life of the medieval hospital, but also, to the clerical eye, seemed tainted with the stain of parturition, were not always welcome in such institutions. Indeed, St Paul's was the only hospital in medieval Norwich specifically to cater for them. The idea that disease and death had been unleashed upon the world through Eve's fatal transgression, and that her daughters were condemned to endure the pain of childbirth and curse of menstruation as a result ('I will greatly multiply thy sorrow and thy conception, in sorrow thou shalt bring forth children': Genesis III, v. 10), fostered a potent strain of misogyny in the Church.[35] Women who died while carrying an unbaptised child might be refused burial in consecrated ground or else buried there secretly without a proper funeral, while parish priests sometimes also denied Christian rites to anyone expiring in or just after a confinement because they too were deemed still to be defiled.[36] St John's hospital in Cambridge specifically excluded a list of undesirables, including lepers, wounded people (*vulnerati*), madmen and pregnant women: as well as being difficult, if not dangerous, to nurse, the leper and the lunatic also displayed very obvious marks of divine retribution for sin, as, in many cases, did those who had engaged in acts of violence. Similar restrictions obtained at the hospital of St John in Bridgwater, where expectant mothers and babies alike were consigned to the category of 'intolerable persons' and refused entry.[37]

This prejudice against pregnant women was no doubt intensified by the fact that many of the poor would be unmarried, perhaps driven by financial necessity into prostitution. Although, in 1240, the keeper of St John's hospital, Oxford, received a gift of £16 6s 8d from Henry III 'to make a chamber for the use of women labouring in childbirth', the hospital statutes refused to help anyone who might be considered 'lewd' or promiscuous. From an economic as well as a moral standpoint 'an unwed mother was an anomaly', whose desperate situation obliged her 'to fill the dual roles of nurturer and provider, to behave as both husband and wife'.[38] Single females who became pregnant often had little alternative but to conform to the worst ecclesiastical stereotypes simply to support themselves and their children. Yet St Mary Magdalen had herself once walked the streets (or so it was believed), and philanthropists such as the London mercer, Richard Whittington, recognised the importance of helping girls 'that hadde done a-mysse' so they could rebuild their lives afterwards. Although none of the City's hospitals provided special facilities staffed by trained midwives, as was the case at the Hotel Dieu in Paris and the hospital of Santa Maria Nuova in Florence, some responded to a pressing social need by admitting pregnant women and caring for the offspring of any who died in labour.[39]

These London hospitals customarily undertook to support and educate any children left orphaned at birth, being able to subsidise their schools because the high standards of tuition attracted private pupils as well. The survival at St Paul's of a tradition of teaching the very young suggests that here, too, the sisters took their responsibilities seriously. As an old man nearing eighty, the London priest, Thomas Salter, left them money in his will of 1558:

> bycause that I have a great truste that they wylle praye for me; and also bycause that a verie good, devowte syster of the said howse of Vincent Norman was the fyrst creature that tawght me to knowe the lettres in my booke: Dame Katherin Peckham was her name; I was skoller seventy-two years ago in the sayde parrysh of St Powle. I beseche Jhesu to have mercye on her sowle.[40]

Dame Katherine's involvement in the education of local children, perhaps even to the extent of running a small hospital school, shows how important the work of the sisters had become. For although the founders had clearly envisaged a mixed community of both men and women, in which the brethren would play a leading part, changes during the third quarter of the fourteenth century led to the emergence of a predominantly female establishment.

The Sisters and other Staff

Such a large and prestigious institution as St Paul's naturally required careful management and a sizeable workforce. According to the early statutes, an unspecified number of lay brothers and sisters were to live under a quasi-monastic regime, which demanded absolute obedience to the master and threatened everlasting anathema upon those who broke the rules, especially with regard to the sale of alms for personal profit. Newcomers had to surrender all their possessions to the master upon arrival, while promising under oath to hand over anything they might earn or acquire in future unless he agreed otherwise. In return, each one was guaranteed 'all things needful' until death, and, presumably, the spiritual benefits of a Christian burial in the neighbouring churchyard afterwards.[41] We may assume that the sisters were expected to tend the sick and the brothers to perform whatever manual or administrative tasks might be required around the precinct and on the estates, but for reasons now unknown this division of labour was eventually superseded. By the mid–1370s the lay brothers had disappeared, leaving a two-tier community of women, made up of 'whole sisters' on full board and 'half sisters', who were fed and clothed but not accommodated by the hospital.

In 1422–23, the date of the first surviving hospital account roll, the house engaged a chaplain, at an annual stipend of 53s 4d, to supervise the daily round of prayers, hear confessions and say mass for the inmates. All the work previously assigned to the brothers was, however, undertaken by a small group of laymen, comprising a cook, a bailiff, a carter and a jobbing labourer, the last of whom appears have been retained on a part-time basis. It was no doubt cheaper and more efficient to hire unskilled workmen as circumstances required, especially since they could be drawn from the larger pool maintained by the Cathedral monks.[42] A change in accounting practice and the method of remunerating servants was instituted at some point during the next decade, with the unfortunate result that it is now impossible to discover how many men remained on the hospital payroll or what they cost. In 1422–23, the wages of the four servants came to just over £4; a further £3 10s 7d was spent on food purchased for their hall; and some of the master's additional outlay of £11 16s 8d on fuel, salt, meat, fish and other such necessities was almost certainly incurred on their behalf as well. But by 1433 the authorities had adopted a different system, whereby virtually all regular expenditure on staff other than the sisters and their priest was met separately and no longer itemised in the annual accounts.

Apart from tithes and altarage, which in 1422–23 produced £43, the hospital's most valuable single source of revenue came from its horses and carts. These could be hired out at a fixed daily rate to tradespeople or landowners, and then raised more than enough (almost £13) to cover the entire outlay on servants. Attracted by the prospect of turning a net profit, the latter readily agreed to sub-contract the carting business themselves: their meals and wages were henceforward financed directly from the proceeds, and no mention of either the sums or the personnel involved was ever made in subsequent accounts. An unexpected shortfall of £15 in revenues between 1423 and 1433 was thus more apparent than real, being simply a consequence of the new procedure, which saw a corresponding decrease in recorded expenditure as well.[43] The master of St Paul's showed no inclination to drive a hard bargain by forcing his workmen to pay for repairs, new equipment and draught animals, even though the stock represented a major investment and proved costly to maintain. In 1434–35, for example, he spent almost £6 on iron-rimmed wheels, three more horses, veterinary bills and fodder; and from 1450 onwards, if not earlier, the bailiff was allowed an extra salary of 66s 8d from the hospital budget for looking after the horses and carts, over and above his usual wage, an annual livery (comprising a suit of clothes) and whatever surplus came his way from renting out haulage.[44]

The dramatic decline in income from the Cathedral Priory's estates during the latter part of the fifteenth century has been partly blamed upon the innate conservatism of previous generations of senior administrative staff. Yet Prior Burnham's decision in the early 1420s to cut his losses by leasing out what remained of the monastic demesnes must have seemed the only viable response to falling agricultural prices and soaring wage rates. In a small way, the servants at St Paul's reaped the benefit of this retreat from direct management, being strongly placed to negotiate advantageous terms for themselves. The bailiff, in particular, contrived to exploit a situation favourable to wage earners rather than employers: a lease drawn up in 1532 between John Ketteringham and the master followed established custom by allowing the new appointee to live free of charge in furnished rooms in the inner court of the hospital, taking seven loaves 'of the greater weight' from the bakery each week and ten gallons of ale at every brewing. He was, moreover, granted the farm of sixteen acres of land outside the city walls, again without charge, for the next seven years.[45] In return, he assumed responsibility for the routine supervision of the hospital estates, the upkeep of property and oversight of repairs (which, as we shall see, might involve considerable sums of money) and the collection of rents. Given that St Paul's could not perform its charitable work without him, such generous recompense may have been entirely justified, although it is unlikely that a lay employer would have been so open-handed. From about 1500 onwards, as it became necessary to cut back on all but the most essential items of expenditure, the bailiff seems to have been obliged to forgo some of his financial perquisites, negotiating alternative recompense instead. Yet other residents, living nearby in the sisters' quarters and the poor house, still had good reason to be envious.

During the fifteenth and early-sixteenth centuries, cash doles of 8d and 3d a week were assigned, respectively, to support each of the 'whole sisters' and 'half sisters', who may, in practice, have received bread, ale and herring to the same value. Assuming that the recipient already had a roof over her head, the higher rate, supplemented by legacies and gifts from pious benefactors and extra pittances distributed on major feast days, provided enough for basic subsistence in fifteenth-century England. Sweeping reforms of the almshouse at Sherborne, in Dorset, for example, ensured that from 1438 onwards the sixteen male and female inmates would each receive food and drink to the value of 7d a week, which was considered sufficient to maintain a respectable pauper without recourse to begging.[46] But the 'half sisters' at St Paul's were evidently expected to supplement their allowance: if they continued to live at home, and simply took one meal a day in the hospital, they would have needed at least 1d a week for rent, another 4d or so for food and money for fuel as well. Some may have found casual work, while others could no doubt rely upon a small income, perhaps left to them as widows or distributed through the auspices of one of the city's many craft mysteries and fraternities.

Charitable relief from the latter source was, however, far from generous. Whereas at the close of the fourteenth century a few of the richer Norwich guilds felt able to promise their members one shilling or more a week in the event of unforseen (but not self-induced) illness or destitution, others would have been hard put to raise a fraction of this sum. In practice, subventions often fell below the rate specified in the regulations, and were sporadic rather than regular. The evidence confidently presented by guilds throughout England in response to a government enquiry of 1388–89 must be used with caution. Even on paper, the Guild of Poor Men of St Augustine's parish, which lay quite near St Paul's hospital, could offer only limited mutual support. The pledge that 'if any brother or sister of this pouere gilde falle in any pouerte or secknesse, or any other meschef be the sendyng of Crist, and he may nought helpe him-self with his owen godis' he or she would receive 3d each week seems unduly optimistic. The large and relatively affluent Guild of St George, with its membership of aldermen and city merchants, only managed to subsidise an average of two or three people a year between 1427 and 1447, albeit in this instance private almsdeeds, intended to respect the sensibilities of 'shamefaced' paupers who had known better times, were no doubt widely forthcoming.[47]

Although it, too, was constrained by difficult financial circumstances, the hospital of St Paul was able to investigate and support a number of deserving cases who may have received no more than occasional alms from a parochial or craft fraternity: in 1433–34, 1450–51 and 1452–53 it was assisting thirteen 'whole sisters' and eleven 'half sisters', which, allowing for sudden death or unforeseen absence, seems to have been the usual complement during the fifteenth century. A similar change, whereby women apparently took priority over men as recipients of institutionalised charity, may be observed in York. All the city's *maisons dieu* accepted women, and by the close of the Middle Ages three hospitals were reserved for them alone. As Patricia Cullum notes, the economic depression of the late fifteenth and early-sixteenth centuries had disastrous consequences for the female labour force, not least because it intensified the restrictive practices of the male craft guilds. Yet, once again, questions of morality may have proved decisive. Poor women of good character and mature years, whose circumstances were known to the local authorities, presented a more acceptable face of poverty than vagrants or unemployed men.[48]

Compared with St Giles's in Bishopgate and many other English hospitals, the ratio of sisters to patients (who can rarely during this period have numbered more than the score or so for which the founders had made provision) seems remarkably high. It is, however, important to remember that all ranked as almswomen, and some would already have been old or infirm. In certain Florentine hospitals, where impoverished single women and widows were pleased to offer their services as nurses and domestic servants in return for the promise of permanent shelter, the sick could rely upon a superabundance of carers who were themselves in need of charitable relief and would, eventually, end their days as patients.[49] During the later Middle Ages, the 'poor sisters' of St Paul's hospital often received modest bequests of a few pence or shillings from Norwich testators, which confirms that, initially at least, they were viewed in the same light. Friction between the civic authorities and the Cathedral monks over the hospital's rights and franchises certainly did not deter laymen and women from giving generously to the sick paupers and especially to their nurses. Nor can the fact that donations of land or rents to the hospital became so few and far between after the late-thirteenth century be taken as evidence of growing indifference to, or even antagonism towards, the needy who found refuge there.

An analysis of the wills made by 615 citizens and 289 secular priests dying in

4. St Elizabeth of Hungary served as a model to all pious women in the later Middle Ages. They were expected to care for the sick and tend the poor as a work of Christian charity especially incumbent upon the female sex. Elizabeth not only founded hospitals, but also performed the most menial duties as a nurse.

Norwich between 1370 and 1532 reveals, for example, that about a third of all testators left at least a few pence to the sisters of St Paul's, sometimes supplementing their bequests with gifts of bedding or furniture.[50] In 1500, for example, John Newman promised 2d to each 'whole' sister and an image of John the Baptist to the others, presumably on the assumption that it would be sold. Some donors were remarkably generous: from John Porter (1499) came 6s 8d to be shared between all the sisters, along with 'a petaunce of vijd every day by the space of vij dayes'; from Richard Albon (1476) doles of 8d each; from Robert Hekelyng (1483) 6d each and no less than 10s for one sister named Isabel Hedde, who may have been a relative; and from John Narborough 'ij peir shetes ... for the beddes of poure pepyll in the almes howse' and 4d for each of their nurses. Most notable of all was Sir Thomas Erpingham's gift, made in 1428, of two separate sums of ten marks (£6 13s 4d), one to 'the sustres and poure folk' of St Giles's hospital Bishopgate and the second to the inmates of 'Normannys'.[51] Perhaps some of these women required no more than temporary assistance: although the surviving statutes assumed that sisters who had sworn the oath of obedience would remain cloistered in St Paul's until they died, the new 'half sisters' were bound by no such restriction. On the contrary, one left the house 'and never returned' in March 1434, having been sent on her way with a subvention of 33s 4d; and another disappeared for months on end during the following year.[52]

The fall in hospital revenues evident by 1475 [TABLES A and B] may have led to stringent economies, for by then payments to a mere twelve sisters, of whom seven received full board, are recorded. Moreover, those who did gain admittance may no longer have been ready to perform menial nursing tasks in return for accommodation. Bishop Goldwell's visitation of 1492 found that each of the sisters, then fifteen in number, had been obliged to pay the master ten marks (the equivalent of Erpingham's munificent legacy) in order to gain admittance, even though such practices were categorically forbidden in the foundation statutes. It was, however, just as well that the women in question possessed some private means, since rents had fallen so badly in arrears that stipends often remained unpaid for upwards of eight or ten weeks.[53] The sale of corrodies (which secured for the recipient board, lodging and perhaps also robes) was then a common practice in almost all the larger English hospitals. It tended to deprive the most vulnerable poor of support originally reserved for them alone, and insidiously changed the nature and purpose of the institutions concerned. Even so, contrary to the trenchant views expressed by contemporary critics, not all the beneficiaries were rich or even moderately well-heeled: although their situation could hardly be compared with that of bedridden paupers or vagrants soliciting alms, some corrodians badly needed help. Elderly widows no longer capable of work, or young ones overburdened with children could not, for example, expect to remain for long above the poverty line, and gladly exchanged what little money or few possessions they had in return for the promise of shelter. If, in some cases, this meant that hospitals could no longer rely upon all their female pensioners to perform nursing duties and even added to the burden of those who still did so, it at least provided a valuable safety-net for individuals with an otherwise uncertain future and thus constituted a legitimate work of charity among the deserving.[54]

None the less, in a period of economic contraction, the temptation to use corrodies as a means of raising money or acquiring land, and thus to sell them competitively on the open market, became increasingly hard to resist. As the author of *Dives and Pauper*, one of many late medieval tracts concerned with the virtues of 'holy poverty', complained, the admission of wealthy boarders and liveried dependents into a hospital or monastery was fraught with practical as well as moral dangers:

> The goodis of holy chirche so wel induyd ben gouyn to helpe of the pore peple and to kepyn hospitalyte, not to sellyn is agen to riche men to mentethin hem in onlusthed and in bodely hese, but that the clerkis that seruyn the chirche schuldyn lyuyn therby and to spendyn the remenant in hospitalyte and in elmesse-geuynge to the pore peple; and so the goodis of that colege ben nout here but as dispensouris, for it ben the pore mennys to whom and for whom it wern gouyn. And be swyche lyuersonys the colegis ben brout to pouert, and the pore folc and the seek folc schuldyn ben holpyn therby ben fraudyt and robbyd of her ryght, and personys ben mad ryche and the comounte mad ouyr-pore. And charite is exylyd out of the congregacion, for whan the monye is payyd the religious that seldyn the lyuersonys desyryn the deth of the byere.[55]

Nor was this all. Commissioners sent to investigate abuses at the hospital of the Holy Innocents, Beverley, in 1316, reported with dismay that the new inmates, who had paid handsomely for admission, felt in no way obliged to spend their days in church. Indeed, they categorically refused to pray for the souls of the royal founders 'as they are bound to do and as the other brethren do'.[56] During the later Middle Ages, St Saviour's hospital in Bury St Edmunds became something of a retirement home for friends, servants and relatives of the abbot, with a long waiting list of affluent townsfolk ready to pledge large sums in anticipation of their future comfort.[57] A potentially serious problem had, meanwhile, developed at St Leonard's York, one of the country's largest hospitals, where, between 1392 and 1409, no less than sixty-six corrodies were sold on the open market, along with forty or so liveries (which cost rather less and brought fewer privileges, but undoubtedly helped the elderly). In principle, funds could be raised quickly in this way to pay off debts or finance costly building projects, but the officials concerned inevitably laid themselves open to charges of profiteering, or worse; and unless great care was taken only to accept elderly or frail corrodians, the hospital could find itself far poorer, saddled with long term commitments to healthy men and women who stubbornly refused to die.[58]

The annual return on a corrody bought competitively on the open market came to about one tenth of the total investment, which meant that if the purchaser survived for more than a decade after making the arrangement the hospital would have to start using its own funds to support him or her. In practice, since many institutions (such as St Saviour's) were either unwilling or unable to engage in long-term financial planning, corrodians became a drain on resources as soon as their money had been spent. The prospect of lost revenues, as much as any diminution of spiritual life, worried episcopal visitors throughout England: in 1387, for example, Bishop Wykeham of Winchester complained that the reserves of St Thomas's hospital, Southwark, had been dissipated 'by indiscreet sales and grantings of liveries and corrodies', and warned that the practice should stop. At the same time, he rebuked some of the nurses, who were probably corrodians, for neglecting their patients.[59]

Although driven by financial necessity to charge sisters the equivalent of four years' support for admission, St Paul's appears to have avoided such flagrant commercialism. It survived the dissolution of the Cathedral Priory, being placed under the immediate direction of a senior nursing sister, who was herself answerable to the newly constituted Cathedral chapter. For three decades after the Reformation (by which time revenues had slumped to less than £30 a year) it provided a refuge for the sick poor and continued to attract bequests from local testators. Surviving wills of the period refer to the 'armesse-house' or 'poore-house' of the hospital, with its 'pore mennys beddys' and sick, paralytic patients, although only a handful were accommodated at any given time.[60] Finally, in 1565, the civic authorities negotiated with the dean and chapter a 500 years' lease

> of all those their chambers, lodginges, howses, buyldynges, gardeyns and yardes of the hospytall of St Powle, commonly called the Normans, scituate and being in the parrisshe of Saincte Powle in Norwiche, as they lately wer in the handes, rule, governement and custodye of one Mystres Agnes Lyon, now departed, somtyme a syster of the same hows or hospytall, and heretofore used for the comfort, relieff and lodgynges of pore straungers, vagrantes, syck and impotent persons, together with all the bedsteddes, beddyng, clothing and stuff belonging to the ... seid hows or hospytall.[61]

Despite a clear undertaking that the buildings in question would still be used as 'allmes howses and lodginges for pore straungers, vagrantes, syck and impotent persons', as had been the case since the early-twelfth century, within a few years St Paul's had been converted into a bridewell for the correction of lazy beggars.[62] The lease does not mention the teaching work of the sisters, possibly because it was done on an informal basis. Whatever their attitude to the menial task of nursing sick paupers, some of the corrodians, such as Dame Katherine Peckham, who had enjoyed the benefits of education (a clear sign of improvements in social status), were prepared to pass on their skills to the young.

The Hospital's Finances

So far as we can tell from the six detailed and eleven short accounts of annual income and expenditure still preserved in the Cathedral archive, St Paul's was managed quite efficiently, at least to the extent of avoiding massive debts or failing to collect its revenues on time. Nor is there any evidence of the ambitious architectural ventures which plunged many such houses into debt by turning them into grand colleges for secular priests with expensive tastes. At St Saviour's, Bury St Edmunds, another monastic hospital, the master was obliged in 1375 to make up a deficit of £38 from his own coffers; and a decade later, at the close of the accounting year 1385–86, expenses (£185) exceeded receipts (£104) by £81. Because of elaborate building works and redecoration in the chapel, expenditure soared to £234 in the following year, while income remained virtually unchanged at £106. It is thus hardly surprising that the authorities used every means at their disposal to raise money, including the short-term expedient of selling corrodies. In 1392, for example, one John Reeve paid 26 marks (£17 6s 8d) towards the cost of the new fabric in return for a lifetime's food and lodging, which was in part to be supplied from a 'poor man's place'.[63]

Problems may, however, have arisen at St Paul's during this period, for we have no information about its late-fourteenth and early fifteenth-century finances beyond two brief statements for 1363 and 1364. These appear in the earliest surviving composite accounts to be compiled from particulars of income and expenditure rendered by each of the twelve obedientiaries of the Cathedral Priory and the heads of its five dependent houses. The master of the hospital ranked among the six highest spending officials, with about three per cent of the monastery's net receipts at his disposal, and was naturally included in the annual *status obedientiarum*. St Paul's evidently overspent by £26 in 1363 and £25 in 1364, which, although by no means as serious as the alarming situation later encountered at St Saviour's, must still have caused some concern, since income fell from £71 to £64 over these two years [TABLE B]. By 1423, the balance had changed completely, with almost £7 in hand, and remained fairly healthy until 1453, when the house again found itself in debt to the tune of almost £25.

On the last occasion, if not previously, apparent overspending was due not to extravagance or bad management but to the cost of essential repairs and building work, necessary to keep property in a viable state for leasing, to protect the fabric of barns and storehouses and ensure that the hospital's churches were decently

TABLE A

The Finances of St Paul's Hospital, 1422-1510

Year	1422-23	1433-34	1434-35	1450-51	1452-53	1509-10
Arrears	8 3 5¼	1 7 0½	-	-	-	5 7 11
Rents	6 8 6	6 13 4	6 12 4	6 1 5	6 1 2	3 10 9
Tithes	43 7 8½	52 14 9	52 6 2	51 3 4½	56 19 10	29 6 10½
Miscellaneous	22 2 10	5 2 2	1 14 2	4 18 10	18 11 4	-
TOTAL INCOME	80 2 5¾	65 17 3½	60 12 8	62 3 7½	71 12 4	38 5 6½
Deficit last year	-	-	7 10 0	14 11 8¼	12 16 3¼	2 2 4
Sisters	14 13 10½	28 2 0	26 2 3	29 14 4	29 18 2	15 7 8
Repairs	14 2 0½	23 10 2	6 1 5	4 2 7½	23 7 4	3 10 9
Miscellaneous	12 17 9¼	16 11 5½	13 15 5	17 17 5	22 9 6¼	20 12 9½
Wages	6 15 2	2 19 0	2 15 8	7 13 1	7 14 3½	-
Servants' Hall	3 10 7	-	-	-	-	-
Equipment	9 8 9½	2 4 8	6 15 8	-	-	-
Bakery, Larder	11 16 8	-	-	-	-	-
TOTAL EXPENSES	73 4 10¾ *	73 7 3½	63 0 5	73 19 1¾	96 5 7	41 13 6½
In hand/deficit	+ 6 17 7	- 7 10 0	- 2 7 9	-11 15 6¼	-24 13 3	- 3 8 0

Norfolk Record Office, DCN 2/5/1-3, 5-7

* A mistake in the account gives expenses of £72 9s 10¾d, and £7 12s 7d in hand.

TABLE B

The Finances of St Paul's Hospital and Norwich Cathedral Priory, 1363-1534

Year	1363	1364	1409-10*	1434-35	1471-72	1475-76	1476-77	1531	1532	1533	1534
St Paul's alone											
Income	71 12 8½	64 5 1	68 17 4½	60 12 8	40 0 0½	36 2 4½	36 9 0½	25 15 10	23 14 9	24 5 5	34 16 9
Expenses	98 2 9½	89 12 11½	82 7 10	63 0 5	46 9 8	43 13 11¼	46 10 2	25 2 11¾	25 7 2½	25 19 0½	25 10 6½
Entire Priory											
Income	2260 12 10¾	2286 14 6	2200 14 9¼	1610 7 3¾	1495 2 3	1521 9 4¾	1518 5 7	1066 1 3	1025 10 3¼	906 12 2	941 0 6¾
Expenses	2773 7 4¼	2815 11 1	2235 10 4¾	1960 17 0¾	1218 12 11	1318 1 11¼	1259 12 7	1084 3 0¼	1161 8 10¾	1160 11 0	951 17 2¾

Norfolk Record Office DCN 1/13/1-6

* Originally dated 1505-6 in the NRO list of Dean and Chapter Records (2 Robert de Catton), this document should be 1409-10 (2 Robert de Burnham).

maintained as the ecclesiastical authorities required. In both 1433–34 and 1452–53 the annual repair bill accounted for about one third of net receipts: on the first occasion, a large new barn had to be constructed at Ormesby to store the grain collected by St Paul's as tithes; and on the second extensive improvements were made to tenements in the hospital precincts. No medieval landowner, however prudent, could afford to let a major source of income fall into decay, but the cost could make serious inroads into an already tight budget. Agricultural and building workers in the 1450s earned enough to purchase twice as much grain as their fourteenth-century predecessors, leaving employers whose rents or tithes were paid in malt or barley at an even greater disadvantage. In addition, a myriad of small expenses – making good storm damage, renewing thatch, replacing broken windows – insidiously ate away any cash surplus.[64]

Faced with a decline of almost fifty per cent in net receipts over the century before the Reformation, successive masters of St Paul's seem to have done their best to effect stringent economies. Once the decision had been made to farm the carting business out to the servants and make them self-supporting, the accounting procedure was considerably simplified. To facilitate analysis here, major items of hospital income and expenditure after 1423 have been grouped into eight basic categories, which correspond roughly with the layout of the original documents [TABLE A]. The hospital drew its revenues from three sources: rents from the Norwich area, including the sheriff's annual payment of Henry I's livery; tithes and altarage from various parts of Norfolk; and 'casual' receipts, raised from the sale of surplus stock and produce, as well as such unpredictable sources as alms and legacies. In 1452–53, for example, the master received £8 13s 4d in charitable donations and a further £8 which was described as 'alms' but had actually been paid by a local resident towards the cost of building works on her own land.[65]

As might be expected, the main charge on the hospital's finances constituted the payment of weekly doles to the sisters. Far smaller sums were assigned for oil to keep their lamps burning, pittances on feast days and occasional modest gifts of a few pence to the patients in their care. Since male servants were neither fed nor paid out of the main budget after 1433, the relatively small wage bill is somewhat deceptive. It includes only the priest's annual stipend of 53s 4d, together with the cost of hoods and coats for lesser clerical staff (who are not otherwise mentioned), rewards to the bailiff and, briefly, the extra fee of 66s 8d allocated to him for looking after the horses and carts. In 1509, when cash receipts had plummeted below £33, these payments were either made from another source or else renegotiated in kind. Purchases of equipment, too, seem to have been reduced as part of a cost-cutting exercise. The hospital was less well able to avoid the host of 'foreign' or outside expenses incurred by any institution: on top of the inevitable legal fees, rents to other landowners and douceurs to local officials came dues to the Cathedral Priory, quite substantial payments (of £6 or more) to the vicar of Ormesby for his cure of souls and travel expenses sustained by members of staff. The master also claimed an allowance for clothing and medical care, although none of the inmates enjoyed the uncertain benefits of professional treatment.

The absence, from 1433 onwards, of any references to the purchase of food suggests that, while the servants supplied their own hall out of the profits made from carting and the sisters were paid their doles, no sustained attempt was being made to succour the wayfaring poor as had previously been the case. We do not know how much the hospital managed to raise in alms and charitable donations made by visitors to St Paul's church, which may have paid for some ad hoc outdoor relief, but the sums involved are unlikely to have been very large. Nor is there much evidence of activity in the *domus dei*, where no more than a few infirm paupers found refuge. Did the gradual rise in working class standards of living discernible after the Black Death make the wholesale distribution of alms unnecessary, or had the Cathedral monks adopted the deliberate policy of restricting their charitable effort to a narrow group of resident, deserving, female poor? Perhaps they had little choice in the matter, for although food shortages and rising levels of poverty and homelessness had already taken their toll in Norwich before the Reformation, St Paul's lacked the resources to cope adequately with the demands of the sisters, let alone to tackle these additional problems.[66]

Whereas Norwich itself was slightly cushioned against recession by developments in the woollen industry, Norfolk as a whole experienced a steady contraction of population up to the 1470s, made worse by successive outbreaks of plague. As noted above, landlords caught between the pincers of rising labour costs and falling grain prices generally chose to lease out their demesne farms to tenants; but since the latter tended to pay rents – and, significantly in this context, tithes to the Church – in barley or malt, their predicament hardly improved. The upturn in the national economy evident between 1470 and 1500 was less pronounced in the barley producing areas of East Anglia, where supply far outstripped demand. Like most local farmers, the Clere family of Ormesby Hall, who must have paid tithes and altarage to the hospital church of Ormesby St Margaret, went in for intensive barley cultivation on their estates. In order to sell in bulk they had to ship their grain as far afield as Newcastle-upon-Tyne and London, thus reducing a shrinking profit margin even further. As rentiers, their neighbours, the Pastons, were obliged either to accept barley rents or wait until their tenant farmers could raise the necessary cash themselves. It was, for example, noted in the early 1440s that one such leaseholder could 'not yet gete monay, for his cornes arn at so litell price that he can not vtter them, and yet ther is noman wole bye it for al the gret chep'.[67]

The depressed state of the local grain market clearly spelt trouble for ecclesiastical landlords, who relied heavily upon tithes and rents in kind. The fortunate survival of eleven statements of account, summarising the finances of the entire Cathedral Priory at various points between 1363 and 1534, enables us to assess the position of St Paul's hospital in a wider context, and thus appreciate the constraints under which the master was forced to operate [TABLE B]. Such an exercise is rarely possible in the case of English hospitals run by monasteries, making it hard to tell how far their economic difficulties were shared with, or even caused by, the mother house. The evidence of these records suggests that St Paul's enjoyed a fairly steady, albeit sometimes inadequate, income until real decline set in during the third quarter of the fifteenth century, as the worsening economic situation began to bite. Certainly, by the 1530s, when revenues hovered around £24 a year, the outlook seemed very bleak indeed, reflecting that of the Priory as a whole. The masters of the hospital quite evidently fell victim to circumstances beyond their control, being required, like all the other obedientiaries, to tighten their belts as revenues dwindled.

In 1533, Sir Thomas More wrote approvingly of the efforts made by the monks of Westminster Abbey to relieve poverty. 'I vse not myche my slefe to go very farre abrode,' he remarked, 'and yet I here some say that there is, and I se som tyme my selfe, so many poore folke at Westmynster at the dolys [doles], of whome, as farre as euer I harde, the munkes vse not to sende awaye many vnserued, that my self for the preace [press] of them haue ben fayn to ryde another waye'.[68] Such crowds are unlikely to have gathered outside St Paul's hospital, where the sisters themselves may sometimes have gone hungry because their stipends fell into arrears.[69] A rather more systematic attempt to feed the poor was still being made at the Cathedral Priory, although it could boast neither the landed income nor, significantly, the royal patronage which made possible the apparent largesse of the Westminster Benedictines. In the accounting year 1532–33, the almoner spent almost £12 on the annual provision of bread and other alms out of a total outlay of £40, which was exactly half the sum set aside for this purpose in 1466–67, but rather more than was customary in the early-sixteenth century because of falling revenues. On the assumption that each quarter of grain bought in 1532–33 produced about 250 standard two-pound loaves (always depending on the density of the grain used), the almoner would then have been able to distribute some 375 wheaten loaves on the anniversary of Bishop Herbert Losinga and a further 6,250 coarser, cheaper ones of mixed corn (usually rye, wheat, barley and even bran) throughout the year.[70]

Two pounds of bread yields just over 2,000 calories and is considered sufficient to sustain one moderately active person for a day at subsistence level. If all the mixed grain purchased in 1532–33 was, in fact, earmarked for baking, a daily average of seventeen 'mixed' loaves would have been produced for almsgiving by the monks, although in practice such factors as the weather and the availability of casual work would have made for marked seasonal variations. The almoner also accounted for 36s 4d spent on cash doles (the equivalent of 8d a week) shared among all comers, in memory of Bishop Herbert. The *Valor Ecclesiasticus*, compiled three years later, records a slightly larger amount of 40s, while noting that no less than £10 was set aside annually on Maundy Thursday to provide the poor with 'bread, herring, drink and money', according to the Bishop's wishes. In addition, and for the same reason, twelve paupers were given dinner and supper each day in the Priory hall at a total annual cost of £16 18s 10d.[71] Yet however superficially generous these last two sums may appear, they constituted only a fraction of overall expenditure [TABLE B]; and confirm the impression, gained by historians from the early years of this century onwards, that voluntary almsgiving by the great English monastic houses was one of the first casualties of the fifteenth century economic crisis, and no doubt also the result of a more discriminating attitude towards the 'naked', migrant poor.[72]

With the exception of the Maundy Thursday doles, required of the house by its founder, Norwich Cathedral Priory was neither sufficiently constrained by the requirements of past benefactors nor, indeed, rich enough to provide relief on anything approaching the scale offered at Westminster or even in many affluent lay households. As an old man, the sixteenth-century chronicler, John Stow, reflected on 'charitable almes in old times given', recording how

> I my selfe, in that declining time of charity, haue oft seene at the Lord Cromwels gate in London, more than two hundered persons serued twise euery day with bread, meate and drinke sufficient, for hee obsuered that auncient and charitable custome as all prelates, noble men, or men of honour and worship his predecessors had done before him.[73]

It would be misleading to make so direct a comparison between the almoner's relatively modest outlay in the 1530s and the impressive annual expenditure of as much as £104 on food and clothing incurred by his predecessors in the 1280s, since their spending power was correspondingly greater and Norwich was expanding dramatically under an influx of rural poor. It is, however, worth noting that up to eighty-three per cent of their budget then went on charitable relief: indeed, so far as we can tell, a fairly steady consumption of 350 to 400 quarters of grain a year was maintained during the late thirteenth century and the first four decades of the fourteenth century, irrespective of fluctuating prices. This would have made possible an *average* daily distribution of between 240 and 274 loaves, although some supplies of grain and flour may have been given directly to impoverished householders for baking, which in itself would represent a more selective type of philanthropy.[74]

Allowing for the fact that other monastic obedientiaries shared some of the burden, an analysis of the 138 surviving almoners' accounts (which begin in 1275) reveals a significant decline in charitable provision over the years between the first outbreak of the Black Death and the Reformation. Some of these rolls give details of the amount of grain actually milled before distribution, and therefore provide a more accurate idea of the quantities available for baking than those which simply record purchases. In the latter case, the almoner might have drawn upon reserve supplies of rye or barley to augment what was bought or, conversely, have chosen to fill his granary at an attractive price. Perhaps he sometimes elected to provide poor local families with grain rather than bread: in 1491–92, for example, only half of the hundred quarters bought at a total cost of £20 went to the miller, although by and large, when they are both available, the two sets of figures correspond quite closely.[75]

With this caveat in mind, it appears that between 1378 and 1391 an average of 132 quarters of grain a year was being milled, the lower and upper limits ranging from a mere fifty-two quarters in 1378–79 to an unusually generous 178 quarters in 1390–91.[76] At the turn of the century (1395–1402) the average annual purchase stood at 115 quarters, which was, in turn, considerably larger than that sustained over the next four decades.[77] Then the average hovered around seventy-six quarters a year, with a high of 140 in 1426–27 and a low of no more than thirty-five in 1423–24, when the last of the monastic demesnes were being leased out to tenant farmers.[78] The middle years of the century, from 1447 to 1469 saw comparatively little change. Although the almoner reverted to his earlier practice of recording exactly what went to the mill, the yearly average of seventy-eight quarters confirms that further economies did not seem necessary.[79] The situation worsened over the next twenty-five years, though, as declining revenues demanded severe cuts across the monastic budget, and the average quantity of grain milled each year fell by almost half to forty-four quarters. Indeed, the exceptionally large consignment of seventy-two quarters milled in 1477–78 was *less* than the average amount generally available for distribution not so long before.[80] This cost cutting exercise continued right up to the Dissolution: from 1499 to 1533 purchases were reduced by about twenty-five per cent, averaging no more than twenty-four quarters a year after 1521. The disastrous effects of the two fires of 1507, which resulted in the loss of over 700 houses in sixteen Norwich parishes, further exacerbated the almoner's plight. Under normal circumstances, he would have lacked the resources to cope with such a great mass of homeless people, and since his own income from city rents had fallen from £10 a year to 19s because of the fire, he was even less able to help. Rebuilding proceeded at a snail's pace, not least because the slump in the overseas worsted market and the rising cost of food had hit the region so badly.[81]

For both the almoner and the master of St Paul's hospital the problems faced by landowners after the Black Death of 1348–49 and subsequent outbreaks of plague may initially have been made easier to bear because of the general rise in living standards experienced by the rural and urban poor, who had less need of their charity. Improvements in diet, health and housing as the population grew smaller must have eased their collective burden, as, quite possibly, may the climatic trends evident between the 1350s and the start of the 'Little Ice Age' in the early seventeenth century, during which period the weather became slightly cooler but more equable.[82] By the end of the fifteenth-century, however, when demographic and economic changes already threatened to upset this settled state of affairs, neither St Paul's nor the Cathedral almonry was in a strong position to assist the growing number of sick, elderly and homeless paupers. On the contrary, it became increasingly difficult for them to do more than perform the absolute minimum required.

END NOTES

1   Kealey, *Medieval Medicus*, pp. 82–106.

2   Brief accounts of the hospital may be found in *The Victoria History of the County of Norfolk, II*, pp. 447–48; Kirkpatrick, *History of the Religious Orders*, pp. 194–220; and Blomefield, *History of the County of Norfolk*, vol. IV, pp. 429–33.

3   Prayers were still being said for their souls in 1535, *Valor Ecclesiasticus*, vol. III, p. 287.

4   During the first half of the twelfth century, Bartholomew, son of the original donor, one Thurstan son of Guy, confirmed that his parents had granted the Cathedral monks 'land and houses next to Fyebridge and land where the Hospital of St Paul is situated' (*The First Register of Norwich Cathedral Priory*, ed. H.W. Saunders (Norfolk Record Society, XI, 1939), p. 65).

5   J. Campbell, *Norwich* (Historic Towns Trust, 1975), pp. 8–9 and Map 3.

6   A lucid account of the marginal position of hospitals may be found in Geremek, *Margins of Society*, pp. 169–79.

7   Kealey, *Medieval Medicus*, pp. 86–87; Cullum, *Cremetts and Corrodies*, pp. 7–9.

8   Norfolk Record Office, DCN 2/5/8. This document has been edited and translated by E.H. Carter, 'The Constitutions of the Hospital of St Paul (Normanspitel) in Norwich', *Norfolk Archaeology*, XXV (1935), pp. 342–53.

9   The hospital of St Cross was founded in about 1136 for thirteen 'poor and impotent men, so reduced in strength as rarely or never to be able to raise themselves without the assistance of another', and for the further provision of a meal each day for one hundred paupers. Since the latter were allowed to take away any leftovers, they would have been able to feed dependents as well (*The Victoria History of the County of Hampshire and the Isle of Wight*, II, ed. H.A. Doubleday and W. Page (London, 1903), pp. 193–94).

10   Both *The Victoria History of the County of Norfolk*, II, p. 447, and A. Jessopp in his edition of *Visitations of the Diocese of Norwich 1492–1532* (Camden Society, new series, XLIII, 1888), p. 43, make this assumption.

11   *First Register of Norwich Cathedral Priory*, p. 63. This charter was misread by Kealey (*Medieval Medicus*, p. 156) as the foundation deed of St Giles's hospital, Bishopgate, which was set up in 1249. A roll of early charters of St Paul's, confirmed by Bishop Salmon in 1301, is printed in full in *The Charters of Norwich Cathedral Priory*, ed. B. Dodwell (Pipe Roll Society, new series, vols XL, 1965–66, and XLVI, 1978–80), vol. I, no. 259.

12   *Charters of Norwich Cathedral Priory*, vol. I, nos 98, 100, 102, 104, 256–57; vol. II, no. 496.

13   Norfolk Record Office, DCN 2/5/1–3, 5–7; *Charters of Norwich Cathedral Priory*, vol. I, nos 99, 101.

14   A. Saltman, *Theobald Archbishop of Canterbury* (London, 1956), no. 188.

15   *Charters of Norwich Cathedral Priory*, vol. I, nos 254, 258.

16   Ibid., p. 65; Campbell, *Norwich*, pp. 8–9; Norfolk Record Office, DCN 40/21A-B (a sixteenth-century list of the hospital's jurisdictions).

17   *Charters of Norwich Cathedral Priory*, vol. I, nos 35, 43 (marginalia), 59 (marginalia), 62, 103, 105; *Letters and Papers Foreign and Domestic, Henry VIII*, ed. J.S. Brewer (4 vols, London, 1920), vol. I, part I, no. 546 (14).

18   *Charters of Norwich Cathedral Priory*, vol. I, nos 259, 310–11, 317.

19   Ibid., nos 257, 259; *First Register of Norwich Cathedral Priory*, p. 87.

20   Blomefield, *History of the County of Norfolk*, vol. IV, p. 431.

21   See above, note 4; and for grants of land in Ormesby, *Charters of Norwich Cathedral Priory*, vol. II, nos 500–15.

22   Ibid., nos 497–99. In Norwich the hospital owned land in the parishes of St Andrew (Norfolk Record Office, DCN 45/3/5), St George (45/13/3), St Olave (45/30/9), St Saviour (45/35/3) and, of course, St Paul (45/31/1–5, 15–21, 24, 33), as well as in Hosiergate (45/3/6), Conisford (45/38/7) and Holme Street (85/1). The hospital's Norwich rental was revised in August 1531 (DCN 2/5/4).

23   *Charters of Norwich Cathedral Priory*, vol. I, nos 255, 259 (12).

24   Norfolk Record Office, DCN 44/13/1, 45/38/7.

25   Blomefield, *History of the County of Norfolk*, vol. IV, p. 431.

26   *Calendar of Papal Registers: Papal Letters, 1362–1404*, ed. W.H. Bliss and J.A. Twemlow (London, 1902), p. 525; *1396–1404*, ed. Bliss and Twemlow (London, 1904), pp. 273–74, 586–87.

27   Harvey, *Living and Dying in England*, pp. 8–9.

28   For the statutes see above, note 8.

29   This definition is, for example, provided in *Omne Bonum*, an encyclopaedia compiled in the mid-fourteenth century by an English Cistercian monk: British Library Department of Manuscripts, Ms. Royal, 6 EVII, ff. 217v–18.

30   Rawcliffe, 'The Hospitals of Later Medieval London', *Medical History*, XXVIII (1984), p. 2.

31   Eadem, *Medicine and Society*, pp. 36–40.

32   *Calendar of Papal Registers: Papal Letters, 1458–71*, ed. J.A. Twemlow (London, 1933), pp. 356–57.

33   A.H. Thompson, *The History of the Hospital and the New College of the Annunciation of St Mary in the Newarke, Leicester* (Leicester Archaeological Society, 1937), pp. 143–58, notably pp. 156–57.

34   *Charters of Norwich Cathedral Priory*, vol. I, no. 255.

35   Rawcliffe, *Medicine and Society*, pp. 7–8, 171–77.

36   C. Erickson, *The Medieval Vision: Essays in History and Perception* (Oxford, 1976), pp. 196–97; Finucane, 'Sacred Corpse, Profane Carrion', pp. 54–55.

37   Carlin, 'Medieval English Hospitals', pp. 25, 33; and Rubin, *Charity and Community*, pp. 158–59, each provide examples of hospitals which excluded pregnant women and of others where they were accepted.

38   *Calendar of Liberate Rolls, 1226–1240* (London, 1917), p. 455; Clark, 'Mothers at Risk of Poverty', p. 141. It is worth noting in this context that, in the thirteenth century, the monks of Beaulieu Abbey, who were generally

discriminating about the recipients of poor relief, would only allow almsgiving to women whom they suspected of being prostitutes in 'times of grave famine'. Otherwise they were sent away empty handed (Dyer, *Standards of Living*, p. 237).

39   Rawcliffe, *Medicine and Society*, pp. 204–5; *Calendar of Close Rolls*, 1343–46 (London, 1904), p. 432; *1349–54* (London, 1906), pp. 414–15.

40   Kirkpatrick, *History of the Religious Orders*, p. 217.

41   See note 8 above.

42   Norfolk Record Office, DCN 2/5/1.

43   Ibid., DCN 2/5/2.

44   Ibid., DCN 2/5/2, 5–6.

45   Ibid., DCN 45/31/34. The estates and finances of the Cathedral Priory during the later Middle Ages are examined by R. Virgoe in *Norwich Cathedral: Church, City and Diocese, 1096–1996*, ed. C. Harper-Bill and E. Fernie (London, forthcoming, 1996), chapter VIII. I am grateful to Dr Virgoe for allowing me to read his text before publication and to Dr Bruce Campbell for discussing the Priory's agricultural problems with me.

46   Dyer, *Standards of Living*, p. 245.

47   *English Gilds*, pp. 40–41. According to the 1388–89 returns, other Norwich guilds then paid at divergent rates: the Tailors offered 7d a week to poor members (pp. 33–36) and St George's Guild 8d (pp. 17–18); the Guilds of St Christopher, the Holy Trinity and St James the Apostle pledged a shilling (pp. 22–26; Public Record Office, C43/47/297); the Pelterers' Guild promised 14d (pp. 28–32), and the Fraternity of the Annunciation at the College of St Mary in the Fields 'a suitable sufficiency' according to the status of the individual (C43/47/290). The three Guilds of St Botolph, St Katherine and the Carpenters levied a farthing from each solvent member (pp. 15–16, 19–21, 37–39) every week for the relief of brothers or sisters who had fallen into poverty. All these bodies insisted that recipients should not have brought misfortune on themselves. For the debate over the reality of such support, see McRee, 'Charity and Gild Solidarity', pp. 195–225.

48   Norfolk Record Office, DCN 2/5/2, 5, 6; P.H. Cullum, '"And Hir Name Was Charite": Charitable Giving by and for Women in Late Medieval Yorkshire', in *Woman is a Worthy Wight: Women and English Society c.1200–1500*, ed. P.J.P. Goldberg (Stroud, 1992), pp. 199–200. At least four late-medieval Parisian almshouses and hospitals reserved places for women, so that in theory some ninety females, more than half of whom had to be widows, were accommodated (Geremek, *Margins of Society*, p. 176).

49   Henderson, 'The Hospitals of Late Medieval and Renaissance Florence', pp. 80–81.

50   N. Tanner, *The Church in Late Medieval Norwich*, p. 134; Kirkpatrick, *History of the Religious Orders*, pp. 210–12.

51   Norfolk Record Office, DCN 69, ff. 13r, 14r, 15r, 26r, 27r; *The Register of Henry Chichele, Archbishop of Canterbury*, ed. E.F. Jacob (4 vols, Oxford, 1943–47), vol. II, p. 386.

52   Norfolk Record Office, DCN 2/5/2, 3.

53   *Visitations of the Diocese of Norwich*, pp. 14–15.

54   Clay, *Mediaeval Hospitals of England*, pp. 213–14. For a perceptive discussion of monastic corrodies, see Harvey, *Living and Dying in England*, chapter VI, notably pp. 193–98, where she evaluates the circumstances of corrodians.

55   *Dives and Pauper*, vol. I, part II, p. 195.

56   *Calendar of Inquisitions Miscellaneous*, vol. II, no. 293. A government enquiry of 1380 into the management of St Bartholomew's hospital, Gloucester, set out to examine charges that 'divers corrodies have been granted by the prior and his predecessors, so that goods do not suffice to maintain the chantries, alms and other works of charity, and brothers and sisters even lack food and clothing' (*Calendar of Patent Rolls, 1377–81* (London, 1895), p. 573).

57   E. Rowland Burdon, 'St Saviour's Hospital Bury St Edmunds', *Proceedings of the Suffolk Institute of Archaeology*, XIX (1927), pp. 270–76; *Charters of the Medieval Hospitals of Bury St Edmunds*, ed. C. Harper-Bill (Suffolk Charters, XIV, 1994), pp. 14, 16–17, 146–51.

58   Cullum, *Cremetts and Corrodies*, pp. 20–28.

59   New College, Oxford, Ms. 3691, ff. 92–92v. I am grateful to Professor Martha Carlin for supplying me with a transcript of this document.

60   *Valor Ecclesiasticus*, vol. III, p. 287; Kirkpatrick, *History of the Religious Orders*, pp. 210–12.

61   Norfolk Record Office, DCN 48/26A/1.

62   *The Norwich Census of the Poor, 1570*, ed. J.F. Pound (Norfolk Record Society, XL, 1971), pp. 91–93, records twenty-four individuals living in thirteen houses maintained 'in the Normans' by the civic authorities. Of these, Joan Gogney, a widow, who was 'lame in one hande' had lately been in hospital.

63   Rowland Burdon, 'St Saviour's Hospital', pp. 269–70; *Charters of the Medieval Hospitals of Bury*, pp. 15, 148; J. Rowe, 'Medieval Hospitals of Bury St Edmunds', pp. 259–62. Additional expenses of £151 were incurred in 1385–86 and of £155 in 1386–87, thus running the hospital even further into debt.

64   Norfolk Record Office, DCN 2/5/2. 6;*The Agrarian History of England and Wales Volume III, 1350–1500*, ed. E. Miller (Cambridge, 1991), p. 436.

65   Norfolk Record Office, DCN 2/5/6.

66   *Visitations of the Diocese of Norwich*, pp. 14–15.

67   *The Agrarian History of England and Wales, Volume III*, pp. 612–14; R.H. Britnell, 'The Pastons and their Norfolk', *Agricultural History Review*, XXXVI (1988), pp. 132–44.

68   Thomas More, *The Apologia*, ed. J.B. Trapp (*The Complete Works of St Thomas More*, IX, 1979), p. 104.

69   *Visitations of the Diocese of Norwich*, pp. 14–15.

70   Norfolk Record Office, DCN 1/6/137. The account for 1466–67 is number 81. The calculations regarding loaves are based on Dyer, *Standards of Living*, pp. 57, 153. H.W. Saunders, *An Introduction to the Rolls of Norwich Cathedral Priory* (Norwich, 1930), p. 125, estimates a mere 80 loaves to the quarter, which seems remarkably low. Ordinances of 1244 for the hospital of St James at Northallerton, Yorkshire, required that bread given to the infirm inmates and an additional thirteen paupers begging each night at the gates was to be of such a weight that each quarter of wheat made 200 loaves; and wheat mixed with rye or barley would have gone further (*The Register of Walter Gray*, ed. J. Raine (Surtees Society, LVI, 1870), p. 181).

71   *Valor Ecclesiasticus*, vol. III, p. 287.

72   The question of monastic almsgiving is discussed by W.T. Mellows and P.I. King in *The Book of William Morton, Almoner of Peterborough Monastery 1448–1467* (Northants Record Society, XVI, 1954), pp. xxv-xxix, xliii, xlvi; and by Harvey, *Living and Dying in England*, chapter I, passim. Almsgiving by the monks of Norwich is currently

being investigated by Miss Claire Noble, in a doctoral thesis on 'Aspects of Life in Norwich Cathedral Priory during the Later Middle Ages', at UEA.

73 John Stow, *A Survey of London*, ed. C.L. Kingsford (2 vols, Oxford, 1908), vol. I, p. 89.

74 Saunders, *Rolls of Norwich Cathedral Priory*, p. 123.

75 Norfolk Record Office, DCN 1/6/108.

76 Ibid., DCN 1/6/18–24.

77 Ibid., DCN 1/6/26–30.

78 These calculations run from 1409 to 1443: ibid., DCN 1/6/39–67. No evidence about grain supplies is presented in the accounts for 1403 to 1408.

79 Ibid., DCN 1/6/68–82.

80 Ibid., DCN 1/6/83–110.

81 Ibid., DCN 1/6/111–137; Ayers, *Norwich*, pp. 92–94.

82 *The Agrarian History of England and Wales, Volume III*, pp. 439–40.

CHAPTER III

The Hospital of St Giles

Quite soon after his consecration as bishop of Norwich, in February 1245, Walter Suffield decided to construct a new hospital in the city on land bounded to the south by the Cathedral Priory and to the north by the river Wensum. He may well have been prompted to do so by members of the mercantile elite, who gave generously to the foundation during its early years. Yet, allowing for this groundswell of lay support, the hospital of St Giles was very much a personal creation, built by the bishop 'for remission of his sins'.[1] At first glance, his choice of location and, indeed, his enthusiasm for this particular project seem rather surprising, since plans were then afoot to build another refuge for the sick poor on the opposite side of Norwich. Shortly before 1248 a priest named John le Brun had endowed a hospital and chapel dedicated to the Virgin Mary in St Stephen's parish, on a site now occupied by the Assembly Rooms (off Theatre Street). The chapel and its short-lived infirmary then lay in open fields very near one of the main city gates and would not have lacked for patients. St Mary's charitable activities were, however, soon abandoned; and it became instead an opulent college and confraternity for secular clergy.[2] Perhaps Bishop Suffield encouraged this development, preferring to direct all the funds newly available for poor relief into a single hospital on his own doorstep and thus ensure a clear separation of philanthropic from liturgical functions. Ironically, however, St Giles's was destined to follow the same path, despite all the meticulous precautions taken by its founder.

Bishop Walter Suffield

The two foundation charters of St Giles's hospital reflect the ideals and preoccupations of a remarkable man, whose striking combination of pragmatism and piety still makes an impression over seven hundred years after his death. The family of Suffield *alias* Calthorpe took its name from a village some fourteen miles north of Norwich, and Walter clearly retained a strong sense of civic pride. His building programme was not simply confined to the hospital, but extended to the very heart of the diocese. As the first stage in an ambitious plan for the redesign of the entire east end of the Cathedral, he replaced the modest apsidal Norman chapel built by Herbert de Losinga with a long rectangular Lady Chapel twice its size. Had circumstances permitted, he would have gone on completely to remodel the semicircular ambulatory, too, giving the presbytery a larger, square end. The chapel was either finished or very near completion when he drew up his will in June 1256, as he then asked to be buried before the high altar. He also arranged for candles to be burnt there in perpetuity in honour of the Virgin Mary and for masses to be said at the altar for the health of his soul. This long and revealing document contains no mention of St William of Norwich, whose shrine lay nearby: if, as has been suggested, he hoped thus to revive a flagging cult, there is no evidence that he himself venerated the young martyr. The Lady Chapel fell victim to Protestant reformers in the sixteenth century, but the surviving arch, which leads from the east end of the apse into what is now the Regimental Chapel, gives some idea of the original design. Had they been implemented by Suffield's successor, Bishop Walton, the rest of the proposed renovations would have produced an effect not dissimilar to that at the east end of Peterborough Cathedral.[3]

Like many other senior clergy of the period, Suffield took his pastoral duties very seriously.[4] Along with his obligation to preserve and improve the fabric of the Church went a responsibility to care for the needy, whose plight exercised him throughout his life and dominates his will. In it he left well over £375 in cash to be spent on the local poor, as well as instructing his two nephews that they were each to feed one hundred paupers every year on the feast of the Assumption of the Blessed Virgin and give a square meal every day to one poor person. The almoner of the Cathedral Priory was likewise assigned sufficient capital to provide annual doles worth 20s on the anniversary of Suffield's death. A major part of the £100 set aside to pay for his funeral was, in addition, to be distributed among the elderly, sick and indigent, while his new hospital received a promise of £200 together with carts, grain, livestock and part of the residue of his estate, which may have been worth even more. Any debts due from poor clergy, tenants or parishioners were to be written off by his executors.[5] Testamentary largesse on this scale might, in some cases, be taken as evidence of a troubled conscience or anxiety about a lifetime's indifference towards the poor of Christ, but Suffield's past record seems to have been unimpeachable. Such was his reputation for philanthropy that centuries later the London chronicler, John Stow (d.1605), coupled him with St Ethelwold (d.984), bishop of Winchester, as one who 'sold all his sacred vessels of the Church' to relieve the hungry. Among the various goods left by him to St Giles's was 'the cup out of which the poor children drank', which suggests that he customarily received paupers in his own home.[6]

The bishop's charitable activities in times of famine were favourably noted by his contemporary, Matthew Paris, who was less flattering about his close relations with the papal court and his efforts to levy taxes from ecclesiastical property.[7] As the senior of the three English prelates charged, in September 1253, with assessing and raising the 'new' tenth on clerical incomes which Innocent IV had granted King

Henry to fund a crusade, Suffield gave his name to the controversial 'Valuation of Norwich'. Already, in 1247, he had come in for criticism as an assessor of the conventional tenth paid by the English Church to Rome; and his association with a scheme designed both to increase and spread the fiscal burden placed him in an invidious position. Enthusiasm for warfare against the heathen was, in practice, muted by unwillingness to support its cost and doubts about Henry's good intentions. Much as he might protest his reluctance to take part in the exercise, Suffield was seen by many religious as the principal agent of an unpopular royal policy which would tighten the screws on those least able to pay. Notwithstanding the comparative leniency of the ensuing assessment, his reputation as a friend of the destitute was compromised. Nor were his efforts any more pleasing to the King, who professed disappointment at the returns. It was, no doubt, with considerable relief that he stepped down in 1255, to be replaced by papal agents chosen for their greater enthusiasm.[8]

For all his sensibilities, Suffield was a man of the world, with an acute awareness of the failings and foibles of humankind. He must also have been an eloquent preacher. When, in 1247, Henry III acquired a crystal phial of the Holy Blood of Christ from the Knights Templars, the honour of celebrating mass and preaching to the assembled crowds at Westminster Abbey fell to the bishop. Matthew Paris's account of this solemn event, at which Henry himself carried the container on foot from St Paul's Cathedral to the Abbey, provides a precis of his sermon, a masterly contribution to royalist propaganda, carefully crafted to strike just the right note of pious nationalism. Henry's rival, Louis IX of France (whom he constantly sought to emulate if not outdo in ostentatious acts of piety), might possess a sizeable piece of the True Cross, but the Blood of Christ was surely far more sacred. If the one provided a means for God to redeem the sinful world, the other constituted the price paid by him to achieve this end. Just as it pleased God to make King Henry, 'the most Christian of all Christian princes', custodian of such a peerless relic, so too England, where 'faith and holiness flourish more than in other parts of the world', was predestined to be its ideal home.[9]

We may reasonably assume that Suffield joined with his learned contemporary, Robert Grosseteste (d.1253), in dismissing as simplistic the reservations voiced at the time by sceptics 'slow of heart to believe' in the authenticity of Henry's acquisition. (Since Christ had risen from the tomb on the third day, and later ascended into heaven, how could so much blood have remained behind?) His devotion to the cult of the Holy Blood seems to have sprung from a sincerely held belief, yet he was shrewd enough to recognise the political and personal advantages to be gained from such a public profession of faith. Although he never earned a reputation as a teacher or theologian, Suffield had himself benefited from a sound academic training and was described in flattering terms by Matthew Paris as a man of letters (*virum eleganter literatum*).[10] His bequest of £5 to 'the poor scholars at Oxford' supports the tradition that he studied there: according to the Norwich

Benedictine, Bartholomew Cotton (d.1298), he also read and lectured in decretals (canon law) at the University of Paris. His skills as a canonist were certainly put to good use over the years and help to account for his early rise in the ecclesiastical hierarchy. The late-twelfth century decretists, whose *summae* of the work of Gratian figured prominently in the university syllabus, had, moreover, devoted considerable attention to the question of poor relief, an issue which preoccupied the bishop throughout his adult life.[11]

In this respect Suffield's career appears remarkably similar to that of Richard Wych (d.1253), his close friend and spiritual mentor, who was elected bishop of Chichester against Henry III's wishes, in 1244, and was eventually canonised.[12] A zealous reformer, he drew up synodal statutes for his diocese which aimed to improve the moral calibre of the clergy, while also emphasising their pastoral responsibilities towards the needy.[13] Suffield freely acknowledged how much he had profited from his guidance and example, although the debt may not have been entirely one-sided. Both men had experienced the intellectual excitement of the Paris and Oxford schools at a time when ideas about the Church's responsibility towards the poor and the nature of their claims upon society were being developed by canonists. Even more dramatic was the impact of the early followers of St Francis (d.1226) and St Dominic (d.1221), whose renunciation of property and identification with the destitute as 'sacred images of Christ' added an entirely new dimension to the growing debate about poverty.[14]

While he was bishop of Norwich Suffield's household included two other noteworthy figures, whose presence provides further evidence of the scholarly milieu in which he lived. His 'companion', Richard of Wendover (d.1252), was a medical practitioner and canon of St Paul's, London, who may have attended Pope Gregory IX (d.1241) as one of his physicians.[15] Lawrence of Somercotes seems also to have served in the papal curia, and went on to become a leading authority on electoral procedure. His great treatise on canonical election appeared in 1253, but he had been collecting material for many years.[16] The two of them probably gave expert advice when the statutes of St Giles's hospital were first drafted, not least with regard to the arrangements for, respectively, choosing nurses and selecting new masters. Wendover's close connexion with the hospital and priory of St Bartholomew in London is especially relevant, as this was one of the first English hospitals to run a school on the premises, initially for orphaned children, but later for other deserving cases.[17] At the time of his death, Suffield owned a substantial collection of books, some of which, on divinity, law and philosophy, he bequeathed to his nephew. That he retained a more than conventional interest in education is evident from the provisions made by him at St Giles's for teaching grammar to poor local boys who showed particular aptitude and might thus be trained for the priesthood.[18]

In common with many medieval churchmen, Suffield combined a successful administrative career, which sometimes placed him on the international stage, with an inner life of great spiritual vitality. Two further examples of this are especially significant in the present context. His new hospital in Norwich was dedicated collectively to the Holy Trinity, the Virgin Mary (whose cult he was then fostering at the Cathedral), her mother, St Anne, and all the saints of God, but first and foremost to St Giles.[19] As the patron saint of lepers, cripples and nursing mothers, St Giles (d.c.710) enjoyed considerable popularity throughout northern Europe. One of Norwich's five civic *leprosaria* also bore his name, as did well over a score of other English hospitals. The Saint's legend contained many elements likely to appeal to

5. A cast of an impression of a late-thirteenth century seal of St Giles's hospital shows the patron saint seated, with a wounded hind seeking refuge at his knee. The legend notes that this is 'the seal of the master and brothers of St Giles's of Norwich', and at the base a mitre surmounts a cross, confirming the house's strong episcopal connections.

Bishop Suffield: as a young man in Greece he had reputedly given away all his possessions to be shared among the poor, and had devoted himself to caring for the sick and destitute. Later on, however, he abandoned the world to live as a hermit near Nimes, being sustained by the milk of a hind sent to him from heaven. While in pursuit of the beast, King Wamba (or some other local ruler, depending on the source) accidentally wounded Giles with an arrow, and in reparation founded an abbey for him at what became known as Saint-Gilles in Provence. Suffield left a mitre, the pastoral staff given to him by his friend and predecessor, William Raleigh, and twenty marks in cash to the abbey, which housed St Giles's shrine and still flourished as an important pilgrimage centre.[20] Besides the many healing miracles attributed to him, Giles was reputed to have interceded with God on behalf of the Emperor Charlemagne, securing divine forgiveness for a sin too terrible to name. The widespread belief that he took the part of sinners who wished to repent and amend their lives, and that devotees of his cult might as a result be saved without first confessing to a priest, contributed further to his popularity among the sick and dying:

> O gracious Gyle, of pore folk chef patroun,
> Medycyne to seke in ther dystresse,
> To alle needy sheeld and proteccyoun,
> Reffuge to wrecchis, ther damages to redresse,
> Folk that were ded restoryng to quyknesse [life],
> Sith thou of God were chose to be so good,
> Pray for our synnys, pray for our wikkidnesse ...
> And as thou were tryacle [theriac: a powerful drug] and medycyne
> To kyng Charlis, whan he in myschef stood,
> Teche us the weye by thi gostly doctryne.[21]

Bishop Suffield's relationship with a second medieval saint was far more immediate and personal. He may possibly have attended lectures by Edmund of Abingdon, who taught theology at Oxford between about 1214 and 1222, and would certainly have encountered him from time to time thereafter. We do not know if the gilt cup which he described in his will as once belonging to 'the blessed Edmund' had been a gift from the saint, or his sometime chancellor, Richard Wych, but it was clearly one of his most precious possessions, and went, appropriately, to the new hospital in Norwich.[22] As celebrated for his generous almsgiving as he was for his commentaries on the Scriptures, Edmund had been made archbishop of Canterbury in 1233 and died in exile (or, more accurately, self-imposed retirement) at Soissy seven years later during the course of a dispute with Henry III. The various contemporary accounts of his life contain many references to his concern for the sick and destitute, which, even allowing for the conventions of medieval hagiography, was manifestly sincere. Although Matthew Paris was mistaken in claiming that he gave all his patrimony to a hospital in Abingdon, he is known to have settled property on that of St John the Baptist, Oxford, and to have run up debts because of his generosity to the poor.[23] Bishop Raleigh had initially played a significant part in fostering the cult of St Edmund, but its chief propagandist was, without doubt, Richard Wych, who had shared the archbishop's last days.[24]

Edmund's body was buried, as he had wished, at the Cistercian monastery at Pontigny, and translated after his canonization in 1246 to a new and splendid shrine within the abbey. Here King Henry came in 1254, one of many pilgrims bearing costly gifts. Suffield himself contributed towards the elaborate decoration of the shrine, and left twenty marks in his will to complete the work he had already started. Of even greater interest is his desire to follow Edmund's example by having his heart removed after his death and placed in a spot 'where his love would ever abide'. The saint had intended in this way to honour (and reward) the regular canons at Soissy, who had cared for him in his last illness: his royal, episcopal and aristocratic imitators likewise saw heart burial as a means of expressing their attachment to particular religious orders or institutions.[25] And among the very first was Bishop Suffield, whose choice fell upon St Giles's hospital. In the event of his dying (and thus being interred) at any distance from Norwich, he asked that his heart should be removed from his body and placed in a cavity made in the wall next to the high altar of the hospital chapel.[26] Did he nurse a secret hope that one day St Giles's or his new Lady Chapel would become a centre for pilgrimage? For a while it looked as if a healing cult to rival those at Pontigny and Chichester might be established at his tomb in Norwich Cathedral, but rumours of early miracles soon died out. Despite the great reputation which he enjoyed in his lifetime for generosity to the poor, Walter Suffield was never canonised.[27] Perhaps his career lacked that element of outspoken defiance so desirable in a saint: his involvement in Henry III's unpopular financial schemes may have done him irreparable harm. Nor did he evidently display the conspicuous asceticism or 'inner consecration of life' so characteristic of Abingdon and Wych. He appears, for example, to have been stout: to his 'faithful and beloved' William Whitewell he bequeathed his 'great belt to gird him with when he grew old', which suggests a comfortably spreading waistline. But the making of a medieval saint was often as much a matter of finance and politics as it was of holiness and self denial. His successors may simply have lacked the necessary funds to embark upon such a long and costly process.[28]

The Hospital Statutes

Three thirteenth-century charters recording the foundation statutes of St Giles's hospital survive. One is undated, and has been said (without any supporting evidence) to have been compiled as early as 1245 or 1246, although a date around 1249 seems more likely.[29] Allowing for a few minor scribal changes, its contents are reproduced verbatim in the letter of confirmation issued by Bishop Walton of

Norwich on 21 June 1265.[30] Both documents are now preserved in the hospital archive. The phrasing and order – but not the substance – of these regulations differ slightly from what may have been Suffield's preferred text: the one dated October 1249 which he eventually submitted for ratification by Pope Alexander IV. He had already secured papal letters of approval and blessing for St Giles's on 24 July 1251, followed, five days later, by a bull, placing the master and brothers under the formal protection of Innocent IV.[31] On the latter's death, in December 1254, it seemed expedient to acquire from his successor new letters in support of the hospital and its work for aged priests, poor scholars and sick and hungry paupers. An entry in the papal registers records the issue of such letters on 10 March 1255, as does a separate, undated *inspeximus* of them by the prior of Bromholm.[32] In addition, a copy of the episcopal foundation charter of October 1249, as confirmed by Alexander, was acquired by the monks of Norwich. It passed into the ownership of the Dean and Chapter, and is still among their muniments.[33] Both the undated hospital regulations and those of October 1249 had first been issued in the presence of Prior Elmham (d.1257) and the Cathedral chapter, probably after lengthy discussions about the legal, financial and ecclesiastical status of their new neighbours. It is also worth noting that Suffield visited the Roman curia in 1249, returning (as Matthew Paris believed) 'with an infamous privilege for extorting money from his diocese': perhaps he outlined his plans for the hospital there as well.[34] That he gave considerable thought to the project, bringing to it his customary blend of acumen and compassion, is evident from the breadth and detail of the statutes, which draw heavily upon what he perceived to be the best aspects of existing models.

Although the master of St Giles's, his four honest chaplains 'instructed in the divine office', his two clerks, deacon and subdeacon were to be recruited from the ranks of the secular clergy, their rule was closely (in a few cases directly) based on that of the Augustinian canons. Emphasis upon the evangelical ideals of poverty, simplicity and absolute obedience combined with a desire for moderation to make this order particularly well-suited for work in hospitals and among the urban poor. Its asceticism contrasted sharply with the laxity of some older Benedictine houses, yet at the same time it permitted the freedom of association and movement necessary for anyone engaged in charitable work.[35] The almoner of the Augustinian priory at Barnwell was, for example, urged to make frequent visits to 'old men and those who are decrepit, lame and blind, or are confined to their beds', and to 'endow with more copious largess pilgrims, palmers, chaplains, beggars and lepers'. Always bearing in mind the words of Christ, he was to keep a stock of warm clothing for distribution to the poor. But his task was not merely to feed, clothe and tend the needy. The sick paupers admitted by him as boarders in the almonry were constantly to be admonished 'respecting spiritual goods, as confession, communion and the welfare of their souls'.[36]

The Augustinians were also noted for their restrained approach to the liturgy, which left them more time (and money) for other activities. As envisaged by Bishop

Suffield, the regulations at St Giles's likewise discouraged elaborate ritual: the master and chaplains were to observe the canonical hours, to sing three masses every day (including one for the soul of the founder) and to offer a weekly mass in honour of the patron saint, but all was to be done *cum cantu et tractu moderato*, neither too loud nor with too elaborate an accompaniment.[37] This requirement was one of the first casualties of expansion. Ceremonial and musicianship came to occupy a place which would greatly have displeased the founder, not least because they diverted attention and resources away from the poor. In order to prevent such an eventuality, and also to foster a tradition of apostolic poverty, Suffield had further insisted that all the hospital clergy should live together, sharing the same spartan accommodation, food and drink, and observing the same fast days as four lay brothers. The latter were expected to undertake manual work, supervise routine business outside the house and attend most of the services. It is interesting to note that the bishop specifically banned esquires and youths from the hospital precincts, since they were most likely to disrupt its tranquil atmosphere with noise and other distractions. Nor, although he was prepared to admit respectable women as occasional visitors, would he countenance female boarders: as noted in the previous chapter, even the most distinguished guests could undermine discipline and disturb the routine of prayer essential for physical and spiritual health.

Within the hospital all goods were to held in common, and everyone had to abide by a draconian code of discipline enforced by the master at weekly chapter meetings. He was himself constrained by an oath of office which demanded almost continuous residence, warned against the dangers of protracted contact with outsiders (especially over meals) and forbade ostentatious display. Bishop Suffield was particularly anxious to limit the number of the master's servants and horses. Although his own household was baronial in size and he kept an impressive stable, along with a pack of hunting dogs, he clearly recognised the problems likely to occur if others followed suit. However austere they may have been in their personal habits, most late medieval English bishops ran large and costly establishments, in keeping with their social and political status.[38] The temptation to emulate them, through the acquisition of a mounted retinue and other trappings of power, was hard to resist and easy to ridicule:

> When he schal oniwer ride oute, yea, thouh it be to visite his pore scheep, he mut ride with foure or fyve score hors proudeli apareilid at alle poyntes, his owne palfrai for his bodi worth a xx or a xxx pound, al bihangid with gliterynge gold as though it were an hooli hors, himself above in fyne scarlet or other cloth as good as that, ... his persones and his clerkis rydynge aboute hem, al in gult harneise, with bastard swerdis overgild bi hire sides hangynge, as thou it were Centurio and his knythes rydynge toward Cristes deth.[39]

Nothing was to distract the master and staff of the new hospital from their round of devotions and charitable work dedicated to the care of the sick poor on earth and the welfare of all Christian souls after death. Suffield's avowed desire to build St Giles's for the remission of his past sins reflects a growing preoccupation on the part of the Church with the doctrine of Purgatory, which it was then seeking formally to define.[40] Yet his scheme for practical relief reflects an awareness of contemporary social problems, indicative of more than a single-minded concern for the fate of his own soul.

Every day, without fail, thirteen paupers were to receive a dole of 'sufficient good bread', a dish of meat or fish, sometimes supplemented with eggs and cheese, and an adequate supply of drink. In summer this was to be distributed outside the hospital gates, but in the cold East Anglian winter the recipients might sit in front of the fire to eat their food. Whenever the bishop visited St Giles's (which may have been quite often, given its proximity to the episcopal palace) the number of meals was to be doubled. In addition, the house was to maintain a poor box for alms to be collected from pious donors and distributed daily, as available, to poor wayfarers. To encourage benefactions during the octave of the feast of St Giles (which fell on 1 September), Walter Suffield offered a perpetual indulgence of forty days' remission of sins each year. Similar attempts at fund raising were made by Bishops Middleton and Walpole in 1279 and 1294 respectively.[41] Although the second indulgence was extended, in a year of especial dearth, to cover the anniversary of the dedication on 3 October and the octave following, the most testing period for the hospital would under normal circumstances have fallen rather earlier, during the months before the harvest when reserves of food were running low. Between 25 March and 15 August extra supplies of bread 'sufficient to assuage hunger' were therefore to be handed out at the ringing of the great bell. The founder's requirement that nobody should be turned away empty-handed on these occasions must sometimes have imposed a considerable strain on the hospital's resources. In the year following his death, a local chronicler recorded that

> there was a great shortage of everything because of the floods of the previous year, and corn, which was very scarce, cost from 15s to as much as 20s a quarter. Famine resulted so that the poor had to eat horsemeat [fodder], the bark of trees and even more unpleasant things. Many died of hunger. In the same year all kinds of grain grew abundantly in the fields but were ruined by the autumn rains. In many places the corn remained in the fields after the feast of All Saints [1 November].[42]

Worse was to come. In the crisis year of 1294, the same writer reported a further increase in the price of corn, adding that continuous heavy rain throughout August and September had once again made it impossible to gather more than a fraction of that year's crop.[43] A run of bad harvests from 1310 onwards gave rise to the devastating famines and cattle murrains of the period 1314–25, which in turn caused mass starvation, epidemics and depopulation. In London over sixty people were killed in the stampede for alms: quite possibly similar scenes took place outside St Giles's and the other Norwich hospitals, none of which could possibly have organised relief on the scale required during this exceptional decade. In his study of the early-fourteenth century agrarian crisis, Ian Kershaw notes that over a hundred hospitals and religious houses were placed under royal protection in the year 1315–16 alone, and that many others complained of dire poverty. If the actual survival of St Giles's was not in doubt, the volume and quality of its food supplies must have declined dramatically just when they were most needed.[44]

Outdoor relief was, moreover, only one of the charitable activities which Bishop Suffield expected his hospital to undertake. He shared with several other thirteenth and fourteenth-century bishops an understandable anxiety about the welfare of poor chaplains in his diocese who could no longer earn a living because of old age, disease or disability.[45] At the time of his death, in 1253, Richard Wych was, for example, involved in setting up a hospital for infirm clerks at Windham in Sussex. It was, predictably, dedicated to St Edmund of Abingdon, and served to house priests who might otherwise 'be exposed to public mendicancy', thus bringing their calling into disrepute.[46] The prospects of the less affluent, unbeneficed clergy, whose income derived largely from their work as chantry priests and curates, often deputising on low wages for absentee placemen, could be very bleak indeed. Without wives or children to care for them as they grew old or ill, they enjoyed neither a guaranteed income nor the security of a permanent home. Many must also have suffered from the health problems likely to result from poor diet and the long-term effects of physical strain: as they grew blind, sick or arthritic it was impossible for them to find employment.[47]

A survey of wills made by some 290 members of the secular clergy in Norwich between 1370 and 1532 reveals that over two-thirds of their number never held a benefice, and that although some were quite wealthy many constituted a 'clerical proletariat', barely subsisting on inadequate stipends.[48] Given that regional levels of clerical mortality were particularly high during the plague of 1349–50, the situation may well have been far worse during the preceeding century. Certainly, the bishop's insistence that, so far as the facilities allowed, aged or debilitated chaplains should be received in his hospital, decently housed and properly fed, addressed a pressing contemporary problem. A number of almshouses for destitute clergy sprang up during this period, while older, established institutions often made a point of reserving a few beds for retired priests. At the beginning of the fourteenth century Abbot Northwold of Bury St Edmunds changed the regulations at St Saviour's hospital to give them priority over the poor women who had previously been admitted as patients: as especially deserving recipients of charity, their intercessionary prayers must have seemed all the more effective.[49]

Walter Suffield did not himself seek to discriminate in this way, and made generous arrangements for the accommodation of infirm paupers 'coming from all parts' in need of help. Thirty beds (or more if funds allowed) were to be permanently available for the sick poor, whose warmth and comfort seem, once again, to have been a matter of particular concern. With sheets and counterpanes, perhaps including the silk coverlets which he left to St Giles's in his will, these beds represented a considerable improvement on the straw pallets provided in some English hospitals.[50] It is, indeed, possible that the bishop further ameliorated the lot of patients by allowing each to occupy a single bed, although the practice of sharing, which was common throughout Europe, had the perceived advantage of reducing the amount of laundry, increasing the space available and also making it easier to keep warm in draughty infirmary halls. In 1272 the Norwich merchant, William Dunwich, who was the hospital's most generous lay patron, bequeathed sums totalling £40 for the support of five sick paupers, 'which poor persons shall lie ... in five beds, so that when any one of them is restored to health or enters the way of all flesh another infirm person shall rapidly be substituted in his place'.[51]

Since a regular turnover of patients was anticipated from the outset, Suffield obviously intended to do more than simply offer a home to the elderly or terminally ill. In other words, his hospital received acute as well as chronic cases. Yet, apart from the requirement that the sick were to be honestly and appropriately tended, we know very little about the sort of physical (as opposed to spiritual) care he envisaged. Nursing duties fell to a minimum of three or four lay sisters 'of good life and honest conversation', who were to be decently clothed in white tunics, grey cloaks and black veils. The Bishop was anxious that they should eat and live apart in their own quarters, which were out of bounds to the rest of the hospital staff, confining their duties exclusively to the hospital infirmary. His recommendation that they should be fifty years old, or not much less, was no doubt intended as a further precaution against sexual irregularity. He may also have hoped to avoid the problems which contemporary medical authorities, such as his friend, Richard of Wendover, associated with menstruating females. As Lanfrank of Milan warned at the end of the century, it was highly dangerous for a 'womman in tyme of menstrue' even to look upon a sick man, while other writers maintained that her breath would be contaminating as well. Nor was it desirable that she should remain in close proximity to the Eucharist, which would, of necessity, be regularly exposed to the gaze of hospital patients.[52]

Allowing for differences in the size of the two establishments, nursing duties at St Giles's hospital were probably quite similar to those described in a 1364 visitation of St Leonard's, York. Here the sisters were expected to perform such basic tasks as feeding and washing the patients, 'leading them about as human necessity requires' and fetching a priest whenever one might be needed to hear confession or administer the last rites. They were also charged with 'ministering to the sick', a rather ill-defined responsibility, which almost certainly involved the preparation and application of medicaments, if not some rudimentary surgery, such as lancing boils, cleaning wounds and setting broken limbs. Despite appearances to the contrary, however, the nurses at St Leonard's seem to have had a comparatively easier life than their counterparts in many other English and continental hospitals. A staff of eight was then considered sufficient to look after between 180 and 206 patients, which, at a ratio of one to twenty-two or even twenty-five, seems very low indeed.[53] Even so, the contrast with St Giles's (a ratio of one to fifteen at the very most), the Lancastrian foundation of St Mary in the Newarke, Leicester (exactly one to ten), or Bishop Farnham's new hospital at Northallerton (just over one to four) is more apparent than real, since menial work of the kind customarily assigned to nursing sisters was allocated at St Leonard's to lay brothers and hired servants. By the early fifteenth century St Giles's paid a laundress, but initially the responsibility for washing all sheets, vestments and clothing fell to the nurses. The onerous and disagreeable nature of this task, which had to be performed all year round, can easily be imagined: laundering sheets was one of the hospital sister's principal and most time-consuming chores, generally undertaken in the open air.[54] Whereas in certain institutions, such as St Paul's, Norwich, some of the female staff were themselves elderly pensioners in receipt of charity, there is no suggestion that Suffield intended his nurses to cross the divide between patient and carer. Like the rest of the hospital staff, their duty was to serve God and the sick poor.

Solicitude for the elderly and feeble went hand in hand with a desire to improve the prospects of poor but able boys, who might prove a credit to the priesthood or be trained as choristers. Despite his reluctance to admit youths and esquires into the hospital precincts, Bishop Suffield was anxious that some of the revenues should be earmarked for the support of seven such scholars, drawn from local song schools (the first rung on the educational ladder). They were presumably to attend the Norwich episcopal school, which was then still controlled by the prior, but from 1288 onwards came under the bishop's direct patronage. Towards the close of the Middle Ages it lay between Holme Street and the river Wensum, on a site immediately to the west of St Giles's.[55] Perhaps Suffield had himself insisted that the two buildings should be separated by a boundary wall in order to preserve the peace and quiet of the hospital, although no such provision appears in the foundation charters. In them it was simply established that, on the schoolmaster's recommendation, the master of St Giles's would select seven promising boys on a rota system, providing them with a daily meal during term time and allowing them to remain until they had been 'conveniently educated' in grammar.[56] If it did not offer assistance to the poor of Norwich from the cradle to the grave, Suffield's new foundation came remarkably close, with its attention to the young as well as the elderly. The financial cost of fulfilling these obligations was high, as was the risk that revenues might be diverted to other uses. Most English hospitals experienced problems with regard to the collection and management of limited (often dwindling) funds, and several openly disregarded the wishes of patrons and founders. St Giles's was no exception.

Expansion and Change

No working institution can remain preserved like a fly in amber, and a degree of change was inevitable. The restructuring, in 1272, of Bishop Suffield's detailed arrangements for the election of new masters, served, for example, to iron out some potential problems.[57] But other developments had far-reaching effects upon the very nature of the hospital. In 1309, the master accepted a gift of property in Erpingham and Calthorpe for the support of two paupers and a clerk on the understanding that the number of staff and patients would never exceed the figure first established by 'the blessed late Lord Walter'. Not only did this effectively disregard Bishop Suffield's plans for acquiring more beds as funds allowed: the additional requirement that any persons suffering from 'an intolerable disease' should henceforward be refused admittance, and that patients who currently gave cause for alarm should be removed elsewhere ran contrary to the tenor of the foundation statutes.[58] Since the Bishop had imposed no restrictions whatsoever upon the type of person he was prepared to accommodate at St Giles's, other than insisting that they should be infirm and poor, we may reasonably assume that he wished to help all deserving cases, irrespective of their medical condition. Such a move towards selectivity brought St Giles's into line with several other English hospitals, and marks an early stage in its gradual emergence as an imposing college for secular priests, dedicated to ritual and the liturgy.

So far as we can tell from the foundation statutes, St Giles's was to possess only a modest chapel, situated across the road from the parish church of St Helen, which then belonged to the Cathedral Priory. In 1270, following a dispute between the monks and their new neighbours, Bishop Skerning awarded all the parochial rights, profits and possessions of the existing church (except the cemetery and anchorhold) to the master and brethren.[59] They promptly demolished it, either rebuilding a new church from scratch on the hospital site, or (as seems more likely) greatly enlarging their own chapel to serve both the parishioners of St Helen's and the sick poor. The former, as well as the latter, were entitled to burial in the hospital cemetery, which lay immediately to the north. As was later the case, the patients probably occupied the west end of the church, separated from the congregation in the nave by screens or even a partial stone partition, but the coming and going of local people must still have proved distracting. The priests and chaplains were, moreover, diverted from their ministry to the sick not only by the additional burden of pastoral duties but also by the increasing demands made upon them to sing masses and maintain chantries for influential patrons.

Shortly before his death, in 1272, William Dunwich, a prosperous Norwich merchant and notable benefactor of the hospital, had arranged for two chaplains to celebrate divine service daily in the hospital church for the health of his soul. One was to officiate at a side altar dedicated to St Katherine, while the other was instructed to sing a mass of the Blessed Virgin 'with solemnity' for the benefit of the sick lying in bed and 'any other bystanders'. By the end of the century many gifts of property and rents had been received to pay for lights burning on an altar of the Virgin Mary, at the Easter Sepulchre and at the High Altar. Later references to altars and lights of St Anne, St Helen, St Peter and St Nicholas and to a separate Lady Chapel and tabernacle of the Blessed Virgin to the north of the church suggest that the hospital chaplains spent most of their time praying for the faithful departed.[60] Indeed, in 1310, in response to the demand, Bishop Salmon sanctioned the addition of four more chantry chaplains to the permanent establishment, thus doubling at a stroke the number of senior clerical staff. Twelve years later, a place formerly occupied by one of the hospital's lay brothers was assigned to yet another chaplain so that he could 'celebrate each day for the souls of founders and benefactors'.[61] A steady stream of patrons now wanted to share in the spiritual benefits of the community, which might be extended to friends, relatives and well-wishers. The dorse [back] of a grant of property to St Giles's made by Sir John de Orreby in 1340 notes, for example, the names of all the family members for whom intercession was to be made.[62] Clergy, in particular, sought to associate themselves formally with such a powerful confraternity. In 1412 the master and brothers contracted with Roger Prat, the vicar of Heigham, that the anniversary of his death would, in due course, be celebrated by the entire community in a solemn manner, while also promising him the more immediate comfort of a dwelling house and stable in the precincts.[63] He later became master of the hospital, but other such arrangements seem harder to justify, at least from the perspective of the sick poor.

Whereas many early gifts of property came as free alms, and could thus be applied to whatever charitable or religious use seemed appropriate to the master, later endowments were hedged about with restrictions. They imposed upon the hospital a precise, often carefully costed obligation to pray for the salvation of the donor, and inevitably accelerated the process of change.[64] It would be tedious to list all the bequests settled upon St Giles's for the upkeep of chantries or the celebration of anniversaries. The most notable were from Hugh and Agnes Cailly (c.1269), Roger de Tybeham (1290), John Cusyn of Norwich (1318), Bishop Salmon (1322), Thomas de Preston, rector of Colby (1331), Mary, the widow of Thomas de Brotherton, earl of Norfolk (1351), Robert de Bungay (1376), Beatrice Godale (1397), Roger Eton, parson of Yelverton (1405), John Derlyngton, archdeacon of Norwich and a former master of St Giles's (1410), John Smyth, one of his successors (1489), Bishop Goldwell, whose brother was also a master (c.1499), John Bettyns (1462) and John Veryes (1521).[65] During the 1320s, the hospital could rely on about £8 a year in cash sums paid on an ad hoc, occasional basis for obits; in 1511 the sacristan accounted for sixty pounds of wax (some scented), 5,000 communion wafers and over fourteen gallons of wine for consumption during the mass.[66]

Towards the close of the fourteenth century an ambitious programme of expansion and embellishment, culminating in the erection of a massive chancel some

6. *Part of the ceiling of the medieval chancel of the church of St Helen, completed in about 1383. The chancel was completely separated from the nave after the Reformation, when women (the ultimate sacrilege) were admitted there as patients.*

sixty feet long and a tall bell-tower on the south-western corner of the infirmary hall, marked a further departure from the founder's wishes.[67] The chancel boasted a magnificent east window and a ceiling composed of at least 252 wooden panels interspersed with carved and gilded bosses, reputedly supplied through the patronage of Bishop Despenser of Norwich. Each panel is said to bear the arms of Anne of Bohemia, who visited Norwich with her husband, King Richard, in 1383, although the eagles have single rather than double heads, and it is now impossible to tell exactly when they were painted. Whether or not it was decorated in honour of the young queen, the east end of the hospital church commanded such a fine acoustic that the subsequent growth of a choir, augmented with boys and salaried laymen from the city, and the acquisition of two or more pairs of organs seemed a natural progression.[68] The pealing of the bells, the thundering of the organs and the singing of the choristers made a profound impression upon Bishop Goldwell and his companions when they carried out their visitation of the hospital in 1492.[69] Some contemporary reformers were as critical of such noise and spectacle as Walter Suffield had been before them:

> Thynke yf Saynt Austyn, Jerome or Ambrose herd our curyouse dyscantyng and canteryng in churchys, what they wold say. Surely they wold cry out apon them, and dryve them out of churchys to tavernys, comedys and commyn plays, and say they were noo thyng mete to kendyl and styr Chrystyan hertys to devotyon and love of celestyal thyngys, but rather to ster wanton myndys to vayn plesure and wordly pastyme wyth vanyte.[70]

Goldwell, on the other hand, did not disapprove of this 'fascyon more convenyent to mynstrellys then to devoute mynystyrys', for soon afterwards he instituted his own brother, the archdeacon of Suffolk, as master and set aside funds for the performance of yet more anniversary masses.

Because of its status as the richest and largest hospital in the county, St Giles's was especially vulnerable to the incursions of episcopal nominees. Walter Suffield had insisted that, even if he held another living, the master should never be absent for more than a few days at a time. The appointment from the 1370s onwards of a new breed of Oxford and Cambridge graduates with a string of benefices and outside interests insidiously corroded the spirit of the foundation statutes, for although many lived in Norwich the majority were too busy to attend to routine hospital business. It is, for example, hard to imagine the nobly-born Oliver Dynham (d.1500), who received his first papal licence to occupy two livings in plurality when he was still a teenager, and sought permission to wear fur-trimmed academic robes as a student at Oxford, actually comforting the sick in the infirmary.[71] The arrival from Cambridge in 1372 of John Derlyngton, a licentiate in canon law and newly appointed vicar general to the bishop, heralded a change in direction for St Giles's.

7. The Bell Tower of St Giles's Hospital, built at the end of the fourteenth-century at a cost of at least £41, and heavily subsidised by John Derlyngton, a former master. Immediately to the west stands the medieval infirmary, which later became the mens' quarters and acquired its distinctive chimney.

Before long he had secured two Norfolk rectories and had become archdeacon of Suffolk; and although he left the hospital in 1376 to take up a canonry at the college of St Mary in the Fields, it was his gift of £23 which subsequently helped to complete the imposing bell tower. This had already cost at least £18, spent over a single year in 1396–97.[72]

A series of ambitious careerists followed in his footsteps. Since St Giles's lay conveniently near the episcopal palace (which could be seen from the west window of the infirmary), offered a useful fee of £4 and a set of robes every year and, more to the point, was gradually turning into an imposing residence worthy of a senior diocesan official, the mastership soon became a coveted appointment. Most of the chaplains now occupied private rooms or suites of rooms, and the master enjoyed an even greater degree of privacy with his own lodgings, stables, garden and domestic servants. Although Walter Suffield would have found these developments unacceptable, his late medieval successors clearly welcomed and encouraged them as a means of providing for senior members of their staff. John Selot, a doctor of canon law from Oxford University, who served as master from 1464 until about 1479, was not only secretary to Bishop Lyhart and chancellor to Bishop Goldwell but also archdeacon of Sudbury throughout the entire period. In addition, he acquired the wardenship of another Norfolk hospital, St Thomas's at Beck, and farmed a third with a group of associates.[73] Together, they paid twenty marks a year for the hospital of St Mary and St Nicholas, Massingham, which was initially worth twice this sum yet by 1475 had fallen into bankruptcy and could no longer support a *domus dei*.[74] Allegations of corruption and partiality made against Selot by various members of the Paston family in the 1460s cannot necessarily be taken at face value. His use of the weapon of excommunication as a means of silencing his critics and his brief sojourn in the Marshalsea prison of the King's bench on a charge of bribing juries do, however, suggest that he could be a formidable adversary, cast in the mould of Bishop Despenser rather than that of the saintly Walter Suffield.[75]

It is, no doubt, a reflection of the hospital's status in the diocese (as well as the importance of its geographical location next to the episcopal palace) that ordination services were held by the bishops' suffragans in St Helen's church from time to time in the fifteenth century. Of even greater interest is the remarkable frequency with which new ordinands entering holy orders as subdeacons, deacons and priests named St Giles's hospital as their 'title' or guarantor of financial viability. Canon law required that every candidate for ordination should possess the means to support himself in an appropriate fashion. Evidence, in the form of private testimonials or, more usually, a guarantee by a monastic house, collegiate church or hospital that he occupied a salaried post and would therefore remain economically independent, was demanded before the ceremony. A recent analysis of ordination lists preserved in the registers of six bishops of Norwich between 1413 and 1486 differs from one made by J.F. Williams in the 1950s, but still concludes that St Giles's hospital awarded by far the greatest number of 'titles' (754) of any religious

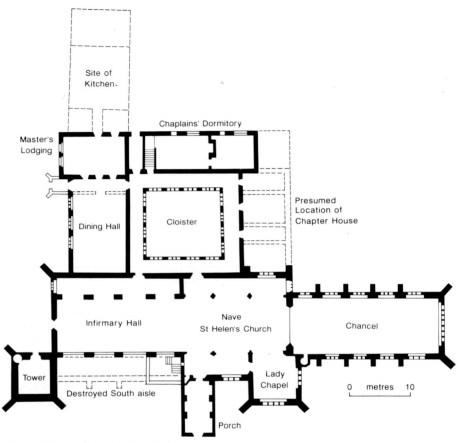

Ground Plan of St. Giles' Hospital

institution in the diocese. Ixworth priory, a moderately prosperous house near Bury St Edmunds, came next (287), and the College of St Mary in the Fields, Norwich, third (183), but none of the great East Anglian monasteries figure significantly on the list. Dismissing as inherently implausible the idea that genuine appointments might have been made, Williams suggested an arrangement, which may have risked the charge of simony, whereby these letters were provided as part of a routine service in return for a modest fee. No evidence that money ever changed hands can, however, be found in the hospital accounts, despite the number of 'titles' issued, so it looks as if the procedure had either become an empty formality or the authorities wished to help ordinands who might otherwise have found it hard to establish their credentials.[76] Activity on this scale – an average of about ten 'titles' issued each year

– had, however, gone far beyond charity to become an established bureaucratic procedure.

Throughout the late-fourteenth and fifteenth centuries, government inquiries into maladministration in English hospitals highlighted the problems caused by absenteeism on the part of masters and wardens. The royal commissioners who investigated a long list of complaints about the mismanagement of the London hospital of St Mary Bethlehem in 1403 discovered wholesale fraud, embezzlement of funds, neglect of the poor inmates (many of whom were insane) and gross dereliction with regard to the religious observances of the house.[77] Almost all these abuses could be blamed upon inadequate supervision, which was such a widespread problem that by 1414 the House of Commons had begun agitating for reform.[78] As we shall see in the next chapter, at least one Norwich hospital went into decline because the revenues were pocketed by a series of ambitious pluralists. At St Giles's, however, the situation was very different: here continued *residence* on the part of masters with high social and professional aspirations meant that a new set of priorities came to the fore. These, in turn, had predictable financial consequences. Although it appears that many of the major building works undertaken to enlarge and beautify the hospital were privately funded by the masters or their patrons, the cost of maintaining the new fabric and of feeding and paying the choristers and chantry chaplains ate into an already limited budget.

Bishops Lyhart and Goldwell, whose respective coats of arms are displayed in the hospital, may well have invested considerable sums in another round of improvements, which saw the enlargement and refurbishment of the nave, the erection of a Lady Chapel on the south side of the church (with roof bosses depicting scenes from the life of the Virgin, the apostles and other saints) and the building of a refectory and cloisters. In addition, projects involving the construction of a new water gate, drains, gutters, walls and outbuildings, as well as the landscaping and planting of gardens began in the precincts at a cost of almost £50 in 1502–3 alone.[79] On the face of things, wealthy masters with powerful relatives or patrons seemed particularly welcome at a time when routine disbursements invariably exceeded receipts. In both 1497 and 1499, for example, Nicholas Goldwell gave sums of £20 towards the repair of tenements damaged by fire; and his successor, John Jullys (1499–1504), paid for extensive work on the master's quarters, new bells and a pair of organs to be placed before the image of St Anne in the hospital church. He also had the old organs mended. William Soper, another early-sixteenth century master, held office for only a short time, but left the house £40 in his will of 1519.[80] The handsome new benches with elaborately carved ends date from the mastership of John Hecker in the 1520s, and bear his initials. Such gifts all came freely as alms, but there was at the same time a more alarming search for long-term credit to underwrite expenses which had themselves been generated by the desire for expansion.

The full extent of these contributions will never be known, but they were

8. *A sketch of the bench end in St Helen's church which depicts St Margaret, the patron saint of women in childbirth, springing unharmed from the belly of the dragon. The initials 'HEC' are of John Hecker, master of the hospital in the 1520s, who probably paid for the carving. Since the church served the parish of St Helen, it would have been frequented by women, unlike the rest of the hospital.*

evidently substantial. An entry at the foot of the accounts for 1502–3 reveals that the hospital currently owed John Jullys at least three times the net income of £80 a year produced by its country estates. In addition to the gifts already noted, he had advanced the staggering sum of £243 'of his own money', partly to meet the customary shortfall between income and expenditure, but also to subsidise important projects which may have included the restructuring of the nave of St Helen's church. His loan had been spent on the 'upkeep and expenses, repairs and buildings specified in the accounts to the honour of God and of St Giles, and for the use and improvement of the hospital'. Overdue rents of £65 collected that year were immediately assigned to him as an interim payment, but since he died soon afterwards the balance seems to have been written off.[81] Jullys was not the only medieval master of a hospital to provide support out of his private coffers. Richard de Ravenser had, for instance, sunk over £400 into maintenance and rebuilding work at St Leonard's, York, during the late-fourteenth century; and the recovery of St Nicholas's hospital near Carlisle after it had been devastated by the Scots not long before was financed out of the master's practice as a surgeon.[82] At least St Giles's did not have to endure the horrors of Anglo-Scottish warfare, although a gradual decline in real landed income, as arrears of unpaid rent rose inexorably during the sixteenth century to exceed anticipated yearly receipts, threatened to pose a serious long-term problem.

The Endowment

At the time of its foundation, in October 1249, St Giles's hospital occupied a relatively small site between Holme Street to the south, the Wensum to the north and land belonging to Isabel de Cressy to the east. In order to support its charitable work, Bishop Suffield made an additional endowment of all the rights and profits of the Norfolk churches of Calthorpe, Costessey, Cringleford, Hardley, St Mary in South Walsham and Seething, which were confirmed to the house, along with their appurtenances, by successive bishops of Norwich. The hospital cartulary, or *Liber Domus Dei*, records 260 early grants, purchases, exchanges and quitclaims whereby the masters and brethren consolidated their holdings in Norwich and other parts of the county, mostly during the second half of the thirteenth century.[83] The spate of transactions involving layfolk of modest means decreased quite dramatically after 1300, in part because of the restrictions imposed by the statute of mortmain of 1279, which forbade perpetual corporations, such as hospitals, from acquiring property without a licence. Support at this level would, in any event, have been hard to sustain during a period of growing economic hardship: the enthusiasm of the initial response reflects local concern about a problem which, by 1315, inspired a feeling of hopelessness rather than a desire for action.

Many citizens and local landowners, anxious to gain spiritual merit and save their immortal souls through almsgiving, settled rents, tenements, small-holdings

9. *The Cow Tower on the bend of the river Wensum and Bishop Bridge marked, respectively, the north-eastern and south-eastern limits of the precincts of St Giles's hospital. Water had strong associations with healing and purification from sin, while bridges symbolised the passage from one world to the next. On a more practical level, hospital patients could solicit alms from travellers entering Norwich on the main approach road from the east.*

and even market stalls in Norwich upon the new hospital as their funds allowed. Successive masters naturally sought to extend the precinct by acquiring all the available plots of land to the east and along Holme Street: it was here that they accumulated their greatest concentration of property in the city. By 1271, thanks largely to William Dunwich and Isabel de Cressy, they had taken possession of all the open fields between the hospital and Bishop's Bridge, some of which were marshy and needed draining. Since Dunwich's grant was conditional upon the payment of fifty-two gallons of wine (later commuted to 40s) a year to the Cathedral Priory, it seems that through him the hospital also acquired the 'Dungeon' or 'Cow Tower' on the bend of the Wensum, and with it the right to collect tolls previously claimed by the prior. The tower stood in a low-lying water meadow known as Cowholme, and was conveyed to the city in about 1378, by which time the fabric had deteriorated badly. Although access to the river made it easy for supplies of foodstuffs, fuel and building materials to be shipped up the Wensum to St Giles's, and even permitted the cultivation of reed beds for thatching, the site was vulnerable to flooding. In January 1290, for example, the next bridge up-river was totally submerged by a torrent of water, which reached the very gates of the hospital and swept away a number of houses.[84] Disasters on this scale were fortunately rare. By the close of the Middle Ages, the hospital precincts resembled a small village, with a walled meadow, orchards, gardens (for recreation as well as growing vegetables and herbs), a horse mill, bakery, slaughterhouse, brewery and kitchen, stables, pigsties, extensive outbuildings and workshops for the carpenters, masons and labourers who found regular employment there. The lay brothers had early on been replaced by paid servants, including a cook, a baker, a laundress, a brewer and a steward, along with their 'boys' and other casual helpers, such as the swan-keeper. In all, at least thirty people (excluding the almsmen and patients) must have been in residence at any given time, while clerks, visiting officials and workmen came and went from day to day.[85]

Other acquisitions in the Holme Street area gave St Giles's a number of tenements, messuages and gardens which could be rented out by the year or for shorter periods according to demand. This part of Norwich had considerable commercial and industrial potential: the old waterfront, near what is now the Adam and Eve public house, had already been redeveloped, and the hospital usually numbered a handful of masons, limeburners and other craftsmen among its tenants. By 1423, the start of an almost complete run of accounts compiled by the hospital's rent collector in Norwich, St Giles's leased out eighteen separate properties, ranging from whole messuages to single chambers, along Holme Street at an annual return of just over £10. Its total income from leasehold in Norwich then stood at £24, the rest coming from tenants in the parishes of St Martin at the Palace Gates, St Simon and St Jude, St Andrew, St Peter Mancroft and St Martin Coslany.[86]

In order to boost his income, the master also let out rooms in the hospital itself. Most of the boarders were chantry chaplains or clergy with business in Norwich, although a few distinguished laymen, such as Sir Thomas Gerberge (who resided there shortly before 1430) were made welcome too. No evidence, beyond a note in the proceedings of the local leet court for 1441, recording a violent affray between two tradesmen in the hospital hall, survives of disorder in the precincts. In this regard, at least, Bishop Suffield's rules appear to have been strictly observed.[87] On the other hand, the practice of charging boys from prominent local families, including the Pastons, Appleyards and Heckers, for accommodation while they were attending the grammar school would have caused him great dismay. An arrangement of 1502, whereby the son of Sir James Hobart, the King's attorney general, was allowed free board because of the valuable legal advice given to St Giles's by his father, was certainly not the kind of subsidised support he had intended.[88]

Lodgers apart, the hospital's annual income from Norwich fell into two basic categories: rents from tenants who negotiated their leases with the master, and were thus subject to the vagaries of the market, and fixed assize rents. The latter offered men and women of relatively limited means an opportunity to endow charitable institutions by setting aside a few shillings, or even pence, to be paid from a specified freehold in perpetuity for pious uses, while retaining the property for themselves and their heirs. Although the recipient had the power to distrain for payment when these rents fell into arrears, in practice the collection of such small sums proved difficult and time-consuming: it was hard to keep track of new owners and expensive to sue defaulters. From time to time, the hospital made an attempt to tackle these problems, but without any real prospect of success. During the early fifteenth century the master hoped to raise £16 a year in assize rents from thirty Norwich parishes, the Bishop's palace and a croft at St Augustine's gate, but £10 of this sum could not be levied without an updated rental. Finally, in 1455–56, by which time the shortfall had reached £234, one was compiled. Debts continued to mount, however, and soon after 1461 (when the accountant stood charged with arrears of £384), it was decided to write off the entire deficit and start afresh. In certain cases, which were noted separately in the accounts, the hospital made a special allowance for paupers who could not afford to pay their rents. In 1464–65, for example, a man and a woman were excused 'because they are beggars and have nothing'. Over the next few years one Robert Munforth was likewise classed as 'insufficient', and another 'mendicant', Hugh Spycer, who owed 16s 4d, obtained a full pardon.[89]

From the turn of the century onwards arrears again began to rise steadily, albeit at a far less alarming rate of about £3 a year. Yet by now the accountant was required to produce no more than £4 in assize rents, and other revenues from the city were falling as well. Whereas during the previous century the combined sums of money available (as net profits) for building work and deliveries of cash to the master had only twice sunk below £20 (in 1459–60 and 1471–72), from 1499 onwards they never rose above £19. The decline was, in fact, quite sudden: between 1474 and 1488 the yearly average of £27 in net receipts had remained consistently higher than at any other point in the century, but in the early sixteenth century it stood at just £16. Indeed, in 1502–3, the accountant overspent by £28 because of extensive improvements being undertaken in the precincts and never made good the balance. Since, for most of the fifteenth century, revenues from Norwich constituted just under a fifth of the master's disposable income, and also funded most of the routine maintenance work at the hospital, this development must have caused some concern.[90]

Although they were, to a certain extent, responsible for the changes which made St Giles's a more expensive place to run, its senior administrative staff lacked neither acumen nor ingenuity. Partly in response to mounting financial pressures and also, no doubt, because of the hospital's development as a secular college at the heart of the diocese, facilities for paying boarders appear to have been improved and expanded during the second half of the fifteenth century. In 1500–1, for example, as much as £18 was raised from twenty-three different individuals staying in the hospital for days, weeks or months. Usually, the annual return from lodgers tended to fluctuate between £5 and £14, which represented a welcome supplement even if it did not fully compensate for rents lost from the city.[91] All the more so, because although St Giles's continued to attract quite substantial endowments throughout the Middle Ages, these came mostly from donors whose overriding concern with their own salvation led them to earmark surplus profits for the upkeep of chantries rather than the support of the sick poor.

It is impossible here to document all the hospital's acquisitions in the Norfolk countryside, but a few deserve specific mention since they added appreciably to its holdings and status as a landowner. Even so, expansion brought problems as well as profits: the cost of fending off predatory neighbours, such as the abbots of St Benet Hulme, could stretch an already tight budget. During the later Middle Ages the masters of St Giles's were rarely out of the ecclesiastical or common law courts, and had to plan accordingly. In 1397 alone legal expenses in London came to almost £7, over and above the sum of £2 spent on seeking professional help locally. It is no coincidence that John Selot, the most litigious and strong-minded of the hospital's medieval masters, was also the most influential, having prudently cultivated the support of the duke of Norfolk and his henchmen.[92] However necessary it may have been for survival, protracted involvement in the murky world of East Anglian politics and the concomitant distribution of bribes were not activities of which Bishop Suffield would have approved. The expense of repairing churches, barns and dwellings was also considerable. In 1366, for example, the accountant responsible for Costessey, who had already overspent by £10 in the previous year, had to pay £14 for constructing a new grange; and in 1441 the bill for roofing the chancel of Thurlton parish church came to almost as much. Rebuilding the entire chancel of Hardley church in the late 1450s cannot have been done for less than £30, although here it was possible to stagger payments over a number of years. In order to increase its income from leasehold property the hospital had first to invest in bricks and

Wickmere
Cathorpe • • Erpingham

Bastwick
Repps • • Rollesby
• South Walsham

Coltishall
Wroxham
Horsford Salhouse
Sprowston
• Thorpe St Andrew
NORWICH Newton
Swannington Colney • Earlham Trowse
Weston Longville Costessey Eaton
Ringland Cringleford Intwood
Hethersett • East Carleton
Hethel
Newton Flotman

Cantley
Limpenhoe
• Reedham
• Hardley
Sisland Loddon Thurlton
Mundham • Hales
Seething
Thwaite

Fobbing Essex

NORWICH

15km

0

The Estates of St. Giles' Hospital

mortar: the master's deficit of £37 in 1397 reflects the cost of constructing new houses in Norwich [TABLE C]. In theory, existing revenues, augmented from time to time with fresh acquisitions, should easily have absorbed these charges, but in most years income failed to keep pace with expenditure.[93]

By the close of the thirteenth century, St Giles's had not only built up substantial estates in the six rural parishes named in the foundation charters, but had also taken possession of others in the Norfolk villages of Sprowston, Repps, Bastwick, Newton Flotman, Rollesby, Wickmere, Erpingham, Ringland, Weston Longville, Thorpe St Andrew, Hales, Intwood, Cantley, East Carleton, Hethel and Reedham.[94] In 1261, Bishop Walton appropriated to the hospital the parish church of Repps and the nearby chapel of Bastwick to help support its spiritual and charitable work. Over the years, existing blocs of property were augmented and further acquisitions made, mostly, as we have seen, to fund chantries and pay for anniversary masses in the hospital. A sizeable amount of arable at Earlham was added in 1318; and the grant of a royal licence permitting the house to acquire land in mortmain to the value of £10 a year facilitated a series of small transactions resulting in the gift or purchase of plots in some fourteen villages, including, for the first time, Loddon, Sisland, Limpenhoe and Thwaite.[95] Bishop Ayermine's endowment of the advowson of Thurlton was conditional upon the hospital's readiness to support three chantry chaplains in the episcopal palace: this proved such a drain on resources that the original terms had eventually to be modified.[96]

Some benefactions, such as Thomas de Preston's gift of £100 for the purchase of the advowson of St Peter's Mundham, were clearly intended to provide immediate assistance for the poor as well as long term spiritual benefits for the donor. Bishop Beck's licence of 1340 permitting the appropriation of this church to the hospital notes that it could no longer afford to help the great number of old and infirm priests, paupers and sick who sought refuge there. This, he explained, was partly because farmland in wet and marshy areas had been so badly damaged by flooding that it had ceased to be productive, but in addition the hospital buildings themselves were in a ruinous state and some 'sons of iniquity' had made matters worse by withholding or making off with revenues, and thus forcing the master to spend money on litigation.[97] Allowing for the somewhat exaggerated claims often made on such occasions, it looks as if St Giles's was already experiencing serious difficulties before the first outbreak of plague in 1348–49. Matters cannot have been helped by the fact that so many of its new acquisitions were set aside for religious rather than overtly charitable purposes.

Fortunately, it proved possible at this point to consolidate holdings just outside Norwich at St Augustine's gate, where the house ran a small farm, known as 'the Lathes'. Here livestock and grain could be sent from the outlying manors and kept until needed in the precinct.[98] Ten years later, in 1351, the countess of Norfolk joined the growing list of patrons, when she made over to St Giles's the advowson of St Lawrence's, the hospital's second living at South Walsham. From its sometime master, John Derlyngton, in 1410, the hospital obtained a generous grant of the advowson of Wickmere and the manor of Cringleford.[99] A more unexpected benefactor, albeit one who characteristically still drove a hard bargain, was the 'cruell and vengible' Norfolk landowner, Sir John Fastolf. Regarded by many of his servants and business partners as being 'for the most parte withoute pite and mercy', he was none the less prepared to assist the hospital to consolidate its possessions in Mundham.[100] The letters which he wrote in 1450–51 to the parson of his living at Castle Combe in Wiltshire suggest that he held the hospital in some regard, although not quite enough to promote the giving of 'almesse'.

> The Maister of St Gylys ... hath been with me for the purchase of Mundham maner, with the appurtenaunce in Cyslond [Sisland], and so I am acorded, and hafe promised him to make a state to such as he wolle name, payeng me CC marc [£133 6s 8d]. And I was not avysed to selle yt, except it goth to good use, for it clere good and servith with avouson, and he wolde I shoulde hafe do almesse on hem and relessed hem som money, but ye may sey [tell] hem the untrouth of the pryour of Hykelyng drawyth awey my devocion in such causes ... Were it not bought for the use of the said place of Seint Gylys, I wold not have sold it yhyt.[101]

None of the four major grants of property settled upon the hospital between 1455 and the Reformation refer specifically to its charitable work. Perhaps both John, duke of Norfolk (d.1461), who made over land in Hethel and East Carleton, and Thomas Wetherby, from whose trustees the hospital finally wrested control of an estate in Colney, Hethersett and Eaton, together with the manor of 'Heylesden' in Cringleford, proposed to found chantries.[102] This was certainly the intention of John Smyth (d.1489), who as master of St Giles's had benefited from the acquisition of the rectory at Coltishall. He also owned land there, which, along with his manor of Rollesby, went to support a priest celebrating for the health of his soul in the hospital church. Last, but by no means least, Bishop Goldwell's chantry there was maintained out of property in Swannington, Horsford, Salhouse, Wroxham, Trowse and Newton, and the Essex village of Fobbing. These were administered separately, and the revenues diverted into a special fund, which also paid the master's annual stipend.[103]

Several of the major acquisitions made by St Giles's were thus intended to find the wages of chaplains or support the cost of requiem masses to be said by the hospital staff. Significantly, the total cost of their fees and liveries had risen from £10 in 1319–20 to over £23 in 1510–11, so extra help was clearly needed.[104] Once this priority had been met, however, any surplus profits would be available for general use, along with the additional income forthcoming from other new properties not encumbered with such charges. Despite the hospital's territorial expansion, net annual income (which could fluctuate in years when substantial legacies or gifts of alms were received) did not rise at a corresponding rate [TABLES C and D]. Depressed land values after the Black Death, escalating labour costs on hospital manors and the problem of mounting arrearages meant that net revenues in 1526–27 were no higher than they had been in 1341–42. In practical terms, then, the grants and purchases listed above served to cushion St Giles's against worsening economic circumstances, but did not bring increased spending power. Indeed, in many cases, the endowment of new chantries, lights and altars actually prompted successive masters to spend far more than they could afford on beautifying the church and enlarging the facilities available for visiting clergy.

Between 1505 and 1527, each surviving annual statement of income and expenditure drawn up by the hospital's senior accountant records all the unpaid arrears then due from his subordinates. Never less than £74, in several instances these sums were considerably higher than anticipated current receipts, and began mounting again after 1519 [TABLE D]. Without doubt, the problem of collecting rents and tithes extended far beyond the city of Norwich, and explains why the total 'charge' laid to the accountant during this period seems so high. Because overspending in one year was, by the same token, included among outgoings in the next, the total annual disbursements (the accountant's 'discharge') during the difficult second and third decades of the sixteenth century also appear inflated. By 1526 the cumulative, inherited shortfall between income and expenditure stood at £88, and constituted a heavy burden which only outside intervention (hitherto in the form of a subvention from the master) could have lifted. Although, by and large, the accountant did his best to keep current expenditure within limits, and ought sometimes (as in 1513–14 or 1521–22) to have ended the year with a few pounds in credit, he was, on the one hand, charged with sums that could not be raised and, on the other, obliged to pay off a backlog of debt, which was insidiously rising. In many English hospitals and monasteries the first casualties of such financial pressure were the poor. Given the way St Giles's was changing, it might be assumed that here, too, stringent cuts were made in charitable relief. But not all Bishop Suffield's ideals were abandoned.

Caring For The Poor

That St Giles's was still performing an important role as a refuge for the destitute, hungry and aged in the 1340s is evident from the wording of Bishop Beck's licence for the appropriation of St Peter's church, Mundham. Did the masters continue to honour this obligation after the upheavals of the Black Death and the hospital's development as a college for secular priests? Royal letters patent of 1411, permitting the alienation in mortmain to the hospital of John Derlyngton's bequest, also refer to a more modest grant of fuel worth 20s a year made by the prior of Horsham St Faith 'to the use and profit of the poor and infirm'.[105] Although tantalisingly little information about these people is to be found in the hospital accounts, which survive in large numbers from 1319 onwards, silence cannot necessarily be equated with neglect. On the contrary, the wills of many Norwich clergy and citizens contain specific bequests to the bedridden poor lying in St Giles's, although it is worth noting that whereas the level of testamentary provision by clergy remained constant between 1370 and 1532, support from the laity declined appreciably after 1440. Throughout this period, about twenty-two per cent of clerical testators consistently left goods or money to the hospital. But whereas thirty-five per cent of the laymen and women whose wills survive before 1439 made some gift, however small, only ten per cent did so thereafter.[106] As early as 1382, one local testator had insisted that his legacy of 15s was to be shared among the poor, rather than the rich (*non divitibus*) dwelling there and at St Paul's. Others may have been disinclined to assist an institution which, to the casual observer, at least, appeared so affluent.[107]

By 1451, when Henry VI allowed the master and brethren to acquire additional estates to the value of £20 a year in mortmain, some economies had been made. The establishment still provided meals at the gate for thirteen paupers every day, housed infirm chaplains and offered a bed for the night to 'other poor people .. from outside, converging on the hospital'. Seven impoverished scholars, now described as choristers, were also accommodated. But the number of nurses had been halved to two, and only eight 'debilitated paupers' were allowed to remain as long-stay patients in the infirmary. Emphasis was, moreover, placed upon the obligation to perform divine service, which evidently constituted a major drain on resources. It may be noted that the hospital paid £32 for this particular licence, in addition to all the other bribes and douceurs which customarily changed hands on such occasions.[108] References in the late medieval accounts to 'le goddeshouse', the '*domus dei*', the '*domus pauperum*' and 'the door for the poor at the gates' suggest that the poor who stayed overnight, and perhaps even the sick as well, were placed in a separate building outside the hospital church. This move would accord with the architectural and liturgical changes discussed above, and would make sense if fewer people were being accommodated.[109] The *Valor Ecclesiasticus* records the presence of just six patients in the hospital, although there were also four almsmen, who may possibly have been elderly chaplains. Between 1465 and 1527 the accounts list modest payments to these 'bedesmen', who never numbered more than three at any given time.[110]

It is, however, apparent that the master and chaplains would occasionally undertake to support other deserving cases out of their own budget. In 1440, the jurors of Holme Street leet complained that one Geoffrey Skinner, a leper, had been permitted to live in the hospital precincts and threatened both him and the master with fines of 20s each unless he left within a few days.[111] No further evidence of the presence of such 'intolerable persons' has yet come to light, but temporary shelter

TABLE C

The Finances of St Giles's Hospital, 1319-1397

Year	1319-20	1320-21	1322-23	1326-27	1327-28	1341-42	1374-75	1396-97
INCOME	115	115	166	127	114	149	181	143
Deficit last year	4	7	8	40	5	-	6	16
Current expenses	118	123	171	92	125	152	175	164
EXPENSES	122	130	179	132	130	152	181	180
Deficit this year	7	15	13	5	16	3	-	37

Norfolk Record Office, case 24, shelf A, box of accounts 1306-97

All sums are in pounds sterling. Accounts run from Michaelmas to Michaelmas (29 September), except for 1396-97, which begins in February and ends in the following January

TABLE D

The Finances of St Giles's Hospital, 1465-1527

Year	1465-66	1483-84	1486-87	1488-89	1499-1500	1500-01	1502-03	1505-06	1506-07	1507-08	1509-10	1510-11	1511-12
Arrears	15	18	-	-	-	-	-	85	91	91	85	74	80
Receipts	102	89	106	109	106	139	83	86	141	160	110	107	79
INCOME	117	107	106	109	106	139	83	171	232	251	195	181	159
Deficit last year	5	10	22	19	39	53[1]	-	-	18	-	9	7	-
Current Expenses	145	117	108	98	111	151	177	106	103	130	107	98	97
EXPENSES	150	127	130	117	150	204	177	106	121	130	116	105	97
Current receipts in hand/overspent	- 48	- 20	- 24	- 8	- 44	- 65	- 94[2]	- 20	+ 20	+ 30	- 6	+ 2	- 18[3]

Year	1512-13	1513-14	1514-15	1515-16	1516-17	1519-20	1521-22	1522-23	1523-24	1524-25	1525-26	1526-27
Arrears	114	114	116	123	130	117	125	138	144	172	174	185
Receipts	94	127	117	122	117	135	133	122	119	117	102	147
INCOME	208	241	233	245	247	252	258	260	263	289	276	332
Deficit last year	37	57	55	61	18[4]	33	78	75[5]	76	50	62[6]	88[7]
Current expenses	114	124	123	130	112	134	125	121	90	122	118	120
EXPENSES	151	181	178	191	130	167	203	196	166	172	180	208
Current receipts in hand/overspent	- 57	- 54	- 61	- 69	- 13	- 32	- 70	- 74	- 47	- 55	- 78	- 61

Norfolk Record Office, case 24, shelf A, boxes of accounts 1465-1501, 1485-1508, 1510-25.
All sums are in pounds sterling.

1. Additional overspending of £9 by the steward added in.

2. The deficit actually stood at £243, but the master underwrote it.

3. The accountant was **said** to have overspent by £37 but the calculations are unclear

4. Because certain arrears of rent were **theoretically** counted as receipts, the accountant's deficit was reduced by £51.

5. Deficits run up by the accountant elsewhere on the hospital manors were added to those in his own account.

6. As number 5

7. As number 5

may customarily have been afforded to them. Nor can we tell how much of the food purchased by the steward or sent to the house from its country estates was intended for charitable purposes. In the absence of information about individual allowances (or 'diets') we must take on trust the claim made in 1536 that seven poor scholars were still being maintained (at an annual cost of £12) and that £19 was spent each year on daily meals for thirteen paupers and the support of six bedridden almsmen. In addition, a total of 280 meals of bread, pottage and eggs or cheese were distributed on the feasts of the Annunciation and St Dunstan.[112]

Among the recipients of charity listed in the *Valor Ecclesiasticus* were the hospital's two nurses, whose task was 'to attend upon the poor coming and going each day'. In return they received board and lodging to the annual value of 52s each, which was a few shillings more than the allowance made for the almsmen. At an early stage in its history, St Giles's had followed the road already trodden by many English hospitals and had begun selling corrodies to women who needed to provide for their old age. In 1309, for example, the widowed Mary de Attleborough settled her late husband's estates in Seething upon the house, being promised a refuge there for life as one of the sisters.[113] Just as St Paul's hospital had established a standard rate for corrodies, so St Giles's appears to have expected a minimum payment for admission. Both Alice Bothumsyll and Elizabeth Ordyng, nurses in residence during the 1520s, handed over 66s 8d in instalments 'as alms' when they first arrived. Alice left the hospital in 1526 to live at Watton, near Thetford, taking her personal possessions with her by cart at the master's expense. Any notions of shared property or monastic hardship had clearly been abandoned by then, although no hint of scandal or impropriety ever attached itself to the sisters.[114]

The will of Richard Hawze, who died in the hospital at this time, provides a further insight into their life and status, which was by no means as humble as might be expected. Far from being an impoverished wayfarer himself, Hawze left behind goods to the value of almost £2: he bequeathed 3s 4d to one of the priests and a similar sum to Dame Elizabeth for her prayers. Elizabeth received an additional 20d 'for helpyng me', which suggests that she had nursed him in his final illness. She must have inspired his confidence, for he named her as executrix, too, and also left a few pence to her servant.[115] The latter, who is otherwise undocumented, may also have been the recipient of alms in return for labour: one of the many potential 'loyterers' who managed to escape vagrancy by taking menial jobs in hospitals and monasteries, where they were paid in kind.[116]

Although St Giles's failed in many respects to follow the rule set down in 1249 by Walter Suffield, the poor were not entirely forgotten. And if, over the years, its development as a secular college, staffed with chantry priests and ambitious careerists, took priority over the care of the sick, some beds were still maintained, meals were regularly distributed and a few needy travellers welcomed. Indebtedness, extravagance and mismanagement are, like poverty, relative concepts: many English medieval hospitals, dogged by unfavourable economic circumstances

10. The south-west corner of the cloister of St Giles's hospital, overlooked by the bell tower. The church of St Helen stands on the south side, and the refectory on the west. Built shortly before the Reformation, the cloister marked a further step in the move from hospital to college.

beyond their control, contrived to make matters worse through chronic overspending, maladministration and absenteeism. The case of the London hospital of St Thomas Acon, which owed £718 to creditors in 1510, and was in such a desperate state of disrepair that the Mercers' Company had to step in to assume control of its finances, shows how bad such problems could become.[117] Since neither the government nor the papacy ever saw fit to send commissioners to investigate charges of misconduct at St Giles's (a fact itself worth noting), we may assume that it remained free from the worst abuses and was felt to perform its proper function. The early Tudor episcopal visitors certainly found little cause for complaint, at least in comparison with the neighbouring monastery, where standards left much to be desired.[118]

The author of *Dives and Pauper*, a popular medieval tract on the subject of poor relief, was critical of men and women whose piety found expression in bricks and mortar rather than almsgiving:

> Me thynkith that it were betere to geuyn the monye to the pore folc, to the blynde and to the lame wose soulys God boughte so dere, than to spendyn it in solempnyte and pride and makynge of heye chyrchis, in riche vestimentys, in curyous wyndowys, in grete bellys, for God is nought holpyn therby and the pore folc myghte be holpyn therby wol mychil [much].[119]

Yet St Giles's late medieval patrons were as anxious to build bell towers, endow chantry chapels and subsidise architectural improvements as the master and brethren were to accept them. For many pious donors, such institutions could barely be distinguished from colleges of priests: they were places for the celebration of divine service, dedicated in all its splendour and musicianship to the salvation of the Christian departed. Here the sick poor, whose intercession had once seemed so important, were now increasingly – sometimes even physically – marginalised. Although benefactors continued to support whatever charitable activities might still be undertaken by the country's older hospitals, there was a move towards other, less formal schemes for poor relief. These could be managed by the laity at a parochial level, and offered far greater opportunities for selectivity and control.

END NOTES

1   As he said in his will. A copy survives in the Norfolk Record Office, case 24, shelf B, no. 2. An English version, heavily edited and with some omissions, appears in Blomefield, *History of the County of Norfolk*, vol. III, pp. 487–92.

2   *The Victoria History of the County of Norfolk*, II, pp. 455–57. As late as the 1280s St Mary's is described as a hospital: Norfolk Record Office, case 24, shelf B, no. 48 (The *Liber Domus Dei*), ff. 31v–32r.

3   D.H.S. Cranage, 'Eastern Chapels in the Cathedral Church of Norwich', *Antiquaries Journal*, XII (1932), pp. 117–26; E.C. Fernie, 'Two Aspects of Bishop Walter Suffield's Lady Chapel at Norwich Cathedral', in *England in the Thirteenth Century*, ed. W.M. Ormrod (Nottingham, 1985), pp. 52–55 and plates; and idem, *An Architectural History of Norwich Cathedral* (Oxford, 1993), pp. 162–63. The chapel measured 72 feet by 36 feet and was 38 feet high at its eaves.

4   Dyer, *Standards of Living*, p. 241, provides some examples of episcopal philanthropy in thirteenth-century England, as does J.R.H. Moorman, *Church Life in England in the Thirteenth Century* (Cambridge, 1945), p. 206.

5   See note 1, above.

6   John Stow, *A Survey of London*, vol. I, p. 90.

7   Matthew Paris, *Chronica Majora*, vol. IV, pp. 555–56; vol. V, pp. 80, 451–52, 638; vol. VI, pp. 296–97. On p. 638 Paris notes that in times of famine Suffield 'expended all his vessels and even his silver spoons (*etiam coclearia argenta*) along with all his treasury on the poor'.

8   W.E. Lunt, *The Valuation of Norwich* (Oxford, 1926), pp. 52–68.

9   Matthew Paris, *Chronica Majora*, vol. IV, pp. 640–44. Paris was actually present on this occasion.

10   Ibid., vol. IV, p. 261.

11   See note 1, above. Bartholomew de Cotton, *Historia Anglicana*, ed. H.R. Luard (Rolls Series, 1859), p. 394. Tierney, 'The Decretists and the "Deserving Poor"', pp. 360–73. A synodal statute drawn up under Suffield's direction may be found in *Councils and Synods II, 1205–1313*, part I, *1205–65*, pp. 498–501; and his note on the role of the archbishop in election procedures at Canterbury Cathedral Priory (1244) in *Anglia Sacra*, ed. H. Wharton (2 vols, London, 1691), vol. I, pp. 174–75.

12   E.F. Jacob, 'St Richard of Chichester', *Journal of Ecclesiastical History*, VII (1956), pp. 174–88, and especially p. 182 for a description of his almsgiving and care for the sick.

13   *Councils and Synods II, 1205–1313*, part I, *1205–65*, pp. 451–67, especially pp. 461, 465.

14   Jacob, 'St Richard of Chichester', pp. 174–88. Wych's will, which is remarkably similar to that of Bishop Suffield, has been edited, with extensive notes, by W.H. Blaauw, in *Sussex Archaeological Collections*, I (1848), pp. 164–92. See pp. 182–85 for his close connexion with Suffield, to whom he left two bequests. For the impact of the mendicants on ideas about poverty, see Mollat, *The Poor in the Middle Ages*, pp. 120–25.

15   See note 1, above; C.H. Talbot and E.A. Hammond, *The Medical Practitioners in Medieval England* (London, 1965), p. 284.

16   F.M. Powicke, *Henry III and the Lord Edward* (2 vols, Oxford, 1947), vol. I, p. 269; J.C. Russell, *Dictionary of Writers of Thirteenth Century England* (London, 1936), pp. 81–82.

17   *Historical Manuscripts Commission Ninth Report*, part I, p. 49. In 1250 Wendover entered the fraternity of St Bartholomew's, in return for gifts of books and ornaments. For the hospital's educational role, see Rawcliffe, 'The Hospitals of Later Medieval London', pp. 2–3.

18   See note 1, above.

19   Norfolk Record Office, case 24, shelf B, no. 1; DCN 43/48.

20   See note 1, above. *The Oxford Dictionary of Saints*, ed. D.H. Farmer (Oxford, 1978), pp. 173–74, provides a short life of the saint and assessment of his influence.

21   *The Minor Poems of John Lydgate*, ed. H.N. MacCracken (Early English Text Society, CXCII, 1911, reprinted 1961), pp. 171–72.

22   See note 1, above.

23   C.H. Lawrence, *St Edmund of Abingdon* (Oxford, 1960), pp. 77, 109, and generally for a reassessment of the hagiographical literature.

24   Jacob, 'St Richard of Chichester', pp. 174–88.

25   E.A. Brown, 'Death and the Human Body in the Later Middle Ages: The Legislation of Boniface VIII on the Division of the Corpse', *Viator*, XII (1981), pp. 228–33, records several cases of heart burial, some of which predate Edmund of Abingdon, although he was especially influential in this regard. In addition, it is worth noting that Roger, earl of Winchester (d.1264), ordered a measure for corn in the shape of a coffin to be placed in the chapel of the hospital of St James and St John, Brackley, near the shrine holding his mother's heart. His own heart and, reputedly, that of the Norman founder, were said to be buried there, too (*The Victoria History of the County of Northamptonshire*, II, ed. R.M. Serjeantson and W.R.D. Adkins (London, 1906), p. 151.

26   See note 1, above.

27   The fame of his miracles is noted by Matthew Paris, *Chronica Majora*, vol. V, p. 638; and by Bartholomew Cotton, the Norwich monk, *Historia Anglicana*, p. 394.

28   Jacob, 'St Richard of Chichester', p. 183. For the bequest to Whitewell, see note 1, above. A sermon of Edmund of Abingdon warns against 'false counsellors, grasping persons, flatterers, the hard of heart and oppressors of the poor. With such people the court of every prince and great man is filled. Whoever, therefore, wishes to lead a good life, let him depart from court.' (Lawrence, *St Edmund of Abingdon*, pp. 131–32.) Suffield was perhaps too much of a curialist.

29   Norfolk Record Office, case 24, shelf B, no. 1. The suggested date of 1245–46 is advanced in *The Victoria History of the County of Norfolk*, II, p. 442, where the hospital regulations are listed, almost in their entirety. It seems that the prior of Bromholm's *inspeximus* of a letter of Alexander IV, issued to the hospital in the first year of his pontificate (1254–55), has been misread as dating from Suffield's first year as bishop (1245–46). See note 32, below.

30   Norfolk Record Office, case 24, shelf B, no. 4.

31   Ibid., N/MC 15/4 (the letter); COL 5/2/1 (the bull).

32   *Calendar of Papal Registers: Papal Letters*, 1198–1304, ed. W.H. Bliss (London, 1894), p. 312; Norfolk Record Office, case 24, shelf B, no. 3.

33   Norfolk Record Office, DCN 43/48. This is the text used by Blomefield, *History of the County of Norfolk*, vol. IV, pp. 382–83.

34   Matthew Paris, *Chronica Majora*, vol. V, p. 80. He had left England just after Michaelmas 1248 '*pro quibus causis secretis*' (ibid., p. 36).

35   Rubin, *Charity and Community*, pp. 154–56; C.H. Lawrence, *Medieval Monasticism* (London, 1989), pp. 163–69.

36   *The Observances in Use at the Augustinian Priory of St Giles and St Andrew at Barnwell, Cambridgeshire*, ed. J. Willis Clark (Cambridge, 1897), pp. 175, 179.

37   Similar regulations about the way mass was to be sung or said were introduced at St John's hospital, Bishop's Lynn, in 1234 (Norfolk Record Office, DCN 84/14), and at the hospital of the Blessed Virgin, Yarmouth, in 1386 (ibid., Phi 623)

38   Moorman, *Church Life in England*, pp. 176–77.

39   R. Owst, *Literature and the Pulpit in Medieval England* (Oxford, 1961), pp. 283–84.

40   Le Goff, *The Birth of Purgatory*, pp. 283–85.

41   Norfolk Record Office, case 24, shelf B, no. 9.

42   *The Chronicle of Bury St Edmunds, 1212–1301*, ed. A. Gransden (London, 1964), p. 22. Monastic chroniclers, who ate wheat bread, may, however, give a misleading impression of the effects of bad weather on barley crops, which were more resilient and constituted a staple of the peasant diet. See H.E. Hallam, 'The Climate of Eastern England 1250–1350', *Agricultural History Review*, XXXII (1984), pp. 124–32.

43   *The Chronicle of Bury St Edmunds*, p. 123.

44   P.H. Cullum, 'Poverty and Charity in Early Fourteenth-Century England', in *England in the Fourteenth Century*, ed. N. Rogers (Stamford, 1993), pp. 140–51, especially pp. 147–48; I. Kershaw, 'The Great Famine and Agrarian Crisis in England 1315–22', *Past and Present*, LIX (1973), p. 31.

45   Clay, *The Medieval Hospitals of England*, pp. 23–25. According to Knowles and Hadcock, *Medieval Religious Houses*, pp. 310–410, a bare minimum of eighteen hospitals made specific provision for 'decayed' clergy, but many others would have accorded them priority.

46   *The Victoria History of the County of Sussex*, II, ed. W. Page (London, 1907) p. 109. Blaauw, 'Will of Richard de la Wych', pp. 172–73, misidentifies Windham as Wymondham in Norfolk, and consequently states that 'no trace' can be found of Wych's hospital (pp. 190–91).

47   N. Orme, 'A Medieval Almshouse for the Clergy: Clyst Gabriel Hospital near Exeter', *Journal of Ecclesiastical History*, XXXIX (1988), pp. 1–15; idem, 'Sufferings of the Clergy: Illness and Old Age in Exeter Diocese 1300–1540', in *Life, Death and the Elderly*, ed. M. Pelling and R.M. Smith (London, 1991), pp. 62–73.

48   N. Tanner, *The Church in Late Medieval Norwich*, pp. 48–51.

49   Rowland Burdon, 'St Saviour's Hospital', p. 264.

50   See note 1, above. Straw was, for example, used for bedding at St John's Hospital, Winchester (D. Keene, *Survey of Winchester* (2 vols, Oxford, 1985), vol. II, p. 815).

51   *Histoire des Hopitaux en France*, p. 123; Norfolk Record Office, case 24, shelf B, no. 7.

52   *Lanfrank's 'Science of Cirurgie'*, ed. R. von Fleishhacker (Early English Text Society, CII, 1894), p. 55; John of Arderne, *Treatises of Fistula in Ano*, ed. D. Power (Early English Text Society, CXXXIX, 1910), p. 88. Suffield may also have had in mind the words of the First Epistle of Paul to Timothy (V, vv. 9–13): 'Let not a widow be taken into the number under threescore years old, having been the wife of one man. Well reported for good works ... if she have relieved the afflicted ... but the younger widow refuse: for when they have begun to wax wanton against Christ, they will marry; having damnation because they have cast off their

faith. And withal they learn to be idle, wandering about from house to house; and tattlers also and busybodies ... '

53   Cullum, *Cremetts and Corrodies*, pp. 7, 15.

54   Thompson, *The History of the Hospital and the New College of St Mary*, pp. 19, 47, 185; *The Register of Walter Gray*, p. 181; Rawcliffe, *Medicine and Society*, pp. 207 13. For some French comparisons, see *Histoire des Hopitaux en France*, pp. 111–12.

55   R. Harries, P. Cattermole and P. Mackintosh, *A History of Norwich School* (Norwich, 1991), pp. 10–15.

56   St Giles's may have served as a model for changes at the hospital of St John the Baptist, Bridgwater. In 1298 it was agreed that, among other things, the master would maintain thirteen poor boys *'habiles ad informandum in grammatica'*, who would study daily in the town, while the schoolmaster would send seven other mendicant scholars for meals at the hospital *(Calendar of the Register of John Dronkesford*, ed. Bishop Hobhouse (Somerset Record Society, I, 1887), p. 268).

57   Norfolk Record Office, case 24, shelf B, no. 5; Phi 516–18.

58   Ibid., box 30E1, no. 12075.

59   Ibid., case 24, shelf B, no. 48 (*Liber Domus Dei*), f. 59v.

60   Ibid., nos 7 and 48, ff. 1r–2v, 6v–8v, 23r–24v, 38v–39r (an arrangement of 1277 for burning a lamp at the high altar all night, which would have benefited the patients as well as the souls of the donors); box 30E1, no. 12083; Norwich Consistory Court Wills, Reg. Doke, f. 36r; Reg. Brosyard, f. 288v; Reg. Alpe, ff. 49v–50r.

61   Ibid., box 30E1, no. 12077; Blomefield, *History of the County of Norfolk*, vol. IV, p. 386.

62   Norfolk Record Office, case 24, shelf B, no. 48 (*Liber Domus Dei*), ff. 13r, 28r–28v, 52v; box 30E1, nos 12095, 12102.

63   Ibid., case 24, shelf B, no. 17.

64   See B. Thompson, 'From "Alms" to "Spiritual Services": The Function and Status of Monastic Property in Medieval England', in *Monastic Studies II*, ed. J. Loades (Bangor, 1991), pp. 227–61, for the background to these changes.

65   Norfolk Record Office, case 24, shelf B, nos 7, 26, 28, 55, 59, 66 and 48 (*Liber Domus Dei*), f. 42r; box 30E1, nos 12083, 12105; Norwich Consistory Court Wills, Reg. Brosyard, f. 288v; Reg. Alblaster, ff. 107v–8r; *Calendar of Patent Rolls, 1317–21* (London, 1903), p. 236; *1321–24* (London, 1904), p. 111; *1350–54* (London, 1907), p. 114; *1408–13* (London, 1909), p. 187; Blomefield, *History of the County of Norfolk*, vol. IV, pp. 386–87.

66   Norfolk Record Office, case 24, shelf A, boxes of general accounts, 1306–98 and 1510–25.

67   For a very general architectural history of St Giles's hospital, see F.W. Bennett-Symons, 'The Hospital of St Giles, Norwich', *Journal of the British Archaeological Association*, new series, XXXI (1925), pp. 55–67. Photographs of the surviving medieval fabric may be found in C. Jewson's pamphlet, *History of the Great Hospital Norwich* (Norwich, 1978), but the text is unreliable.

68   Testamentary evidence enables us to date the building of the choir to 1381 (Norfolk Record Office, Norwich Consistory Court Wills, Reg. Heydon, ff. 196r–96v), and its completion to 1383 (Reg. Harsyk, ff. 5r–5v).

69   *Visitations of the Diocese of Norwich*, pp. 12–13.

70   Thomas Starkey, *A Dialogue between Cardinal Pole and Thomas Lupset*, ed. J.M. Cowper (Early English Text Society, extra series, XXXII, 1878), p. 137.

71   Emden, *Biographical Register of the University of Oxford to 1500*, vol. I, pp. 618–19.

72   Idem, *Biographical Register of the University of Cambridge*, pp. 185–86. His gift for the tower is recorded in the account for 1397 (Norfolk Record Office, case 24, shelf A, box of general accounts, 1306–98).

73   Emden, *Biographical Register of the University of Oxford to 1500*, vol. III, p. 1667.

74   *Calendar of Close Rolls, 1461–68* (London, 1949), p. 178; *The Victoria History of the County of Norfolk*, II, pp. 386–87.

75   Selot figures prominently in the Paston correspondence, largely because he sat in judgement in a case between the Pastons and the Duke of Norfolk, whom he was alleged to favour. In 1465, for example, Margaret Paston complained about 'alle the demenyng and parcialte of master John Salatt' and one of the hospital chaplains (*Paston Letters and Papers of the Fifteenth Century*, ed. N. Davis (2 vols, Oxford, 1971–76), vol. I, pp. 320–21); Norfolk Record Office, case 8, shelf A, no. 11 (a transcript of Public Record Office, KB 27/793, rot. 103); *Calendar of Papal Registers: Papal Letters, 1471–84*, ed J.A. Twemlow (London, 1956), p. 727.

76   E.C.K. Underwood, 'Fifteenth-Century Clergy in the Diocese of Norwich' (Tasmania University PhD thesis, 1993), table XI, p. 580; J.F. Williams, 'Ordination in the Norwich Diocese during the Fifteenth Century', *Norfolk Archaeology*, XXXI (1956), pp. 347–58.

77   Public Record Office, C270/22.

78   See below, p. *****.

79   For expenditure on the precincts in 1502–3, see Norfolk Record Office, case 24, shelf A, roll of accounts for Norwich, 1485–1509.

80   Ibid., (for the year 1497–98) and box of general accounts, 1485–1508 (for the years 1499–1501).

81   Ibid., box of general accounts, 1485–1508 (for the year 1502–3). Jullys had previously provided as 'alms' 161 sheep, thatch, money for building projects, 28,000 tiles, ten combs of rye, five of malt and quantities of fish.

82   Cullum, *Cremetts and Corrodies*, p. 28; *Calendar of Inquisitions Miscellaneous*, vol. II, no. 1456; vol. III, no. 6; *Calendar of Patent Rolls, 1348–50* (London, 1905), pp. 175–76; Talbot and Hammond, *The Medical Practitioners in Medieval England*, pp. 345–46.

83   Norfolk Record Office, case 24, shelf B, no. 48 (*Liber Domus Dei*), ff. 1–70v.

84   Ibid., ff. 2r–2v, 59r; B.S. Ayers, R. Smith and M. Tillyard, 'The Cow Tower, Norwich: A Detailed Survey and Partial Reinterpretation', *Medieval Archaeology*, XXXII (1988), pp. 191–92; Cotton, *Historia Anglicana*, p. 172.

85   Norfolk Record Office, case 24, shelf A, boxes of accounts for Norwich, 1415–60, 1465–1501, roll for 1485–1509, box for 1510–28.

86   Ibid., box of accounts for Norwich, 1415–60 (for the year 1423–24).

87 Ibid., DCN 79/3 (Although it was reported, in 1526, that two of the chaplains disrupted services by arguing: *Visitations of the Diocese of Norwich*, pp. 206–7).

88 Ibid., case 24, shelf A, box of general accounts, 1485–1508.

89 Ibid., boxes of accounts for Norwich, 1415–60, 1465–1501.

90 Ibid., boxes of accounts for Norwich, 1465–1501, roll for 1485–1509, box for 1510–28.

91 Ibid., boxes of general accounts for Norwich, 1465–1501, 1485–1508, 1510–28.

92 Ibid., box of general accounts, 1306–98 (for the period January to September 1397); and note 75, above.

93 Ibid., case 24, shelf C, roll of accounts for Costessey, 1338–74, m. 4; shelf B, no. 51; F. Woodman, 'Hardley, Norfolk, and the Rebuilding of its Chancel', in *Studies in Medieval Art and Architecture Presented to Peter Lasko*, ed. D. Buckton and T.A. Heslop (Stroud, 1994), pp. 203–10.

94 Norfolk Record Office, case 24, shelf B, no. 48 (*Liber Domus Dei*), ff. 45v–47r, 49r–57v; Phi 292–93, 519, 600; box 30E1, nos 12056, 12058.

95 Ibid., case 24, shelf B, nos 3, 7, 15, 54, 57; *Calendar of Patent Rolls, 1317–21* (London, 1903), p. 236; *1330–34* (London, 1894), pp. 148, 151; *1377–81* (London, 1895), p. 604.

96 *Calendar of Patent Rolls, 1334–38* (London, 1895), p. 21; Norfolk Record Office, box 30E1, nos 12087–89; case 24, shelf B, nos 50, 52.

97 *Calendar of Patent Rolls, 1334–38*, p. 113; Norfolk Record Office, box 30E1, nos 12083, 12085; case 24, shelf B, no. 14; Phi 525.

98 Norfolk Record Office, box 30E1, no. 12097; Phi 378; case 24, shelf B, no. 48 (*Liber Domus Dei*), ff. 58r–58v.

99 *Calendar of Patent Rolls, 1350–54* (London, 1907), p. 114; *1408–13*, p. 187; Norfolk Record Office, case 24, shelf B, no. 55; box 30E1, no. 12108.

100 K.B. McFarlane, *England in the Fifteenth Century* (London, 1981), p. 192.

101 Quoted by Blomefield, who owned the letters, *History of the County of Norfolk*, vol. IV, pp. 388–89. In his nuncupative will of 1459 Sir John planned the endowment of a college of seven priests and seven 'porefolke' to pray for his soul and the souls of members of his family. Each of the almsmen was to receive 40s a year (*Paston Letters and Papers*, vol. I, p. 88).

102 Norfolk Record Office, Phi 99, 621; box 30E1, no. 12111; case 24, shelf B, no. 29.

103 Ibid., case 24, shelf A, roll of accounts for Fobbing etc., 1521–28; shelf B, no. 26; DCN 9/4; Blomefield, *History of the County of Norfolk*, vol. VI, p. 309.

104 Norfolk Record Office, case 24, shelf A, boxes of general accounts, 1306–98, 1510–25.

105 *Calendar of Patent Rolls*, 1408–13, p. 187.

106 N. Tanner, *The Church in Late Medieval Norwich*, p. 222.

107 Norfolk Record Office, Consistory Court Wills, Reg. Heydon, ff. 183r–84r.

108 *Calendar of Patent Rolls, 1446–52* (London, 1910), p. 475.

109 Norfolk Record Office, case 24, shelf A, box of accounts for Norwich, 1465–1501, roll for 1485–1509, box for 1510–28.

110 *Valor Ecclesiasticus*, vol. III, pp. 291–92; Norfolk County Record Office, case 24, shelf A, boxes of general accounts, 1465–1501, 1485–1508, 1509–25.

111 Norfolk Record Office, DCN 79/3. In 1443 (79/4) one John Wrenne, another leper, was presented by the jurors of the leet court, although they did not state where he lived. Stephen de Hospital was then charged with staying in the leet for a year without joining a tithing: perhaps he had found refuge at St Giles's.

112 *Valor Ecclesiasticus*, vol. III, pp. 291–92.

113 Norfolk Record Office, Phi 311.

114 Ibid., case 24, shelf B, box of general accounts, 1509–25.

115 Ibid., Norwich Consistory Court Wills, Reg. Alpe, ff. 49v–50r.

116 Sir Thomas More believed that in providing work for vagrants monastic houses gave the most socially useful and morally acceptable type of alms (*The Apologia*, p. 105).

117 Rawcliffe, 'The Hospitals of Later Medieval London', p. 16.

118 *Visitations of the Diocese of Norwich*, pp. 206–7, 271. One of the chaplains complained about the presence of married servants, in 1532, and urged that they and their wives should be removed. In this respect, at least, Bishop Suffield's regulations were still taken seriously.

119 *Dives and Pauper*, part I, pp. 189–90.

CHAPTER IV

Small Hospitals before the Reformation

As will already have become apparent, the cost of running even a small hospital and maintaining the endowment was so great that many establishments collapsed under the burden, either vanishing altogether or abandoning their charitable functions to become chantry chapels or fraternities for secular priests. Long before the Black Death took its devastating toll on the city, a number of Norwich's hospitals had already disappeared: only a passing mention in the sources, perhaps of nothing more than a pious intention on the part of the donor, now yields any trace of these short-lived institutions. Yet, in terms of their tenuous finances, uncertain prospects of survival and modest size, they are probably more representative of the English medieval hospital than the two larger and more celebrated houses of St Paul and St Giles Bishopgate, whose history is so well documented. Between the mid-twelfth century and the Reformation at least nine or ten smaller hospitals and hospices were planned, if not actually set up, by the residents of Norwich, partly in response to the city's rapid expansion and also because of the growing number of poor, often desperately sick pilgrims seeking temporary refuge as they trudged across East Anglia from one shrine to another.

One of the earliest and most pressing reasons for the foundation of hospitals was the need to accommodate penurious wayfarers. In sixth-century France conciliar decrees repeatedly reminded senior clergy of their responsibilities in this quarter; and hospices quickly sprang up along the main trade routes, as well as on the roads carrying hordes of pilgrims to Rome and later Compostella.[1] Most English hospitals accepted a similar obligation: at least 136 were specifically endowed for the benefit of travellers during the Middle Ages, priority generally being accorded to pilgrims.[2] The hospital of St John the Baptist, Basingstoke, was, for example, originally established for the support of 'sick folk and wayfarers': although new statutes of 1235 afforded admission to aged and infirm priests, Bishop Merton of Rochester still insisted that 'the wayfaring poor of Christ' should continue to find a welcome there.[3] The temptation to cut back on hospitality was, however, considerable, especially when institutions became more interested in operating commercially as schools or chantry chapels. Another house dedicated to St John, at Bridgwater in Somerset, had originally accommodated thirteen paupers and such 'pilgrims and religious' as might be passing through the town. The recruitment of more chaplains and a growing involvement in education gave rise to allegations that wayfarers were being deprived of hospitality; and in 1325 the Bishop of Bath and Wells himself intervened to investigate abuses.[4] A century later William, Lord Lovell, the patron of the hospital of SS James and John at Brackley in Northamptonshire, took similar action, complaining that it had been 'formerly decently built and founded and sufficiently endowed for the reception of pilgrims and sick and other miserable persons, and adorned with laudable statutes', but that 'by the negligence of the masters ... it had suffered so much both in governance and in means that it was feared to be on the point of ruin'. Among the many reforms instituted at his behest was the acquisition of a 'decent house' with half a dozen beds 'for the free relief of poor travellers for one night or longer'.[5]

It was, none the less, one thing to receive genuine pilgrims, who had either elected to make their journey in poverty as a mark of repentance or were truly indigent, and quite another to support idle vagabonds. The constant, nagging fear (especially pronounced after the upheavals of 1348–49 and the Peasants' Revolt of 1381) that hospitals might encourage able-bodied beggars to persist in a life of vice, led many houses to accept only the transient poor and then for two or three days at most. Besides pegging wages at pre-plague rates, the Statute of Labourers of 1349 had prohibited, under pain of imprisonment, the giving of alms to anyone capable of work 'so that thereby they may be compelled to labour for their necessary living'.[6] As the problem of vagrancy grew worse during the late-fifteenth and early-sixteenth centuries, so civic authorities throughout Europe became even more cautious with regard to the provision of accommodation in hostels and pilgrim hospitals. Yet even at Ypres, where reformers aimed to force back to work those who 'idely, lascyvyously and dissolutely are wonte ... to go roune and wander aboute lyke vacaboundes', the claims of sick and needy wayfarers upon the public purse were recognised:

> For suche as ar weryed we prouyde meate and drinke and beddes and ther necessaryes in comen hospytalles. And suche as be sycke and by the reason of sycknesse haue nat strengthe suffyciente to performe theire iourney we entreate fauourablye confortynge and refresshinge them ij, iij or iiij dayes or somtyme longer tyll they waxe stronge and be able to performe their begon vyages.[7]

Since, by and large, English pilgrim hostels were comparatively small, poorly endowed and prey to many vicissitudes, historians have tended to underestimate their importance. Perhaps, too, an abiding image of the medieval pilgrim derived from Chaucer's robust band of storytellers in *The Canterbury Tales* has led us to forget that many of the men and women who left home each year at the start of the 'season' were barely able to put one foot in front of the other. The widespread belief that disease, suffering and deformity came ultimately from God, either as a

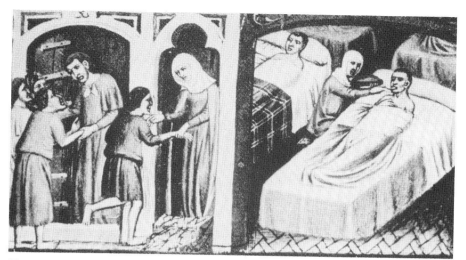

11. Weary and sick travellers are received at the gates of a hospital by the master and matron, then given food, drink and rest, in accordance with Christ's teaching.

punishment for sin or as a means of purifying the soul on earth, encouraged medieval men and women to invoke the intercessionary help of saints and holy relics when they fell ill. So also did the high cost, extreme discomfort and unpredictability of many types of conventional medical treatment, which might well make even minor ailments worse and could do little to alleviate chronic pain.[8]

Along with pilgrims who simply wanted a change of scene, or sought to improve their own or their deceased relatives' spiritual health, the sick, crippled, blind and mentally disturbed flocked to shrines in search of more immediate relief. Long before the Reformation, a perceived tendency on the part of the Church to exploit the faith of vulnerable people, and make handsome profits out of their adversity aroused criticism. Followers of John Wycliffe, including well over half the sixty-one heretics tried in Norwich between 1428 and 1431, shared the conviction that 'no maner of pylgrymages owith to be do to ony seyntes, but the expenese whiche shuld be do and made in suche pilgrimages shuld be yoven to pore puple'. Some went even further: in the words of one woman from the Norfolk village of Loddon, 'all pilgrimage goyng servyth of nothyng but oonly to yeve prestes good that be to riche, and to make gay tapsters and proude ostelers'.[9] Since she herself lived on one of the major thoroughfares through the county, along which travelled visitors from every part of England, we may assume that she spoke from personal observation.

Reports of miraculous cures were carefully compiled by the shrine keepers: besides presenting evidence of sanctity, this practice served to attract greater crowds and the gifts of cash, plate and jewels they brought with them. Pilgrims also made *ex voto* offerings of appropriate 'ymages' fashioned in wax or even precious metals, an aspect of devotion seized upon by satirists and reformers. While staunchly upholding 'the wonderfull worke of God' effected through the medium of his saints, Thomas More recognised how easily the sick might be deceived:

> Some preste to brynge vp a pylgrymage in his parysshe may deuyse some false felowe, faynyng hym selfe to come seke a saynt in his chyrche, and there sodeynly say that he hathe gotten his syght. Then shall ye haue the belles rong for a myracle. And the fonde folke of the countrey soone made foles. Then women commynge thyther with theyr candels. And the person byenge of some lame begger iij or iiij payre of theyr olde crutches, with xij pennes spent in men and women of wex thrust thorowe dyuers placys ... wyll make his offeryngys for one vij yere worth twyse his tythes.[10]

He did not exaggerate. Papal commissioners visiting the tomb of Thomas Cantelupe at Hereford Cathedral in 1307, during the course of the canonisation process, recorded 2,000 such models of whole bodies or human limbs, 108 discarded walking-sticks and crutches, ninety-five childrens' shifts and 'an uncountable quantity of eyes, breasts, teeth and ears'. On returning a few months later, they found that nearly a hundred more items had been deposited by new visitors who either hoped to be cured or wished to give thanks for deliverance.[11]

Norwich as a Place of Pilgrimage

Through the efforts of a Benedictine monk named Thomas of Monmouth, Norwich briefly became the centre of a similar healing cult, dedicated to William, the child martyr. Although he was never actually canonised, the boy was popularly held to be a saint; and news of his posthumous miracles, which were catalogued in considerable detail by Thomas at various points between 1150 and 1173, drew large numbers of pilgrims to the city. *The Life and Passion of St William the Martyr of Norwich* constitutes an important source for the study of local charitable and medical provision during the twelfth century, not least because it provides the only known reference to Brichtiu's hospital, about which no further information survives. Here lay an impoverished and dsfigured woman

> who had been suffering for a long time from her sickness and was quite helpless. All her body was swollen and ulcerated, as though afflicted with elephantiasis *(ac tanquam elephantino perculsa)*; she presented a miserable and horrible spectacle to all beholders. When she had been

suffering for more than a year from this great sickness, the blessed martyr William came to her in a vision of the night and said: 'Because I have compassion upon thy misery, woman, I pity thee, and I come to bestow on thee a saving remedy for all thy sufferings'.[12]

Having described how the woman was able to return home and lead a normal life, Thomas does not mention the hospital again, although his account suggests that it accepted the terminally sick and may well have been a *leprosarium*. Contemporary works on leprosy were firmly grounded in humoral theory and distinguished four basic types, of which 'elephancia' (the generic name given to the disease in Classical times) was one.[13] But whatever her presumed condition, she had clearly been admitted on a permanent basis, and was being nursed accordingly.

Sick visitors, on the other hand, needed no more than a few days' assistance while they stayed in Norwich to pray for a cure at William's tomb. Public interest in the rather implausible figure of the young apprentice leather-worker had initially been aroused by a series of translations. The body was moved in 1150 from the monastic cemetery to the chapter house (against the Prior's better judgement), thence to a more prestigious site within the Cathedral and finally, four years later, once the crowds began to swell, to the martyrs' chapel north of the high altar.[14] Although largely regional, in so far that most of William's miracles were reported by people from East Anglia, at its height the cult attracted some desperate cases from further afield. One man, who travelled over 180 miles, who was

> very weak throughout his body, guided his steps and supported his feet and frame on two sticks such as are commonly called crutches. ... He set out from York as best he could and, journeying slowly, spent many days over his long pilgrimage, supported on the way by faith and drawn on by hope.[15]

Thomas of Monmouth records the arrival of children in litters, on stretchers and even slumped in wheelbarrows. A poor woman from Bury St Edmunds 'walking with trestles, which she held in her hands, made the best of her way to Norwich bent double'; while another reputedly took two and a half months to drag herself 'slower than any tortoise' the thirty miles from Langham, near Holt. She had previously been taken to shrines 'laid like a sack across a horse' by the local parson, who fed, clothed and housed her as an act of charity, but on this occasion she felt the need to offer an additional proof of faith. On her long and painful journey she would, presumably, have been sheltered by the many householders who believed it was their Christian duty to assist pilgrims ('I was a stranger and ye took me in': Matthew XXV, v. 35). She may also have stayed in some of the small hospices which sprang up in and around Norwich to cater for sick wayfarers.[16]

According to Thomas, sufferers from heart disease, dropsy, cancer, fevers,

139

demonic possession, swollen limbs and eyes, wasting sickness, sleeplessness, paralysis, convulsions, epilepsy and crippling deformities, as well as the deaf, the blind, the dumb and the lame, were restored to health by the saint, sometimes at home on their sickbeds, but mostly while at prayer beside his remains. Few shrines were, however, able to sustain more than limited local interest for very long. Once William lost his enthusiastic champion and his novelty value began to diminish, the public, always in search of something new, moved on. A few pilgrims continued to invoke his help, but from the thirteenth century onwards Norwich was for most people a staging-post on the way to other destinations. Because of the proliferation of healing shrines throughout East Anglia, which boasted international centres at Ipswich, Bury St Edmunds and Walsingham, as well as dozens of parish churches associated with miraculous cures, the city continued to welcome large numbers of pilgrims right up to the Reformation, lodging them as they trekked across the region. Some would have found accommodation in the various inns which were springing up around the city, but others were too poor or too sick to make use of this facility. A promise of spiritual benefits extended by Bishop Gray in 1201 to those who supported St Paul's hospital in its work for the sick poor specifically mentions pilgrims, the majority of whom would already have been heading elsewhere[17] Despite repeated attempts to acquire new relics and win back their share of the pilgrimage trade, the cathedral monks never managed to recapture the heady days of the 1160s, when the sick had camped out in the apse. After a fairly promising start, devotion to Bishop Suffield (d.1257) lapsed, and although new chapels, shrines and images generated a respectable income from offerings none became the focus of a healing cult.[18]

Even if they may occasionally have outshone him in piety, it is unlikely that any medieval English pilgrims consistently spent as much as Henry III on their journeys. At least some of the money helped to stimulate the local economy: in 1240, for example, the sheriff of Norfolk was ordered to buy 1,000 pounds of wax, to be burnt in tapers at Bury St Edmunds and Walsingham for the health of the King's soul; and ten or so years later Henry himself bought candles to the value of almost £18 while staying in Norwich. But this remarkable outlay enriched the city's chandlers rather than its monks, who must have cast envious glances at their fellow Benedictines in Bury. There, on one single visit, Henry had donated silver candlesticks worth £30 to the shrine of St Edmund, had paid £20 for a new altar front, and had provided each of the town's parish churches and larger hospitals with a new chalice. The poor, too, had benefited to the tune of £20, while a further £10 went on plate for the shrines at Walsingham and Bromholm, which also figured on the royal itinerary.[19]

From 1223 onwards hundreds of sick travellers had as their objective the Cluniac priory of Bromholm (near North Walsham), which lay directly north of Norwich on the coast. It was then that the house first exhibited a sizeable piece of the true cross, purchased under rather dubious circumstances, shortly after the sack of Constantinople by the crusaders in 1204, from the medieval equivalent of a travelling salesman. The investment paid off handsomely, making it possible to rebuild the delapidated church and provide a more appropriate setting for such a precious relic.[20] The chronicler, Roger of Wendover, recounts how, then and there, 'the dead came alive, the crippled recovered their mobility, the flesh of lepers was cleansed, the possessed were freed from their demons, and every single invalid who approached the said wood [of the cross] with faith withdrew again whole and well'.[21] Norfolk remained *par excellence* the county of pilgrims, with at least nineteen well-known shrines famous for their healing powers. Three of them lay within easy walking distance of Norwich and one in the city itself: although their appeal remained essentially regional, they must have added appreciably to the number of needy, infirm people seeking alms there.

Comparatively little is known about the shrine of St Albert at Cringleford, a village just two miles south west of the medieval city and now part of suburban Norwich. Since he was reputedly a king of the East Angles he may have had less popular appeal than St Walstan, who was venerated throughout Norfolk as a 'petitioner for labourers'.[22] Several churches fostered his cult, but the major pilgrimage centre lay at Bawburgh (west of Norwich). Although he offered his especial protection to agricultural workers, Walstan's intercessionary powers were widely invoked by the sick:

> Blind men made to see and look upon the sunne,
> Crooked both and lame right up for to goe,
> The deafe man perfectly his hearing hath wonne,
> Damned spirit cast out of man also,
> Leprosy, fevir, palsy, with many sicknesses mo,
> Be cured and healed in this holy place.[23]

A few travellers from other parts of England might be found among the pilgrims who visited his shrine and holy well. One such was a Canterbury weaver 'sore vexed of bone ach both day and night', whose first recourse was naturally to St Thomas Becket. Disheartened by the ineffectiveness of his prayers, he followed the advice of a Norfolk man and came on crutches to Bawburgh, clutching a wax image of his leg as an offering. The pain left him and he was miraculously cured on the way.[24]

Although it was once regarded as a purely local phenomenon, the cult of Richard Caister (d.1420), the saintly vicar of St Stephen's church in Norwich, seems to have had far wider appeal. Margery Kempe visited his tomb in order to pray for a cure for one of her clerical acquaintances in Lynn; and John Howard made a personal offering of 6s 8d here in August 1483, shortly before becoming Duke of Norfolk. Pilgrim badges, which show Caister preaching from his pulpit, have been found in London and Salisbury. The depiction on them of the dove of the Holy Spirit and of God the Father suggests that the convent of Holy Trinity (which owned the living of St Stephen's) was anxious to advertise its connection with the shrine. If the Cathedral monks failed to turn Caister into a second William, they were at least able to attract visitors to the dependent cell of St Leonard's, which had been founded by Bishop Losinga just across the Wensum to the east of the city. Notable as 'a place after the manner of a pylgrimage for resort of people for dyvers diseases', the church possessed images of the Virgin Mary, the Holy Cross and St Anthony of Egypt (a healing saint to whom hospitals were often dedicated, and whose help was especially sought during outbreaks of plague).[25] The growing popularity of the cult of Henry VI (d.1471) led the monks to acquire 'a famous image' of the Lancastrian martyr as well, although none of the 174 miracles attributed to him between 1481 and 1500 evidently took place there.[26] Even so, the prospect of a cure at St Leonard's provided yet another inducement for pilgrims to make the journey across Norfolk, using a network of special hospices which included St James's, Horning (near the shrine of St Theobald at Hautbois), a hostel outside the gates of the nearby Benedictine abbey of St Benet Hulme, another at the college of St John the Baptist, Rushford, the hospital of SS Mary and Julian by the bridge at Thetford and a Franciscan refuge in Walsingham. The Bury St Edmunds chronicler, Jocelin of Brakelond, noted that St Saviour's, the second and largest of the town's seven hospitals, was endowed by abbot Samson in about 1184 'that it might provide food for the poor and accommodation for travellers'.[27]

The Institutional Response

Some of Norwich's smaller hospitals seem also to have been founded in response to this influx of sick, often indigent pilgrims. Others offered succour to the more deserving of the homeless rural poor, who arrived in large numbers during the two centuries before the Black Death, in need of food, lodging and medical care. Even if they were operating at full capacity, it is unlikely that the hospitals of St Paul and St Giles Bishopgate could have accommodated more than about one hundred patients and a score or so of boarders between them. Yet a far greater number of men and women, not least among the aged and infirm citizenry, required help, which could sometimes best be supplied in modest almshouses or hostels at a parish level. The scale and nature of this provision is now impossible to assess, since many of the more temporary shelters have probably left no written or archaeological record whatsoever.

Were it not for a transcript made by the antiquary, Thomas Tanner, of the Carrow Priory cartulary (which has since been lost), nothing at all would, for example, be known about the hospital of SS Mary and John. This was an obscure foundation, apparently attached to a church of that name, and run by a community of female religious. A royal charter of 1137, granting land worth 25s a year in the fields of Norwich to the church, confirms the existence of a nunnery there, although no mention is made of any nursing activities.[28] Nine years later, however, King

Stephen and the bishop of Norwich apparently joined with two nuns from the hospital in founding Carrow Priory outside the Conisford gate to the south east of the city. An entry in the cartulary refers to their calling as professed sisters (*fundata est domus Sanctae Mariae de Carhowe ... per Seynam et Lescelinam, sorores moniales de hospitalis Sanctae Mariae et Sancti Johannis in Norwico*), and although the authenticity of this claim is open to question the possibility that St Mary's Carrow developed from a small community of women who specialised in charitable work seems reasonable enough.[29] Nuns played an active part in almsgiving and running hospitals, so perhaps the Carrow Benedictines followed the example of their founders by continuing to support the indigent. The great priory church, which dominated one of the major approaches to the city, would have served admirably as a stopping place for pilgrims.[30]

For a while, at least, poor travellers entering Norwich through the Conisford gate could expect more permanent assistance at Hildebrand's hospital (also known as Ivy Hall) in King Street. One of the very few city hospitals to be founded by a layman, it was set up, as the name implies, by Hildebrand le Mercer, a wealthy local merchant, at the very beginning of the thirteenth century. Bishop Gray's claim that the resources of St Paul's were already overstretched may have prompted him to make the endowment, using land acquired specially for the purpose in what was then a relatively undeveloped, open part of the city.[31] Initially intended as a hostel for 'poor people wanting lodging', Hildebrand's comprised houses and a common hall with a private chamber for the master on a compact site immediately to the south of the cemetery of St Edward's parish church, from which it was separated by a narrow lane. In addition, a small private lady chapel, where the master could celebrate mass for the spiritual health of the boarders whenever he wished, stood at the west end of St Edward's church. He may also have served as a chantry priest for the founder's family and other residents of King Street. A conveyance of 1308, whereby one Hildebrand de Norwich and his wife, Maud, left two acres of land in St Michael's parish, Conisford, to the neighbouring Austin friary, stipulated that the friars were to pay a chaplain to say masses for their souls at the hospital, evidently for many years to come if not in perpetuity. No doubt because it concerned the chapel rather than the hospice, the deed refers to 'the hospital of St Mary', although the location next to St Edward's church rules out any ambiguity.[32] In 1368 the chapel possessed its own missal, a breviary, two vessels for use in the mass, a vestment, assorted cloths and a chest, which suggests that it still functioned effectively, albeit perhaps more for the benefit of the wealthy departed than than the poor almsmen. Ninety years later, a newly-made vestment was left to the chapel by a female parishioner, who asked to be buried there and arranged for the floor to be paved with 'brod Flaundryssche tyle'.[33]

The union of the two King Street churches of St Edward and St Julian and their joint appropriation to the hospital in about 1269 provided the inmates with an alternative source of spiritual consolation. Both churches supported female recluses, who spent their lives in prayer for the souls of other Christians, alive and dead, while also offering guidance to those who sought their advice. Dame Julian of Norwich (b.1342), the city's most famous anchoress and one of the greatest English mystics, occupied an anchorhold at St Julian's Church, which lay just a short distance to the north of the hospital within easy reach of all but the most incapacitated boarders.[34] Personal experience of suffering may have made her a sympathetic counsellor to men and women who, like her, inhabited a marginal world at the edges of society. In the *Revelations of Divine Love* she tells of her longing to be vouchsafed physical pain of the intensity endured by Christ on the cross, and of her desire to approach the point of death. It was thus, while prostrate, that she experienced the visions or 'showings' described so eloquently in her book:

> I desyrede a bodylye syght, whare yn y myght have more knawynge of bodelye paynes of oure lorde oure savyoure, and of the compassyonn of oure ladye and of alle his trewe loverse that were be levande his paynes that tyme and sythene; for ... I wolde aftyr be cawse of that schewynge have the more trewe mynde in the passionn of Cryste. For the seconnde, come to my mynde ... a wylfulle desyre to hafe of goddys gyfte a bodelye syekenes, and I wolde that this bodylye syekenes myght have beene so harde as to the dede, so that I myght in the sekenes take alle my ryghtynges [the last rights] of halye kyrke, wenande my selfe that I schulde dye, and that alle creatures that sawe me myght wene the same, for I wolde hafe no comforth of no fleschlye nothere erthelye lyfe. In this sekenes I desyrede to hafe alle manere of paynes, bodelye and gastelye, that I schulde dye, alle the dredes and tempestes of feyndys, and alle manere of othere paynes, safe of the owghte passynge of the sawlle ...[35]

The physical requirements of boarders at Hildebrand's hospital were less well served than their spiritual needs. Indeed, even allowing for the priority invariably given to the souls rather than the bodies of the deserving poor, the level of provision seems to have become extremely frugal. It was understood that 'hospitality' and 'a certain quantity of fuel' would be provided by the master, but as revenues declined steadily from an estimated £8 in 1274 to £5 in 1368, the inmates bore the brunt. By the Reformation net receipts stood at a mere 14s, and since the endowment then evidently comprised no more than one messuage, a yard and a garden, there is reason to suspect that resources had been misappropriated or squandered.[36] Although it never attracted patronage on the scale enjoyed by St Paul's hospital, or St Giles's in Bishopgate, Hildebrand's seems at first to have received its fair share of local support. The founder's descendants proved quite generous, making over a rent of 8s a year from a linen draper's stall in the city market in 1277–78, and another of 8s 6d from a property across the road from the hospital at some point before 1289.

By then other benefactors had granted modest annual sums from tenements in Cordwainer Row, from the area next to the Castle, and thence down King Street in the parishes of St Andrew and St Peter Parmentergate. Hildebrand's also owned land in Conisford: in 1262–63 the master leased one plot to a barber surgeon named Master Adam de St Albans, the only medical practitioner known to have had any connection with the hospital.[37]

A papal indult of 1291, allowing one year and forty days' remission of penance to persons visiting the chapel at Hildebrand's hospital on the four annual feasts of the Blessed Virgin, its patron saint, was clearly intended to encourage almsgiving.[38] Charitable donations of food, clothing and money were all the more important because most of the house's regular landed income went to support the master, who, from the time of Bishop Simon Walton (1257–65), if not before, was an episcopal nominee. In 1274 the citizens of Norwich, with support from King Edward, sued Bishop Skerning for the right to present to the mastership themselves, but failed in their attempt.[39] When the see of Norwich fell vacant, or, as was the case in 1385, the temporalities had been confiscated because of Bishop Despenser's irregularities, the Crown made the appointment. In this instance, two royal clerks were chosen in quick succession; and although one resigned a previous living at Hastings in Sussex to take up the post, neither had any local connexions.[40] It is unlikely that the bishops' appointees showed much more interest in the hospital or assumed personal responsibility for the welfare of the inmates. Certainly, by 1429, at least one prominent citizen had grown so critical of the way it was being run that he apparently withheld the revenues he or his ancestors had given to support the poor. Among the many philanthropic bequests then set out in the will of William Setman, a former mayor and Member of Parliament for Norwich, was a provision concerning the rent from two houses, one near the College of St Mary in the Fields and another close by in Upper Newport, which had previously been paid to the hospital. Their restoration was made conditional upon the master's readiness to hold 'discussions' with Setman's executors and a subsequent promise that he would 'submit to and effectively observe the old regulations of the hospital'.[41]

Since we do not know what was in these statutes, or how they had been broken, we can only assume that, as was often the case in other English hospitals of the period, the claims of sick and homeless paupers had given way to other priorities. The early-fifteenth century House of Commons was especially exercised on this score. At Leicester, in 1414, it had petitioned Henry V for a national investigation into abuses arising from the misappropriation of funds set aside by pious donors with the sole purpose of helping such unfortunates. 'And now as things stand', the Members complained, 'the majority of hospitals in your said realm are fallen into decay, and their goods and profits diverted and put to other use, as much by clergy as by layfolk. Whereby many men and women have died in great misery for want of help, livelihood and succour, to the displeasure of God and peril of the souls of those who spoil and spend what belongs to the poor.'[42] That King Henry took the petition to heart is evident from his instructions to the University of Oxford at this time. Delegates to the council at Constance were to be supplied with articles 'concerning the reformation of the Universal Church', one of which dealt with the malversation of hospital revenues by senior clergy.[43]

Some improvements may have been made at Hildebrand's, which continued to function as a hospice, albeit with only very limited assistance from the people of Norwich. In 1440 the rector of St Edward's and St Julian's, whose connexion with the hospital could hardly have been closer, left a green coverlet, a pair of blankets and a pair of sheets, presumably for the use of the inmates; and about twenty years later Alice Grey, the widow of an alderman, set aside two shillings for the repair of the beds.[44] Further evidence of testamentary bequests or other charitable gifts from local people remains wanting, however, and the impression from then onwards is of unremitting decline. The appointment to the mastership of John Jullys, who served from 1497 to 1504, confirms that the post had become a sinecure, for besides occupying the livings at Coltishall and Blickling, he was also master of St Giles's hospital Bishopgate, where he had previously served as a chaplain and accountant. Such a longstanding association with Norwich set him apart from many of his predecessors at Hildebrand's, although the liturgical and administrative demands made upon him elsewhere left little time for a small, poor and relatively insignificant hospice for indigent travellers arriving in Conisford.[45]

The City's Almshouses

Dissatisfaction with the state of hospitals owned or run by the Church was an important factor in promoting the foundation of private almshouses or *maisons dieu* by late medieval benefactors. These might be managed on a daily basis by secular clergy, who would be needed to minister to the souls of the residents, but would otherwise remain firmly under the control of an urban elite, a corporate institution (such as a guild or fraternity) or, as was often the case, the founder's own family. When endowing a refuge for twelve poor women at Nimes, in 1313, the wealthy merchant Pierre Ruffi stipulated that his descendants or their nominees should enjoy complete autonomy, free of intervention from outsiders, whether lay or clerical.[46] His approach was typical of benefactors throughout England as well as France. It has been calculated that just over fifty-five per cent of the 1,103 hospitals listed by Knowles and Hadcock in their survey of the medieval religious houses of England and Wales were intended to support almsmen and women; and of these a significant proportion constituted a lay reponse to the problem of long term poor relief.[47]

The 'expression of self-help in religious life', often by experienced individuals confident of their own judgement and ability, led to the implementation of charitable schemes which kept the role of the ecclesiastical establishment to a minimum, and excluded the monastic orders altogether. Thus, a leper hospital founded in 1361 by the influential Cambridge burgess, Henry Tangmere, was entrusted to the management of Corpus Christi College rather than the nearby hospital of St John, which had effectively abandoned its charitable functions.[48] A lifetime's involvement in politics and local administration similarly led Roger Thornton, one of the richest merchants in fifteenth-century Tyneside, to choose his relatives and fellow-burgesses as the most suitable governors of the almshouse built by him in Newcastle. It is, however, significant that not even he fully appreciated how much the project would cost. His original endowment proved inadequate, and he had to seek permission from the Crown, in 1424, to make another.[49] In London, too, philanthropists turned to the rulers of the city livery companies as reliable and competent trustees for their new foundations, and as suitable agents for the reform of older, decaying institutions.[50]

Attempts by merchant capitalists and leading members of the landowning classes to provide a more efficient and less indiscriminate system of care for the sick and aged poor have received considerable attention from historians. Yet for every affluent, established and well-documented almshouse, of the kind which inevitably attracts the most notice, there were many short-lived housing projects, destined either by accident or design to offer relief on a very small scale indeed. Such was the case in Norwich, where, for a variety of reasons, no attempt seems to have been made to set any of these schemes on a permanent footing with formal support from the city guilds or corporation. Lack of money, or more precisely of a guaranteed annual income sufficient to maintain the fabric and inmates, meant that at least one projected almshouse did not even get beyond the planning stage.

Towards the end of the thirteenth century, Richard de Breccles (*alias* Herman), a local chaplain and absentee vicar of Nafford in Worcester, decided to endow a hospital dedicated to St Saviour in Coslany, an area in the western part of Norwich, just north of the Wensum. By a deed of 1298, which describes him as the founder, he acquired a bread stall in the market place for his almshouse; and, as he lay on his deathbed eight years later, all the necessary legal arrangements were in place for him to settle a messuage, ten shops and an annual rent of two shillings upon it. In June 1305 the master and brethren had sued out royal letters patent allowing them to acquire the property in mortmain: this was an expensive business, which involved the holding of an official enquiry in Norwich and would not have been undertaken lightly.[51] Yet within a few months, Breccles' executors found that the revenues from his estate simply did not suffice to support such an ambitious venture, not least because he had 'been negligent and omitted certain debts' when drawing up his will. The next heir, his nephew, was therefore obliged to enter an agreement allowing them to divert whatever assets remained after his creditors had been satisfied to 'a more appropriate place', and all plans for the 'proposed' hospital were abandoned.[52]

The chance survival of this document shows how misleading the evidence of testamentary records can be, at least when taken at face value. Pious intentions could easily be set down on parchment and even translated into the formal language of the patent rolls, but the energy, commitment and resources needed to put them into practice often proved wanting. In 1418, for example, the brothers John and Walter Danyell drew up a joint will providing for the repair and upkeep of an almshouse 'of new construction and ordinance' set up by them in the parishes of St Stephen and St Katherine, Norwich.[53] Walter, the survivor, made a long and detailed will of his own six years later, which supplies rather more information about the foundation. Ten separate properties worth over £750 (at his own valuation) were to be sold and the proceeds distributed among the local poor. But his executors were to permit the paupers from St Stephen's parish then living in a 'tenement, messuage and place' near the Needham gate to remain, and were to make available another 'small messuage and renter' in the same parish for this purpose. The second hostel was to be managed at their discretion according to regulations already implemented at the first: since Danyell left no instructions regarding the sale, reversion or alternative use of either property we may reasonably assume that he intended to establish a permanent refuge.[54] It is, however, unlikely that the almshouse continued for more than a few years. Once the two founders were dead support may have waned, and no evidence of interest in the project at either a parochial or civic level survives. Significantly, none of the many wills made by people living in this part of Norwich mentions either the home or its inhabitants.

A few other late medieval almshouses appear fleetingly in antiquarian histories of Norwich, without leaving much, if any, trace behind them in the local records. A *maison dieu* in St Giles's parish, Lower Newport, was apparently founded by one John le Grant during the reign of Edward I and conveyed to the church by his son, Thomas, in 1310. Claims that Bishop Lyhart (d.1472) saved it from collapse, restored the fabric and then chose the almsmen cannot now be substantiated. Nor, despite the many pious bequests which it contains, does his will provide any hint of his involvement in what must have been a costly and time-consuming exercise.[55] Since the leper hospital of St Giles lay on the other side of the city gates, some confusion about the names and dates of patrons may possibly have occurred, but this remains a matter for speculation. Not far away, between the churches of St Margaret and St Swithin in Westwick, was another, even more obscure almshouse, said to have been endowed in 1292 by Robert de Aswardby.[56] A few decades later, perhaps after Aswardby's refuge had ceased to function, a merchant named Hugh Garzoun, whose investments in the property market made him one of the richest men in Norwich, established a third home for the local poor across the street in the parish of St Benedict.[57] The need for almshouses in this part of the city during the late thirteenth and early fourteenth centuries must have been acute: the nearest hospitals of any size lay some distance away, and the area was becoming heavily populated as poor immigrants flooded in from the countryside. Yet the necessary steps to ensure continuity of funding seem never to have been implemented. Witness the case of St Christopher's hospice, which was little more than a tenement belonging to the hospital of the Blessed Mary of Rouncivalle in London. It flourished briefly in the 1360s before passing into the ownership of the Dominican friars, who did not see fit to support its charitable work.[58]

We cannot now tell how many of the 742 English almshouses listed by Knowles and Hadcock functioned effectively for any appreciable length of time, although the evidence from Norwich suggests that the average survival rate might best be calculated in years rather than decades. In her study of hospitals and charitable provision in medieval Yorkshire, Patricia Cullum argues convincingly that the smaller *maisons dieu* were never intended to offer more than temporary, even partial relief to the sick and aged poor. Far from comparing them unfavourably with the larger monastic foundations of the twelfth or thirteenth centuries, and dismissing them as failures because they lasted for no more than a short while, we should see them as an attempt by pious individuals (often of relatively modest means) to continue subsidising private acts of philanthropy for only so long as their limited resources might permit. Dr Cullum's analogous reference to chantries, most of which were established for a finite period in keeping with the financial status of the donor, seems particularly apt.[59] Yet, even allowing for the short-term pragmatism of those who wished to assist the poor in this way, and the attendant problem of documenting their efforts, in Norwich such schemes aroused little interest. York could boast between twelve and eighteen late medieval almshouses, eleven of which were founded by local people during the late-fourteenth and early-fifteenth centuries, as well as a further five hospitals run under the auspices of civic guilds and fraternities. Hull, with a population of some 2,300 adults in 1377, had at least fifteen.[60] In comparison, by the close of the Middle Ages hospital provision in Norwich seems to have been greatly reduced. In the 1380s the city had at least eighteen guilds, and although some, such as the fraternities of St James and of the poor men of St Augustine's parish, were obviously in no position even to contemplate setting up a hospice others might well have done so.[61] Did the citizens actively discriminate against the sick paupers in their midst? Or did they prefer other, less institutionalised systems of relief?

END NOTES

1   *Histoire des Hopitaux en France*, pp. 24–28.

2   Knowles and Hadcock, *Medieval Religious Houses*, pp. 310–410; Carlin, 'Medieval English Hospitals', p. 24.

3   *The Victoria History of the County of Hampshire*, II, p. 208.

4   *Calendar of the Register of John Dronkesford*, p. 268.

5   *Calendar of Papal Registers: Papal Letters*, 1417–31, ed. J.A. Twemlow (London, 1906), p. 469; *1431–47* (London, 1913), pp. 98–100.

6   Mollat, *The Poor in the Middle Ages*, pp. 8, 89–91; *Statutes of the Realm*, vol. I, 23 Ed. III, cap. 5, clause VII.

7   *Some Early English Tracts on Poor Relief*, p. 64. For earlier examples of the importance placed upon hospitality and the distinction made between those who needed temporary shelter rather than continuous alms, see Tierney, 'The Decretists and the "Deserving Poor"', p. 367.

8   Rawcliffe, *Medicine and Society*, chapter I.

9   *Norwich Heresy Trials, 1428–1431*, ed. N. Tanner (Camden Society, fourth series, XX, 1977), pp. 11, 47, 71, 74, 81, 116, 127, 131, 135, 142, 148, 154, 158, 160, 166, 170, 177, 179, 183, 185, 190, 194, 197, 205.

10   Thomas More, *A Dialogue Concerning Heresies*, ed. T.M.C. Lawler and others (*The Complete Works of St Thomas More*, VI, 1981), p. 85.

11   R.C. Finucane, *Miracles and Pilgrims* (London, 1977), p. 98.

12   Thomas of Monmouth, *The Life and Miracles of St William of Norwich*, p. 148.

13   Bartholomaeus Anglicus, *Properties of Things*, vol. I, pp. 423–27.

14   Thomas of Monmouth, *The Life and Miracles of St William of Norwich*, p. xc.

15   Ibid., p. 271.

16   Ibid., pp. 205–6, 242–46, 275. Tales of long journeys, desperate illness and, significantly, the powerlessness and even venality of the medical profession are a standard feature of this genre, and are by no means unique to the tale of little William. See B. Ward, *Miracles and the Medieval Mind* (Aldershot, 1987), p. 35.

17   Norfolk Record Office, DCN 43/9.

18   J.R. Shinners, 'The Veneration of Saints at Norwich Cathedral in the Fourteenth Century', *Norfolk Archaeology*, XL (1987), pp. 134–41; N. Tanner, *The Church in Late Medieval Norwich*, pp. 88–92.

19   *Calendar of Liberate Rolls, 1240–45* (London, 1931), p. 9; *1245–51*, (London, 1937), pp. 343–44.

20   F. Wormald, 'The Rood of Bromholm', *Journal of the Warburg Institute*, I (1937–38), pp. 31–45.

21   Roger of Wendover, *Flores Historiarum*, ed. H.G. Hewlett (3 vols, Rolls Series, 1886–89), vol. II, pp. 274–76. See also Ralph de Coggeshall, *Chronicon Anglicanum*, ed. J. Stevenson (Rolls Series, 1875), pp. 202–3.

22   R. Hart, 'The Shrines and Pilgrimages of the County of Norfolk', *Norfolk Archaeology*, VI (1864), pp. 277–94.

23   M.R. James, 'Lives of St Walstan', *Norfolk Archaeology*, XIX (1917), pp. 238–67, especially p. 258.

24   Ibid., pp. 262–63.

25   B. Spencer, *Medieval Pilgrim Badges from Norfolk* (Norfolk Museums Service, 1980), p. 25; *The Household Books of John Howard, Duke of Norfolk, 1462–1471, 1481–1483*, ed. A. Crawford (Stroud, 1992), part II, p. 447; British Library, Department of Manuscripts, Ms. Harley 1576, f. 251v; Blomefield, *History of the County of Norfolk*, vol. IV, pp. 426–28.

26   *The Miracles of King Henry VI*, ed. R. Knox and S. Leslie (Cambridge, 1923), passim.

27   *The Victoria History of the County of Norfolk*, II, pp. 330–36, 435, 440, 451, 459. Jocelin of Brakelond, *Chronicle*

of the Abbey of Bury St Edmunds, ed. D. Greenway and J. Sayers (Oxford, 1989), p. 43. The great guest house or hospice at the Norfolk abbey of St Benet Hulme, which must have welcomed thousands of pilgrims over the years, was badly damaged by fire in the 1340s, thus adding to the accommodation problems faced by travellers (Norfolk Record Office, DCN Reg. 1, book 3, ff. 74v–75r).

28 *Gesta Regum Anglo-Noramannorum 1066–1154, III*, ed. H.A. Cronne and R.H.C. Davis (Oxford, 1968), no. 615.

29 W. Rye, *Carrow Abbey* (Norwich, 1889), Appendix I; T. Tanner, *Notitia Monastica*, p. 347.

30 S. Thompson, *Women Religious* (Oxford, 1991), p. 49. For a plan of the priory, see R. Gilchrist and M. Oliva, *Religious Women in Medieval East Anglia*, (Studies in East Anglian History, I, 1993), p. 41.

31 Brief, not always accurate, histories of this hospital appear in *The Victoria History of the County of Norfolk*, II, pp. 446–47; Kirkpatrick, *History of the Religious Orders*, pp. 230–36; and Blomefield, *History of the County of Norfolk*, vol. IV, pp. 69–72.

32 Norfolk Record Office, DCN 45/29/1.

33 *Inventory of Church Goods Temp. Edward III*, p. 24; Kirkpatrick, *History of the Religious Orders*, p. 234.

34 Gilchrist and Oliva, *Religious Women*, pp. 74–78, 97–99.

35 *A Book of Showings to the Anchoress Julian of Norwich*, ed. E. Colledge and J. Welsh (2 vols, Pontifical Institute of Medieval Studies and Texts, Toronto, 1978), vol. I, pp. 202–4.

36 Kirkpatrick, *History of the Religious Orders*, pp. 230–36; *Valor Ecclesiasticus*, vol. III, p. 293.

37 Norfolk Record Office, DCN 45/3/4, 9/1, 33/22, 24, 34/3, 4, 6, 10.

38 *Calendar of Papal Registers: Papal Letters, 1198–1304*, ed. W.H. Bliss (London, 1893), pp. 533–34.

39 Kirkpatrick, *History of the Religious Orders*, pp. 230–36.

40 *Calendar of Patent Rolls, 1381–85* (London, 1898), p. 528; *1385–89* (London, 1900), pp. 22, 41.

41 Setman's will is printed in full in N. Tanner, *The Church in Late Medieval Norwich*, pp. 243–44. These rents may have included the four shillings a year from a messuage in Upper Newport reserved to the hospital in 1306 by the executors of Walter le Spoteshale, a mercer (Norfolk Record Office, DCN 45/33/41).

42 *Rotuli Parliamentorum*, ed. J. Strachey and others (6 vols, London, 1767–77), vol. IV, pp. 19–20. These concerns echoed an earlier desire for reform expressed at the Councils of Ravenna in 1310 and of Vienne in the following year, when Pope Clement V had issued directives for the investigation of abuses in hospitals (*Histoire des Hopitaux en France*, pp. 69–72; Mollat, *The Poor in the Middle Ages*, p. 181).

43 *Concilia Magnae Britanniae et Hiberniae*, ed. D. Wilkins (4 vols, London, 1737), vol. III, p. 365.

44 Norfolk Record Office, Norwich Consistory Court Wills, Reg. Doke, f. 144r; Reg. Betyns, f. 49r.

45 For Jullys's ecclesiastical career, see Norfolk Record Office, case 24, shelf B, nos 26 (3), 27 B; *Calendar of Papal Registers: Papal Letters, 1471–85*, ed. J.A. Twemlow (London, 1955), p. 738; Blomefield, *History of the County of Norfolk*, vol. III, pp. 487–92.

46 *Histoire des Hopitaux en France*, p. 77.

47 Knowles and Hadcock, *Medieval Religious Houses*, pp. 310–410. Carlin, 'Medieval English Hospitals', p. 23, gives this percentage as sixty-seven, but is corrected in Gilchrist, 'Christian Bodies', p. 102.

48 M. Rubin, 'Development and Change in English Hospitals', pp. 54–55.

49 *The History of Parliament, the House of Commons 1386–1421*, ed. J.S. Roskell, L. Clark and C. Rawcliffe (4 vols, Stroud, 1993), vol. IV, pp. 596–98. See also the biography of John Plumptre (pp. 92–93), who endowed a similar institution in Nottingham.

50 Rawcliffe, 'The Hospitals of Later Medieval London', pp. 1–21.

51 *A Short Calendar of Deeds Relating to Norwich, 1285–1306*, ed. W. Rye (Norwich, 1903), p. 67; Public Record Office, C143/51/13; *Calendar of Patent Rolls, 1301–1307* (London, 1898), p. 343.

52 *Records of the City of Norwich*, vol. II, pp. 17–18.

53 Norfolk Record Office, Norwich Consistory Court Wills, Reg. Hyrning, ff. 32v–33r. This joint will relates almost entirely to the almshouse, and is followed by John Danyell's own will, made in his name alone.

54 Ibid., ff. 148v–150r.

55 Blomefield, *History of the County of Norfolk*, vol. IV, p. 245. Lyhart's will is Public Record Office, Probate Court of Canterbury, Reg. Wattys, ff. 51v–52r.

56 Blomefield, *History of the County of Norfolk*, vol. IV, p. 250.

57 Ibid. Garzoun's property investments (but no reference to his almshouse) figure prominently in *Calendar of Norwich Deeds, 1307–1341*, passim.

58 William Dugdale, *Monasticon Anglicanum*, ed. J. Caley and others (6 vols, London, 1817–30), vol. VI, p. 1785. Dugdale also notes Croom's almshouse as being in existence before 1516 (ibid.), but no other pre-Reformation record of it evidently survives

59 Cullum, 'Hospitals and Charitable Provision', pp. 318–45. The point is reiterated in Cullum and Goldberg, 'Charitable Provision in Late Medieval York', pp. 31–32.

60 Ibid., Appendix.

61 See chapter II, note 47, for references to the guilds of Norwich.

Conclusion

On the strength of the evidence considered in the previous four chapters, it seems that hospital provision for the sick paupers of Norwich was, by the close of the Middle Ages, very limited indeed. Of the six specialist houses for lepers, the one at Sprowston had effectively ceased to function, while the five at the city gates could accommodate no more than a handful each of men and women, albeit now mostly drawn from the ranks of the infirm poor. Although these establishments were consistently supported by over a third of local testators, the quality of care does not appear to have been high, and by the sixteenth century abuses were rife. Three of the six hospitals founded before 1250 (that is St Mary in the Fields, SS Mary and John and Brichtiu's) did not survive for very long; and only one of the later almshouses noted by local historians has left any significant trace in the records. Of the rest, Hildebrand's hospital still offered minimal facilities to a few destitute boarders during the fifteenth century, but possessed little in the way of resources and did not inspire confidence among the citizenry. St Paul's was, meanwhile, forced by depressing economic circumstances rather than mismanagement to implement stringent cuts from the 1470s onwards. Although they may well have faced an uncertain future in the outside world, the nursing sisters were no longer paupers but corrodians who could afford to pay the equivalent of a skilled craftsman's annual wage for admission; and there is no evidence to suggest that they had many patients to tend. The changes which took place at St Giles's, as the hospital became a college for secular clergy, meant that here, too, the poor increasingly took second place. Charitable relief continued, but the number of indigents to whom it was given fell, and facilities in the infirmary were reduced.

Specific economic factors, most notably the devastating impact of the 1348–49 outbreak of plague on the city and its long-term consequences for the region's ecclesiastical landowners, clearly had serious implications for Norwich's older hospitals. So too did the agricultural problems of the late-fifteenth century, which hit the barley growers and rentiers of East Anglia especially badly. The two fires of 1507 also left their mark for decades, creating an urban wasteland in some parishes and exacerbating the incipient signs of depopulation already observed by the civic authorities. Resources which might otherwise have been available for poor relief were diverted into building schemes, and the slump in the textile market, evident from the early 1530s onwards, led to another protracted period of recession. Yet for all these reversals, Norwich remained the second most populous city in England; and although upwards of sixty per cent of its inhabitants may then have lived near, on or below the poverty line, a small mercantile elite enjoyed great wealth and privilege. In 1523, for example, thirty-two men were assessed for taxation purposes on possessions worth £100 or more, one grocer (the alderman, Robert Jannys) being evaluated at £1,100, a sum only slightly below the return made for the *entire* taxable population of Rochester.[1]

Since the aldermen of late medieval Norwich lacked neither the funds nor the expertise to replace or reorganise their hospitals (as many London merchants elected to do), and were certainly rich enough to endow modest almshouses had they so wished, their apparent lack of enthusiasm for such projects cannot, like the plight of many monastic houses, be explained in terms of financial hardship. It is, indeed, possible to cite some remarkable examples of individual generosity to the sick and impotent poor of Norwich by men and women who wished to help in a more immediate, personal way. Walter Danyell (who continued to support the *maison dieu* founded by his brother) instructed his executors to sell an estate valued by him at £750 and use most of the proceeds to assist any poor neighbours in the city or tenants on his country estates in need of food, money or clothing. Of particular significance are his bequests of one shilling each to the bedridden paupers in his own parish of St Stephen's, of 4d to each sick person begging there, of 2d a week for one year to every old, blind, paralysed or otherwise infirm parishioner and of 20s to be distributed every Friday for a year among the most deserving and crippled residents of Norwich.[2]

A few years later, in 1429, William Setman, whose concern about the fate of Hildebrand's hospital is noted in the previous chapter, left the substantial sum of £20 to be shared among 'the most needy poor of Norwich and other towns around' immediately after his death. A further £10 was to be dispensed weekly over the next three years in doles of 3d each to 'the poor and especially the lame, the blind or the severely disabled *residing continually in Norwich*', while £26 13s 4d was promised 'to the most needy poor' of fourteen Norfolk villages. Setman willed, moreover, that the residue of his estate should be sold by his executors for the benefit of 'the blind, widows, orphans and others showing the greatest necessity', the relative merits of each case to be determined at their discretion.[3] For Danyell, Setman and the great majority of their fellow-citizens charity began at home, or at least on the doorstep. In common with the rulers of other English and Continental cities, they were selective philanthropists, anxious that their money should be used carefully under the direction of trustees or executors capable of evaluating the personal circumstances of each recipient.[4]

Although, at best, such an approach offered no more than ad hoc, sporadic relief, it gave the donor sufficient flexibility to help those who might otherwise fall outside the very small and fragile safety net extended by most hospitals. Thus, for example, 'shamefaced' paupers, reluctant to beg openly in the streets or take refuge in an institution, were more likely to receive alms. So too, in theory, might those who had work of sorts, but could not earn enough to support themselves and their dependents. Few English hospitals recognised any formal obligation towards the rapidly expanding group of relatively young and able-bodied men and women known collectively as 'the labouring poor': larger houses, such as St Giles's in Bishopgate, provided meals for workmen employed on the precincts, but otherwise lacked the resources, and almost certainly the will to extend their remit in this way.[5] The practical response to the problem of comparative poverty, as experienced by a substantial part of the workforce, was, in general, somewhat muted. If, as was often the case, the wealthier citizens of late medieval Norwich showed considerable sympathy for the widows, orphans and elderly kindred of their poor neighbours, the collective attitude towards this large and sometimes disruptive sector of the population was very different. In many respects it was influenced by the general distrust of beggars, vagrants and other dubious 'outsiders', which accelerated the shift in patronage away from the hospital, with its open doors, to the comfortable safety of the parish.

Not without reason, the ruling elite of medieval Norwich was wary of the urban proletariat, and had no wish to encourage 'idleness and vice' in the city through the wholesale distribution of alms. As a result of chronic labour shortages and the ensuing rise in wages after the Black Death, the English government had attempted to force 'right myghti and strong beggars' back to work at fixed rates by making it illegal to support such individuals with alms.[6] The problem seems to have been especially acute in Norwich, a city so badly afflicted by pestilence that piles of ordure and filth still lay uncollected in the streets in 1352. It had proved impossible to implement a royal edict ordering the citizens to pave the major thoroughfares, which were like quagmires in winter, repair the walls and remove the dung heaps because they had 'a great want of servants and workmen for this, while many men and women, strong and able, roam about the city, idle and refuse to work'. In response, King Edward authorised commissioners to force the unemployed to undertake these tasks.[7] A tendency to see the active poor as potential troublemakers, even criminals, intensified over the next three decades. The flashpoint occurred in 1381, when those who had managed to escape the worst degradation of extreme poverty as demographic pressures eased reacted against the escalating demands of royal taxation. Their violent protest confirmed the fears of the landowning and mercantile classes, who grew even more distrustful of charitable schemes not directly under their control.

East Anglia had been briefly, but profoundly shaken by popular discontent during the Peasants' Revolt of 1381. Events at Bury St Edmunds, where the townspeople made common cause with the insurgents in attacking the abbey and killing the prior, tend to overshadow the disturbances in other parts of the region. But Norfolk, too, was the scene of widespread disaffection. Rebels from the east of the county banded together on Mousehold Heath outside Norwich under the leadership of their 'king', a dyer named Litster. On 17 June they entered the city in triumph 'with pennons flying and in warlike array'. Having pillaged the homes of some local notables, they proceeded (in the words of the monastic chronicler, Thomas of Walsingham) to extort protection money from others 'on the pretext of saving [them] from slaughter, fire and plunder'. Litster's plan to secure a charter of pardon from King Richard was dashed at North Walsham. Here, nemesis, in the person of Bishop Despenser, hot-foot from his victory over the rebel forces at Peterborough and Cambridge, brought the uprising to an end.[8] Walsingham's account of the 'warrior bishop', who at Peterborough Abbey had personally directed the slaughter of men seeking refuge on the altar steps, is justly famous. The brutal suppression of disorder in the eastern counties won Despenser many plaudits, and marks a further hardening of attitudes towards the unruly poor. Historians have been at pains to stress that most of the protestors who took up arms in 1381 came from the ranks of taxpaying peasants and craftsmen. These were men whose burgeoning social and economic expectations had been disappointed, rather than downtrodden, hopeless paupers. Inevitably, however, the latter were also viewed with suspicion by those in a position of authority, who did not always distinguish between relative degrees of poverty.[9] Over the next few decades the ruling elite grew narrower, increasingly hierarchical and faction-ridden as it pursued a policy of retrenchment.

Fear of a rebellious underclass tainted by the sin of envy bred on itself, and created what Michel Mollat has described as 'a generation frightened by pauperism'.[10] Along with this growing sense of unease went a reluctance to help outsiders, who might also threaten to upset the social order. During the 1380s further repressive legislation empowered local authorities, including 'mayors, bailiffs, constables and other governors of towns', to examine and take security from 'divers people ... wandering from place to place, running in the country more abundantly than they were wont to do in times past'. Suspected criminals and those unable to offer securities for good behaviour were to be incarcerated until the next sessions of gaol delivery, which might involve imprisonment for years rather than months.[11] Although, in practice, these measures were not consistently enforced, the implicit assumption that poverty and crime went hand in hand served to buttress existing prejudices. It is worth noting in this context that when the priest who helped Margery Kempe to write her spiritual autobiography was approached by a young stranger 'compleynyng of pouerte and disese' she warned him not to solicit alms on the stranger's behalf. His offer to approach a wealthy merchant and his wife for help led Margery to protest that 'thei haddyn many powyr neybowrys whech thei knewyn wei a-now hadyn gret nede to ben holpyn and relevyd'. Although her views accorded ill with Christ's teaching on the subject of charity, they reflected a widespread belief in the spiritual merit of giving to needy friends and neighbours rather than outsiders. 'It was mor almes to helpun him that thei knewyn wel for wel dysposyd folke and her owyn neybowrys', she urged, 'than other strawngerys whech thei knew not'. Margery was, in fact, reiterating an argument first put forward by St Ambrose (d.397) and debated at length by successive generations of theologians and canonists. But the practical advantages of providing assistance for people whose need and moral worth could easily be established seemed obvious in an age of economic and social upheaval, at least so far as the donors were concerned.[12]

These ideas found practical expression in schemes for poor relief such as the *Forma Subventionus Pauperum*, begun at Ypres in 1525 and soon taken up in England by a circle of reformers at Court. As the translation made by William Marshall ten years later explained: 'we preferre oure citizens whose persons and maners we knewe before straungers with whom we haue none acquaintance. For we are cheifly bounde to regarde theym bycause they be membres with vs of one politicall body'.[13] The local, resident poor might, then, be accorded a lowly but necessary place as the hands, feet or lesser organs in the body politic, but the vagrant still remained a threat against which that body would be advised to defend itself. An obvious corollary of these developments was the desire 'to privilege those who are familiar and similar', confining charitable relief to people whose circumstances were not too distressingly different from those of the donor.[14]

For Margery Kempe and her contemporaries another, crucial point at issue was the moral worth of the individual to whom alms were being given. The mere fact of assisting the needy *en masse*, as hospitals were originally expected to do, no longer seemed appropriate, and might, indeed, prove injurious to the soul of the donor. A more sophisticated refinement of the Church's doctrine on purgatory prompted ordinary men and women to doubt the efficacy of prayers uttered on their behalf by people who were either living in a state of mortal sin (and thus denied the ear of God) or who simply repeated their devotions by rote, without any real concern as to the fate of their benefactors.[15] The reflective among them, given to thought about the meaning and purpose of prayer, felt that there was little spiritual merit to be gained by paying unknown paupers to chant *Aves* and *Pater Nosters*, especially when they could more easily purchase the heartfelt prayers of deserving neighbours.

> Geve to vertuous men that haue nede,
> That to God wole for the pray:
> The pore manny's erande, God doth spede.
> God will not here what glosere [flatterer] wole say.[16]

Changing beliefs about the best means to salvation had obvious practical consequences for the sick and indigent, since they encouraged, and to a certain extent justified, the growing preference for more personalised forms of charity. It would, however, be a gross simplification to dismiss the declining appeal of Norwich hospitals as little more than a move by disenchanted investors from one low-interest account to another which promised a better return in paradise. Then, as now, a combination of motives, in which compassion, fear, self-interest and civic pride each played a part, led individuals periodically to reassess the nature of their obligations towards the sick and indigent in their midst.

There can be little doubt that the charitable bequests recorded in wills represent only a very small proportion of the alms which would have been dispensed each week or even every day by the people of Norwich. In practice, most relief comprised spontaneous gifts of food, fuel, clothing or accommodation made, as the Church required, in response to particular circumstances. However much it may have been qualified or reinterpreted, this aspect of Christ's teaching was still held up to all but the very poor as a prerequisite of salvation. As one historian has recently observed: 'offering hospitality and distributing excess food were social obligations incumbent upon the wealthy, and the ethic of informal assistance seems to have been shared by people of limited means'.[17] In practice more was expected of women. Homiletic literature and *exempla* taken from the lives of saints, such as Elizabeth of Hungary, portrayed charity as a virtue especially becoming to the female sex. Nursing the sick, attending poor women in labour and feeding the hungry figured high on the list of commendable activities.[18] We know that Norwich possessed at least four informal communities of religious women, one of which, 'dwelling in Westwyk', may perhaps be identified with either Aswardby's or Garzoun's almshouse or have performed a similar function during the early fifteenth century. Quite possibly the younger, fitter members of these small groups helped to care for the sick poor of the parish, while the others may themselves have been taken in as patients.[19]

The chance survival of accounts from the household of Katherine, the relict of Walter de Norwich, sometime treasurer of England, suggests that the contribution made by women (and especially widows) of her social class must also have been considerable. She left her Suffolk manor of Mettingham in January 1337 to spend several weeks at the family residence in Norwich. Throughout the entire period thirteen paupers received a dole each day of herring and bread, specially baked in batches of 200 loaves made from her own grain. Additional food was distributed on Good Friday and the anniversary of her husband's death. She was thus providing exactly the same number and type of daily meals for the poor as St Giles's hospital, albeit from a far smaller budget. In the following century, Isabella, Lady Morley, who also lived in the city, bought Westphalian cloth and fuel as alms, although at a cost of exactly 8s, in 1463–64, her outlay constituted less than one fifth of the bill submitted by her physician.[20] Such survivals are, however, rare, and do little more than hint at the existence of a loosely organised system of welfare provision, firmly based in the local community.

That community and parish were often synonymous is apparent from the strong sense of loyalty and attachment to the latter displayed by the residents of late medieval Norwich. The structure of the city, with its forty-six parish churches, many of which had been spectacularly extended, embellished or rebuilt during the two centuries before the Reformation, helped to foster these sentiments. Of all the pious bequests a citizen might make when drawing up his or her will, the parish church would almost always come first; and charitable effort, likewise, concentrated increasingly upon a small, circumscribed area where donors and recipients were well-known to each other.[21] A feeling that the city's older hospitals had either failed to discharge their proper function, or were less likely to target the truly deserving, resident poor encouraged this trend. Support for the sisters of St Paul's or the nurses at St Giles's, who continued to attract modest bequests throughout the later Middle Ages, confirms that when they were, in fact, seen to perform a valuable service by assisting the impoverished widows or spinsters of Norwich, hospitals could still attract benefactors. But the focus of interest had changed. With an average population of well below three hundred souls during the fifteenth century, the city parish constituted a manageable unit where deserving cases could easily be identified and given succour appropriate to their needs by neighbouring relatives, friends or social superiors.[22]

With very circumscribed help from the institutions endowed by their ancestors, and little in the way of new foundations, the citizens of Norwich thus contrived for many years to maintain an informal system of poor relief based on self-help and individual effort. Such ad hoc measures, dependent on the good will of ordinary men and women, might just suffice while both the population and the coinage remained relatively stable, while the problem of vagrancy could be contained and while there was enough food to go round.[23] But already, by 1520, warning bells had begun to sound. The price of wheat was then higher than it had been since the 1440s, and since it showed no sign of falling the city authorities stepped in for the first time one year later to provide supplies for the poor. Further attempts at regulation followed, including ordinances of 1532 designed to prevent victuallers from cornering the market and causing further shortages ('the poore people is like to be in gret ieoberdye off ffamysshing oneles remedye weere therfore brevaly provided').[24] The rigorous implementation in Norwich during the 1530s and 1540s of parliamentary statutes for the licensing of beggars and the obligatory provision of 'benevolent almes' for the deserving poor marked the start of a new era. Henceforward, the civic authorities were legally bound by draconian poor laws to feed, house and clothe the sick and aged paupers within the walls, to licence beggars and punish work-shy vagabonds.[25]

As part of this programme, St Giles's hospital in Bishopgate, which had narrowly escaped dissolution under the Second Chantries Act of 1547, was taken into the hands of the mayor and aldermen. The south aisle of St Helen's church and part of the infirmary, as well as much of the surrounding property, had been destroyed by Kett's rebels as they swept through the city in 1549; and it seems more than likely that the shock of the 'commoyson' galvanised the corporation into adopting an even firmer attitude towards the control of the poor. In its new, reformed state, the hospital was to comprise a curate for St Helen's, another priest with responsibility for the prisoners in the Guildhall and a small staff of servants. Four nurses, the complement originally envisaged by Walter Suffield, were to 'make the beddes, washe and attende upon' forty poor inmates, at a salary of 24s 4d a year each. A schoolmaster and his assistant, both capable of teaching Latin to local boys, together drew almost £17, and maintained the tradition of scholarship so dear to the founder. Out of an estimated annual budget of £224, a sum of £160 was earmarked for the care of the sick paupers, while just £13 went to the two priests.[26] Under the name of 'God's House' or 'the House of the Poor in Holme Street', St Giles's thus came nearer to fulfilling Bishop Suffield's intentions than it had for the best part of two centuries. Now, however, through the influence of humanist reformers, who were interested in schemes of civic improvement, hospitals were required to serve a secular rather than a spiritual purpose. The removal of potential sources of infection and disease, of political disaffection, of immorality and of crime had become their primary concern, as had the education in such places of a docile workforce. Physicians and surgeons were provided to treat the sick and where possible make them fit again as productive members of society. Labour, rather than prayer, was the debt rendered by the poor for food, clothing and shelter. So too was invisibility. As William Marshall recommended, 'nowe charite shall stande if the poore holde their tonges'.[27]

END NOTES

1   J.F. Pound, 'The Social and Trade Structure of Norwich 1525–1575', *Past and Present*, XXXIV (1966), pp. 50–51. Pound's estimate of the level of poverty in urban society at this time is considerably higher than that put forward by Pythian-Adams, *Desolation of a City*, pp. 131–34. And see ibid., pp. 283–84, for evidence about depopulation.

2   Norfolk Record Office, Norwich Consistory Court Wills, Reg. Hyrning, ff. 148v–150r.

3   N. Tanner, *The Church in Late Medieval Norwich*, pp. 243–44. Setman also left £13 6s 8d for the repair of St Giles's hospital in Bishopgate and 20s to one of the lay sisters there, so he was certainly not indifferent to the provision of institutional care.

4   See, for example, J.A.F. Thomson, 'Piety and Charity in Late Medieval London', *Journal of Ecclesiastical History*, XVI (1965), pp. 182–84.

5   For a general discussion of the problem, see Mollat, *The Poor in the Middle Ages*, pp. 164–77, 183–90.

6   *Statutes of the Realm*, vol. I, 23 Ed. III, c. 5. For background to this legislation, see *The Black Death*, ed. R. Horrox (Manchester, 1994), parts VI and VII.

7   *Calendar of Patent Rolls*, 1350–54 (London, 1907), pp. 283–84.

8   Documents relevant to the East Anglian rising may be found in *The Peasants' Revolt of 1381*, ed. R.B. Dobson (second edn, London, 1983), part IV, passim. See also, E. Powell, *The Rising in East Anglia in 1381* (Cambridge, 1896), pp. 26–40, which is far less reliable.

9   See, for example, Rubin, *Charity and Community*, pp. 50–51.

10   Mollat, *The Poor in the Middle Ages*, pp. 231–32.

11   *Statutes of the Realm*, vol. II, 7 Ric. II, c. 5.

12   *The Book of Margery Kempe*, p. 56; Tierney, 'The Decretists and the "Deserving Poor"', pp. 360–73. This 'aversion to public beggary' had been expressed by William Langland, see Shepherd, 'Poverty in *Piers Plowman'*, pp. 170–75.

13   *Some Early Tracts on Poor Relief*, p. 63.

14   Rubin, 'Imagining Medieval Hospitals', p. 23.

15   E. Duffy, *The Stripping of the Altars, Traditional Religion in England 1400–1580* (Yale, 1992), pp. 363–36.

16   *Twenty-Six Political and Other Poems*, ed. J. Kail (Early English Text Society, CXXIV, 1904), p. 20.

17   M.K. McIntosh, 'Local Resposes to the Poor in Late Medieval and Tudor England', *Continuity and Change*, III (1988), p. 214; Cullum and Goldberg, 'Charitable Provision in Late Medieval York', pp. 35–37.

18   Rawcliffe, *Medicine and Society*, pp. 205–6; Cullum, 'Charitable Giving', pp. 182–211.

19   Gilchrist and Oliva, *Religious Women in Medieval East Anglia*, pp. 71–73 and Table 3.

20   *Household Accounts from Medieval England*, ed. C.M. Woolgar (Records of Social and Economic History, new series, XVII, 1992), pp. 200–27; (XVIII, 1993), pp. 577 79.

21   According to N. Tanner's analysis of wills made by laymen and women in Norwich, ninety-five per cent of testators put their parish church first in their lists of pious bequests (*The Church in Late Medieval Norwich*, pp. 136, 223). For the sense of community in rural England, and the desire to exclude 'outsiders', see Clark, 'Social Welfare', passim.

22   This figure is based upon an estimated population of just over 11,000. See King, 'The Merchant Class and Borough Finance', p. 27.

23   An argument advanced for the country as a whole by McIntosh, 'Local Responses to the Poor', pp. 213–25.

24   *Records of the City of Norwich*, vol. II, pp. xcvii, 116–18.

25   Ibid., pp. xcviii, xcix-c, 126, 153–54, 161–62, 167, 173–75.

26   British Library, Department of Manuscripts, Ms. Harley 1576, ff. 251–59; Norfolk County Record Office, case 24, shelf B, no. 34.

27   *Some Early Tracts on Poor Relief*, p. 73. For attempts in Norwich to treat the sick poor so that they could work, see Pelling, 'Illness among the Poor', pp. 282–83; eadem, 'Healing the Sick Poor', passim.

APPENDIX

The Hospitals of Medieval Norwich

For Lepers:

ST MARY MAGDALEN, SPROWSTON: Founded by Herbert de Losinga, first bishop of Norwich (d.1119), about half a mile to the north of the city outside the Magdalen gate, and run by an episcopal nominee as master. In 1535 its landed income stood at £10 a year. The stone chapel (or more probably the infirmary hall at its west end) still survives, and is now a public library.

ST STEPHEN: Situated just outside the Needham (St Stephen's) gate to the south west of the city, near what became the site of the Norfolk and Norwich Hospital. Its master was appointed by the prior of Horsham St Faith, on whose land it was built. In 1315, four 'leper cottages' stood in the precincts, where there was also a chapel. The hospital had become a poor house by 1469; and after the Reformation (in 1541) the master stood accused of supplying fraudulent credentials to healthy beggars.

ST GILES'S: Situated at St Giles's gate, one of the major western points of entry to Norwich. In 1308 it comprised at least 'seven cottages where leprous people dwell'. By 1541 it had also been redesignated a 'sykehouse', and the proctor likewise faced charges of abusing his position.

SS MARY AND CLEMENT: Stood outside St Augustine's gate, just off the north-west approach road to Norwich. It was allegedly founded by one of the early bishops, but letters of 1529 appointing a proctor to beg throughout England on behalf of 'the infirm and lepers lying in the said house' refer to Margaret, countess of Lincoln, as the foundress. This was probably Margaret de Lungespee, who died shortly before 1310, but an earlier namesake died some fifty years earlier.

ST BENEDICT: Took its name from St Benedict's gate, to the west of Norwich, and due north of St Giles's. It evidently owned property as it possessed a common seal. This *leprosarium* had become a 'sykehouse' by 1541, and was then in the charge of 'an heile and clene' master, rather than a leper or sick pauper.

ST LEONARD: Lay directly north of Norwich outside the Magdalen (Fye Bridge) gate, and on the way to Sprowston. It consisted of a few wooden houses, which in 1335 needed repair. Plans were afoot in the 1440s to rebuild the chapel. Some of the patients were buried in the cemetery of All Saints' Church, within the walls, and perhaps in other city cemeteries, too.

For the Sick Poor

ST PAUL (NORMAN'S): Begun during the early-twelfth century by the prior and monks of Norwich Cathedral Priory, on open land given to them in the north east of the city. Losinga's successor, Bishop Everard (res. 1145), is generally credited (and described himself) as the founder, but he had generous support from Richard Beaufo, sometime archdeacon of Norwich. The parish church of St Paul was built at about the same time and appropriated to the hospital in 1198, as part of a far larger endowment. The hospital was originally intended to accommodate fourteen poor men and aged residents of both sexes, but by the late-thirteenth century the number had been increased to twenty. The house then also offered over-night shelter and food to poor travellers, and facilities for 'the sick, infirm and child-bearing poor of the city'. By the early-fifteenth century only sisters (some full-board, others half-board) were admitted on a permanent basis. They were responsible, under the direction of a wardeness, for running an almshouse for the poor and possibly a school. The master was always a Benedictine monk from the priory, and accounted as one of the senior obedientiaries. Annual income fell from £72 in 1363 to about £25 in the 1530s.

SS MARY AND JOHN: A cartulary of Carrow Priory (now lost) apparently noted that the priory was founded in 1146 by the bishop of Norwich and two nuns, who were sisters of this hospital. King Stephen had made a grant of land 'in the fields of Norwich' to the church of SS Mary and Stephen nine years earlier, but his charter does not mention a hospital.

BRICHTIU'S: According to Thomas of Monmouth, one of the patients, a woman suffering from 'elephantiasis', was cured miraculously by William of Norwich in, or just after, 1150. No further references to the place survive: it may well have been a *leprosarium*, and certainly admitted long-stay, chronic cases.

HILDEBRAND'S (ST MARY'S OR IVY HALL): Founded by Hildebrand (or Hildebrond), a citizen and mercer of Norwich, in about 1200, along with a separate chapel dedicated to the Virgin, which adjoined St Edward's church, King Street. It lay to the south-east of the city near the Conisford gate, and gave hospitality to 'poor people wanting lodging', many of whom would have been pilgrims. The church was appropriated to the hospital, and subsequently united with the parish church of St Julian in about 1269. Revenues fell from £8 a year in 1274 to £5 in 1368, and continued to decline. Concern about the enforcement of the statutes was voiced in 1429, but a few paupers were still being cared for in the later fifteenth century.

ST MARY IN THE FIELDS: A hospital and chapel were set up in St Stephen's parish, on the south-western margins of the city, by John le Brun, a priest, before 1248. The original purpose soon changed, however, and the house became a wealthy and important college for secular clergy.

ST GILES: Founded in 1249 by Walter Suffield, bishop of Norwich, with thirty beds for the infirm poor and additional accommodation for elderly or sick clergy. Thirteen paupers were to be fed each day, and seven boys 'able to learn' were to be supported while they studied grammar. Additional food was to be distributed before harvest time, and when the bishop himself visited the house. There were to be four chaplains, two clerks, a deacon, subdeacon, four lay brothers and four or five nurses (over fifty) but these numbers fluctuated over the years. Although complex arrangements were made for the election of the master, he effectively remained an episcopal nominee. The appointment of ambitious placemen from the 1370s onwards hastened a change whereby the hospital assumed a collegiate status, with growing emphasis on the liturgy. The extensive hospital complex lay to the north east of the Cathedral, within a bend of the river Wensum. The priory church of St Helen was demolished and rebuilt here c.1270, the western end being used as an infirmary. A large, elaborately decorated chancel was added to the east end c.1381. The hospital's Norwich and Norfolk properties together produced about £120 a year just before the Reformation, which was not much less than receipts two centuries earlier. But the appearance of financial stability is deceptive: even though many new properties had been acquired, the masters were sometimes obliged to underwrite expenses. St Giles's has been in constant use since 1249, and a substantial part of the medieval fabric survives.

Later Almshouses:

GOD'S HOUSE (ST MARGARET): Founded as a refuge for the poor, in 1292, by Robert de Aswardby to the west of the city, between St Margaret's church, Westwick, and St Benedict's gate.

ST SAVIOUR: In 1305 the master and brethren of this hospital obtained a royal licence to hold property left to them by Richard de Breccles (*alias* Herman), the founder. Breccles had been planning his almshouse since 1298, with the intention of helping the poor of Coslany, an area to the north west of Norwich, but in the event funding proved insufficient. Because his estate was burdened with debt, the project was abandoned in 1306.

GOD'S HOUSE (ST GILES): Founded before 1306 by John le Grant as an almshouse in Lower Newport near St Giles's gate, and reputedly rebuilt by Bishop Lyhart (d.1472). The bishops of Norwich claimed the right to nominate the inmates. Perhaps the house took over from the *leprosarium* of the same name, with which it may have been confused.

DANYEL'S ALMSHOUSES: Endowed by the brothers, John and Walter Danyell, both of whom were former mayors of Norwich, in the parishes of St Stephen and St Katherine to the south of the city, and described in their joint will of 1418. Nothing more is heard of this foundation after the 1420s.

GARZOUN'S (GARESOHN'S) ALMSHOUSES: Founded by Hugh Garzoun, a wealthy citizen and rentier of Norwich, during the early-fourteenth century. It lay in St Benedict's parish, near Westwick.

ST CHRISTOPHER: Mentioned only in the index of William Dugdale's *Monasticon Anglicanum*, ed. J. Caley and others (6 vols, London, 1817–30), vol. VI, p. 1785. Evidently no more than a tenement belonging to the hospital of the Blessed Mary of Rouncivalle, London (itself a cell of the convent of Nuestra Senora de Roncesvalles in Navarre), it was acquired after 1369 by the Black Friars of Norwich, but did not continue as an almshouse.

CROOM'S: Also noted by Dugdale (ibid.) as being in existence before 1516.

BIBLIOGRAPHY

A. Manuscript Sources:

British Library Department of Manuscripts

Add. Ch. 26726; Ms. Harley 1576; Ms. Royal 6 EVII

Norfolk Record Office

Archive of the Dean and Chapter of Norwich Cathedral:
DCN 1/6/1–137; 1/10/1–38; 2/5/1–8; 9/4; 40/21A-B; 43/9, 48; 44/13/1,
22/5–8, 126/3; 45/3/4–6, 9/1, 13/3, 29/1, 30/9, 31/1–5, 15–21, 24, 33–34, 33/22,
24, 41, 34/3, 4, 6, 10, 35/3, 38/7, 85/1; 48/26A/1; 69; 79/3–4; 84/14; Reg. 1,
book 3

Miscellaneous Deeds:

Box 30E1; COL 5/2/1; Misc 1/5; N/MC 15/4; Phi/95, 99, 292–93, 311, 516–19,
525, 600, 621, 623

Records of the Great Hospital, Norwich:
Case 24 shelves A, B and C.

Wills Proved in the Consistory Court, Norwich:
Alblaster, ff. 107–8; Aleyn, f. 9; Alpe, ff. 49v–50; Betyns, f. 49; Brosyard, f. 288;
Doke, ff. 36, 144; Harsyk, ff. 5–5v; Heydon, ff. 183–84, 196–96v; Hyrning, ff.
32–33, 148–150; Jekkys, ff. 43, 169

New College, Oxford

Ms. 3691

Public Record Office

C1/46/158; C43/47/290, 297; C143/51/13; C270/22; E368/280; KB 27/793;
Probate Court of Canterbury, Reg. Wattys, ff. 51–52

B. Printed Primary Sources:

Acts of the Parliament of Scotland (12 vols, Edinburgh, 1844–75)

Anglicus, Bartholomaeus, *On the Properties of Things: John Trevisa's Translation of Bartholomaeus Anglicus' De Proprietatibus Rerum,* ed. M.C. Seymour (3 vols, Oxford, 975–88)

Arderne, John of, *Treatises of Fistula in Ano*, ed. D. Power (Early English Text Society, CXXXIX, 1910)

Barnum, P. Heath, ed. *Dives and Pauper* (Early English Text Society, CCLXXV, 1976, and CCLXXX, 1980)

Bracton, Henry, *De Legibus et Consuetudinibus Angliae*, ed. T. Twiss (6 vols, Rolls Series, 1878–83)

Brakelond, Jocelin of, *Chronicle of the Abbey of Bury St Edmunds*, ed. D. Greenway and J. Sayers (Oxford, 1989)

Brewer, J.S., ed. *Letters and Papers Foreign and Domestic, Henry VIII* (4 vols, London, 1920)

Brinklow, Henry, *Complaynt of Roderyck Mors*, ed. J.M. Cowper (Early English Text Society, extra series, XXII, 1874)

Brooke, R.B., ed. *Scripta Leonis, Rufini et Angeli Sociorum S. Francisci* (Oxford, 1990)

Calendar of Close Rolls

Calendar of Fine Rolls

Calendar of Inquisitions Miscellaneous

Calendar of Liberate Rolls

Calendar of Norwich Deeds, 1307–1341, ed. W. Rye (Norwich, 1915)

Calendar of Papal Registers: Papal Letters

Calendar of Patent Rolls

Calendar of the Register of John Dronkesford, ed. Bishop Hobhouse (Somerset Record Society, I, 1887)

Celano, Thomas de, *Vitae I et II* (First and Second Lives of St Francis of Assisi, *Analecta Franciscana*, X, 1926–41)

Chaucer, Geoffrey, *The Works of Geoffrey Chaucer*, ed. F.N. Robinson (Oxford, 1970)

Chauliac, Guy de, *The Cyrurgie of Guy de Chauliac*, ed. M.S. Ogden (Early English Text Society, CCLXV, 1971)

Clark, J. Willis, ed. *The Observances in Use at the Augustinian Priory of St Giles and St Andrew at Barnwell, Cambridgeshire* (Cambridge, 1897)

Coggeshall, Ralph de, *Chronicon Anglicanum*, ed. J. Stevenson (Rolls Series, 1875)

Collins, A. Jefferies, ed. *Manuale ad Usum Percelebris Ecclesie Sarisburiensis* (Henry Bradshaw Society, XCI, 1960)

Cotton, Bartholomew de, *Historia Anglicana*, ed. H.R. Luard (Rolls Series, 1859)

Councils and Synods, 1066–1204, ed. D. Whitelock, M. Brett and C.N.L. Brooke (Oxford, 1981)

Councils and Synods II, 1205–1313, ed. F.M. Powicke and C.R. Cheney (2 parts, Oxford, 1964)

Crawford, A., ed. *The Household Books of John Howard, Duke of Norfolk, 1462–1471, 1481–1483* (Stroud, 1992)

Cronne, H.A. and Davis, R.H.C., eds *Gesta Regum Anglo-Normannorum, 1066–1154, III* (Oxford, 1968)

Curtis, R.L., ed. *The Romance of Tristan* (Oxford, 1994)

Davis, N., ed. *Paston Letters and Papers of the Fifteenth Century* (2 vols, Oxford, 1971–76)

Dobson, R.B., ed. *The Peasants' Revolt of 1381* (London, second edn, 1983)

Dodwell, B., ed. *The Charters of Norwich Cathedral Priory* (Pipe Roll Society, new series, vols XL, 1965–66, and XLVI, 1978–80)

Douie, D.L. and Farmer, H., ed. T*he Life of St Hugh of Lincoln* (2 vols, London, 1961–62)

Dugdale, William, *Monasticon Anglicanum*, ed. J. Caley and others (6 vols, London, 1817–30)

Eadmer, *Historia Novorum in Anglia*, ed. M. Rule (Rolls Series, 1884)

Fleishhacker, R. von, ed. *Lanfrank's 'Science of Cirurgie'* (Early English Text Society, CII, 1894)

Foreville, R. and Keir, G., eds *The Book of St Gilbert* (Oxford, 1987)

Gransden, A., ed. *The Chronicle of Bury St Edmunds, 1212–1301* (London, 1964)

Hale, W.H. and Ellacombe, H.T., eds *Account of the Executors of Richard, Bishop of London 1303, and of Thomas, Bishop of Exeter, 1310* (Camden Society, new series, X,1874)

Harper-Bill, C., ed. *Charters of the Medieval Hospitals of Bury St Edmunds* (Suffolk Charters, XIV, 1994)

Hingeston-Randolph, F.C., ed. *The Register of Walter de Stapledon, Bishop of Exeter* (London, 1892)

Historical Manuscripts Commission Eighth Report (London, 1881)

Historical Manuscripts Commission Ninth Report (London, 1883)

Horrox, R., ed. *The Black Death* (Manchester, 1994)

Hudson, W., ed. *Leet Jurisdiction in the City of Norwich during the Thirteenth and Fourteenth Centuries* (Selden Society, V, 1892)

Hudson, W. and Tingey, J.C., eds *The Records of the City of Norwich* (2 vols, Norwich, 1906–10)

Hudson, W. and Tingey, J.C., eds *The Revised Catalogue of the Records of the City of Norwich* (Norwich, 1898)

Jacob, E.F., ed. *The Register of Henry Chichele, Archbishop of Canterbury* (4 vols, Oxford, 1943–47)

Jessopp, A., ed. *Visitations of the Diocese of Norwich 1492–1532* (Camden Society, new series, XLIII, 1888)

Kail, J., ed. *Twenty-Six Political and Other Poems* (Early English Text Society, CXXIV, 1904)

Kempe, Margery, *The Book of Margery Kempe,* ed. S.B. Meech (Early English Text Society, CCXII, 1940)

Knowles. D., ed. *The Monastic Constitutions of Lanfranc* (London, 1951)

Knox, R. and Leslie, S., eds *The Miracles of Henry VI* (Cambridge, 1923)

Larking, L.B., ed. *The Knights Hospitallers in England: The Report of Prior Philip de Thame, 1338* (Camden Society, LXV, 1857)

Langland, William, *Piers Plowman by William Langland: An Edition of the C-Text,* ed. D. Pearsall (York Medieval Texts, second series, 1978)

Losinga, Herbert de, *The Life, Letters and Sermons,* ed. E.M. Goulburn and H. Symonds (2 vols, Oxford, 1878)

Luders, A. and others, eds *Statutes of the Realm* (11 vols, London, 1810–28)

Lydgate, John, *The Minor Poems*, ed. H.N. MacCracken (Early English Text Society, CXCII, 1911, reprinted 1961)

Malmesbury, William de, *Gesta Regum Anglorum*, ed. W. Stubbs (2 vols, Rolls Series, 1887–89)

Monmouth, Thomas of, *The Life and Miracles of St William of Norwich*, ed. A. Jessopp and M.R. James (Cambridge, 1896)

More, St Thomas, *A Dialogue Concerning Heresies*, ed. T.M.C. Lawler and others (*The Complete Works of St Thomas More*, VI, 1981)

More, St Thomas, *The Apologia*, ed. J.B. Trapp (*The Complete Works of St Thomas More*, IX, 1979)

Morton, William, *The Book of William Morton, Almoner of Peterborough Monastery 1448–1467*, ed. W.T. Mellows and P.I. King (Northants Record Society, XVI, 1954)

Nangis, Guillaume de, *Chronique Latine de Guillaume de Nangis*, ed. H. Geraud (2 vols, Paris, 1843)

Norwich, Julian of, *A Book of Showings to the Anchoress Julian of Norwich*, ed. E. Colledge and J. Welsh (2 vols, Pontifical Institute of Medieval Studies and Texts, Toronto, 1978)

Owen, D.M., ed. *The Making of King's Lynn* (Records of Social and Economic History, new series, IX, 1984)

Paris, Matthew, *Chronica Majora*, ed. H.R. Luard (7 vols, Rolls Series, 1872–84)

Pound, J.F., ed. *The Norwich Census of the Poor*, 1570 (Norfolk Record Society, XL, 1971)

Raine, J., ed. *The Register of Walter Gray* (Surtees Society, LVI, 1870)

Rye, W., ed. *A Short Calendar of Deeds Relating to Norwich, 1285–1306* (Norwich, 1903)

Salter, F.R., ed. *Some Early Tracts on Poor Relief* (London, 1926)

Strachey, J. and others, eds *Rotuli Parliamentorum* (6 vols, London, 1767–77)

Salu, M.B., ed. and trans. *The Ancrene Riwle* (Exeter Medieval English Texts and Studies, 1990)

Saunders, H.W., ed. *The First Register of Norwich Cathedral Priory* (Norfolk Record Society, XI, 1939)

Skeat, W.W., ed. *Chaucerian and Other Pieces* (Oxford, 1959)

Small, J., ed. *English Metrical Homilies* (Edinburgh, 1862)

Smith, T., Smith, L.T and Brentano, L., eds *English Gilds* (Early English Text Society, XL, 1890)

Starkey, Thomas, *A Dialogue between Cardinal Pole and Thomas Lupset*, ed. J.M. Cowper (Early English Text Society, extra series, XXXII, 1878)

Stow, John, *A Survey of London*, ed. C.L. Kingsford (2 vols, Oxford, 1908)

Tanner, N., ed. *Norwich Heresy Trials, 1428–1431* (Camden Society, fourth series, XX, 1977)

Valor Ecclesiasticus (6 vols, London, 1810–34)

Viard, J., ed. *Grandes Chroniques de France* (10 vols, Paris, 1920–53)

Walsingham, Thomas, *Gesta Abbatum Monasterii Sancti Albani*, ed. H.T. Riley (3 vols, Rolls Series, 1867–69)

Watkin, A., ed. *Inventory of Church Goods Temp. Edward III* (Norfolk Record Society, XIX, 1947–48)

Wendover, Roger of, *Flores Historiarum*, ed. H.G. Hewlett (3 vols, Rolls Series, 1886–89)

Wenzel, S., ed. *Fasciculus Morum: A Fourteenth-Century Preacher's Handbook* (Pennsylvania, 1989)

Wharton, H., ed. *Anglia Sacra* (2 vols, London, 1691)

Whittaker, W.J., ed. *The Mirror of Justices* (Selden Society, VII, 1895)

Wilkins, D., ed. *Concilia Magnae Britanniae et Hiberniae* (4 vols, London, 1737)

Woolgar, C.M., ed. *Household Accounts from Medieval England* (Records of Social and Economic History, new series, XVII, 1992, XVIII, 1993)

C. Printed Secondary Sources:

Alexander, J.W., 'Herbert of Norwich, 1091–1119: Studies in the History of Norman England', *Studies in Medieval and Renaissance History*, VI (1969)

Amundsen, D.W., 'Medieval Canon Law on Medical and Surgical Practice by the Clergy', *Bulletin of the History of Medicine*, LII (1978)

Amundsen, D.W., 'The Medieval Catholic Tradition', in *Caring and Curing, Health and Medicine in the Western Religious Tradition*, ed. R.L. Numbers and D.W. Amundsen (London, 1986)

Atkin, M., 'Medieval and Clay-Walled Building in Norwich', *Norfolk Archaeology*, XLI (1991)

Ayers, B., *Digging Deeper: Recent Archaeology in Norwich* (Norfolk Museums Service, 1987)

Ayers, B., Smith, R. and Tillyard, M., 'The Cow Tower, Norwich: A Detailed Survey and Partial Reinterpretation', *Medieval Archaeology*, XXXII (1988)

Ayers, B., *The English Heritage Book of Norwich* (London, 1994)

Beeching, H.C. and James, M.R., 'The Library of the Cathedral Church of Norwich', *Norfolk Archaeology*, XIX (1917)

Bennett-Symons, F.W., 'The Hospital of St Giles, Norwich', *Journal of the British Archaeological Association*, new series, XXXI (1925)

Blaauw, W.H., 'Will of Richard de la Wych', *Sussex Archaeological Collections*, I (1848)

Blomefield, F.B., *An Essay towards a Topographical History of the County of Norfolk* (11 vols, London, 1805–10)

Bourgeois, A., *Lepreux et Maladreries du Pas-de-Calais* (Arras, 1972)

Britnell, R.H., 'The Pastons and their Norfolk', *Agricultural History Review*, XXXVI (1988)

Brody, S.N., *The Disease of the Soul: Leprosy in Medieval Literature* (Cornell, 1974)

Brown, E.A., 'Death and the Human Body in the Later Middle Ages: The Legislation of Boniface VIII on the Division of the Corpse', *Viator*, XII (1981)

Bynum, C.W., *Holy Feast and Holy Fast: The Religious Significance of Food to Medieval Women* (University of California, 1987)

Campbell, B.M.S., 'Population Pressure, Inheritance and the Land Market in a Fourteenth-Century Peasant Community', in *Land, Kinship and Life-Cycle*, ed. R.M. Smith (Cambridge, 1984)

Campbell, J., *Norwich* (Historic Towns Trust, 1975)

Carlin, M., 'Medieval English Hospitals', in *The Hospital in History*, ed. L. Granshaw and R. Porter (London, 1989)

Carter, E.H., 'The Constitutions of the Hospital of St Paul (Normanspitel) in Norwich', *Norfolk Archaeology*, XXV (1935)

Clark, E., 'Some Aspects of Social Security in Medieval England', *Journal of Family History*, VII (1982)

Clark, E., 'Mothers at Risk of Poverty in the Medieval English Countryside', in *Poor Women and Children in the European Past*, ed. J. Henderson and R. Wall (London, 1994)

Clark, E., 'Social Welfare and Mutual Aid in the Medieval Countryside', *Journal of British Studies*, XXXIII (1994)

Clay, R.M., *The Mediaeval Hospitals of England* (London, 1909, reprinted 1966)

Cockayne, G.E., *The Complete Peerage*, ed. V. Gibbs and others (12 vols, London, 1910–59)

Cranage, D.H.S., 'Eastern Chapels in the Cathedral Church of Norwich', *Antiquaries Journal*, XII (1932)

Cullum, P.H., 'Leperhouses and Borough Status in the Thirteenth Century', in *Thirteenth Century England III*, ed. P.R. Coss and S.D. Lloyd (Woodbridge, 1991)

Cullum, P.H., *Cremetts and Corrodies : Care of the Poor and Sick at St Leonard's Hospital, York, in the Middle Ages* (University of York, Borthwick Paper, LXXIX, 1991)

Cullum, P.H., '"And Hir Name Was Charite": Charitable Giving by and for Women in Late Medieval York', in *Woman is a Worthy Wight: Women in English Society c.1200–1500*, ed. P.J.P. Goldberg (Stroud, 1992)

Cullum, P.H., 'Poverty and Charity in Early Fourteenth-Century England', in *England in the Fourteenth Century*, ed. N. Rogers (Stamford, 1993)

Cullum, P.H. and Goldberg, P.J.P., 'Charitable Provision in Late Medieval York: "To the Praise of God and the Use of the Poor"', *Northern History*, XXIX (1993)

Darby, H.C., *The Domesday Geography of Eastern England* (Cambridge, 1971)

Dawes, J.D. and Magilton, J.R., *The Cemetery of St Helen-on-the-Walls, Aldwark* (York Archaeogical Trust, 1980)

Dawtry, A.F., 'The *Modus Medendi* and the Benedictine Order in England', *Studies in Church History*, XIX (1982)

Demaitre, L., 'The Description and Diagnosis of Leprosy by Fourteenth-Century Physicians', *Bulletin of the History of Medicine*, LIX (1985)

Doubleday, H.A. and Page, W., eds *The Victoria History of the County of Hampshire and the Isle of Wight*, II (1903, London)

Doubleday, H.A. and Page, W., eds *The Victoria History of the County of Norfolk*, II (London, 1906)

Duffy, E., *The Stripping of the Altars, Traditional Religion in England 1400–1580* (Yale, 1992)

Duncan, K., 'Climate and the Decline of Leprosy in England', *Proceedings of the Royal College of Physicians of Edinburgh*, XXIV (1994)

Dyer, C., *Standards of Living in the Later Middle Ages* (Cambridge, 1989)

Elton, G.R., 'An Early Tudor Poor Law', *Economic History Review*, series two, VI (1953–54)

Emden, A.B., *Biographical Register of the University of Oxford to 1500* (3 vols, Oxford, 1957–59)

Emden, A.B., *Biographical Register of the University of Cambridge* (Cambridge, 1963)

Erickson, C., *The Medieval Vision: Essays in History and Perception* (Oxford, 1976)

Farmer, D.H., ed. *The Oxford Dictionary of Saints* (Oxford, 1978)

Fernie, E.C., 'Two Aspects of Bishop Walter Suffield's Lady Chapel at Norwich Cathedral', in *England in the Thirteenth Century*, ed. W.M. Ormrod (Nottingham, 1985)

Fernie, E.C., *An Architectural History of Norwich Cathedral* (Oxford, 1993)

Finucane, R.C., *Miracles and Pilgrims* (London, 1977)

Finucane, R.C., 'Sacred Corpse, Profane Carrion: Social Ideals and Death Rituals in the Late Middle Ages', in *Mirrors of Mortality: Studies in the Social History of Death*, ed. J. Whaley (London, 1981)

Foucault, M., *Madness and Civilisation*, trans. R. Howard (London, 1971)

Geremek, B., *The Margins of Society in Late Medieval Paris*, trans. J. Birrell (Cambridge, 1987)

Gilchrist, R., 'Christian Bodies and Souls: the Archaeology of Life and Death in Later Medieval Hospitals', in *Death in Towns: Urban Responses to the Dying and the Dead, 100–1600*, ed. S. Bassett (Leicester, 1992)

Gilchrist, R. and Oliva, M., *Religious Women in Medieval East Anglia* (Studies in East Anglian History, I, 1993)

Le Goff, J., *The Birth of Purgatory*, trans. A. Goldhammer (London, 1984)

Hallam, H.E., 'The Climate of Eastern England 1250–1350', *Agricultural History Review*, XXXII (1984)

Hammond, E.A., 'The Westminster Abbey Infirmarers' Rolls as a Source of Medical History', *Bulletin of the History of Medicine*, XXXIX (1965)

Harper-Bill, C. and Fernie, E., eds *Norwich Cathedral: Church, City and Diocese, 1096–1996* (London, forthcoming 1996)

Harries, R., Cattermole, P. and Mackintosh, P., *A History of Norwich School* (Norwich, 1991)

Hart, R., 'The Shrines and Pilgrims of the County of Norfolk', *Norfolk Archaeology*, VI (1864)

Harvey, B., *Living and Dying in England 1100–1540: The Monastic Experience* (Oxford, 1993)

Haskins, S., *Mary Magdalen: Myth and Metaphor* (London, 1994)

Henderson, J., 'The Hospitals of Late Medieval and Renaissance Florence: A Preliminary Survey', in *The Hospital in History*, ed. L. Granshaw and R. Porter (London, 1990)

Henderson, J. and Park, K., '"The First Hospital among Christians": The Ospedale di Santa Maria Nuova in Early Sixteenth Century Florence', *Medical History*, XXXV (1991)

Honeybourne, M.B., 'The Leper Hospitals of the London Area', *Transactions of the London and Middlesex Archaeological Society*, XXI (1967)

Horden, P., 'A Discipline of Relevance: The Historiography of the Later Medieval Hospital', *Social History of Medicine*, I (1988)

Imbert, J., ed. *Histoire des Hopitaux en France* (Toulouse, 1982)

Jacob, E.F., 'St Richard of Chichester', *Journal of Ecclesiastical History*, VII (1956)

Jacquart, D., *Le Milieu Medical en France du XIIe au XVe Siecle* (Hautes Etudes Medievales et Modernes, series 5, XLVI, 1981)

James, M.R., 'Lives of St Walstan', *Norfolk Archaeology*, XIX (1917)

Jewson, C., *History of the Great Hospital Norwich* (Norwich, 1978)

Kealey, E.J., *Medieval Medicus: A Social History of Anglo-Norman Medicine* (Johns Hopkins, 1981)

Keene, D., *Survey of Winchester* (2 vols, Oxford, 1985)

Ker, N.R., 'Mediaeval Mss from Norwich Cathedral', *Transactions of the Cambridge Bibliographical Society* I (1949–53)

Kershaw, I., 'The Great Famine and Agrarian Crisis in England 1315–22', *Past and Present*, LIX (1973)

King, E., *Peterborough Abbey 1086–1310* (Cambridge, 1973)

Kirkpatrick, J., *History of the Religious Orders and Communities of the Hospitals and Castle of Norwich, Written about the Year 1725* (London, 1845)

Knowles, D. and Hadcock, R.N., *Medieval Religious Houses, England and Wales* (London, 2nd edn, 1971)

Langmuir, G.I., 'Thomas of Monmouth: Detector of Ritual Murder', *Speculum*, LIX (1984)

Lawrence, C.H., *St Edmund of Abingdon* (Oxford, 1960)

Lawrence, C.H., *Medieval Monasticism* (London, 1989)

Lipman, V.D., *The Jews of Medieval Norwich* (London, 1967)

Lunt, W.E., *The Valuation of Norwich* (Oxford, 1926)

Lyons, A.S. and Petrucelli, R.J., eds *Medicine: An Illustrated History*, (New York, 1978)

McFarlane, K.B., *England in the Fifteenth Century* (London, 1991)

McIntosh, M.K., 'Local Responses to the Poor in late Medieval and Tudor England', *Continuity and Change*, III (1988)

McRee, B.R., 'Charity and Gild Solidarity in Late Medieval England', *Journal of British Studies*, XXXII (1993)

Maddicott, J.R., *The English Peasantry and the Demands of the Crown 1294–1341* (Past and Present Supplement, I, 1975)

Magilton, J. and Lee, F., 'The Leper Hospital of St James and St Mary Magdalene, Chichester', in *Burial Archaeology: Current Research, Methods and Documents*, ed. C.A. Roberts, F. Lee and J. Bintliff (British Archaeological Report, British Series, CCXI, 1989)

Manchester, K., 'Tuberculosis and Leprosy in Antiquity: An Interpretation', *Medical History*, XXVIII (1984)

Manship, H., *History of Great Yarmouth*, ed. J. Palmer (Yarmouth, 1854)

Miller, E., ed. *The Agrarian History of England and Wales Volume III* (Cambridge, 1991)

Mollat, M., *The Poor in the Middle Ages*, trans. A. Goldhammer (Yale, 1986)

Moore, R.I., *The Formation of a Persecuting Society (Oxford, 1987)*

Moore, R.I., 'Heresy as a Disease', in *The Concept of Heresy in the Middle Ages*, ed. W. Lourdaux and V. Verhelst (Mediaevalia Louaniensia, series 1, IV, 1976)

Moorman, J.R.H., *The Sources for the Life of S. Francis of Assisi* (Manchester, 1940)

Moorman, J.R.H., *Church Life in England in the Thirteenth Century* (Cambridge, 1945)

Moorman, J.R.H., *A History of the Franciscan Order* (Oxford, 1968)

Mundy, J.H., 'Hospitals and Leprosaries in Twelfth and Early Thirteenth-Century Toulouse', in *Essays in Medieval Life and Thought*, ed. J.H. Mundy, R.W. Emery and B.N. Nelson (Columbia, New York, 1955)

Nuthall, T., *Lazar House: From Hospital to Library* (Norwich, 1993)

Orme, N., 'A Medieval Almshouse for the Clergy: Clyst Gabriel Hospital near Exeter', *Journal of Ecclesiastical History*, XXXIX (1988)

Orme, N., 'Sufferings of the Clergy: Illness and Old Age in Exeter Diocese 1300–1540', in *Life, Death and the Elderly*, ed. M. Pelling and R.M. Smith (London, 1991)

Owst, G.R., *Literature and the Pulpit in Medieval England* (Oxford, 1961)

Page, W., ed. *The Victoria History of the County of Sussex*, II (London, 1907)

Park, K., 'Healing the Poor: Hospitals and Medical Assistance in Renaissance Florence', in *Medicine and Charity before the Welfare State*, ed. J. Barry and C. Jones (London, 1991)

Pelling, M., 'Healing the Sick Poor: Social Policy and Disability in Norwich 1550–1640', *Medical History*, XXIX (1985)

Pelling, M., 'Illness among the Poor in an Early Modern English Town: The Norwich Census of 1570', *Continuity and Change*, III (1988)

Pound, J.F., 'The Social and Trade Structure of Norwich 1525–1575', *Past and Present*, XXXIV (1966)

Powell, E., *The Rising in East Anglia in 1381* (Cambridge, 1896)

Powicke, F.M., *Henry III and the Lord Edward* (2 vols, Oxford, 1947)

Pythian-Adams, C., *Desolation of a City: Coventry and the Urban Crisis of the Late Middle Ages* (Cambridge, 1979)

Rawcliffe, C., 'The Hospitals of Later Medieval London', *Medical History*, XXVIII (1984)

Rawcliffe, C., *Medicine and Society in Later Medieval England* (Stroud, 1995)

Richards, P., *The Medieval Leper and his Northern Heirs* (Cambridge, 1977)

Roberts, C.A., 'Leprosy and Leprosaria in Medieval Britain', *Museum of Applied Science Centre for Archaeology*, 1 (1986)

Roskell, J.S., Clark, L. and Rawcliffe, C., eds *The History of Parliament, The House of Commons 1386–1421* (4 vols, Stroud, 1993)

Rowe, J., 'The Medieval Hospitals of Bury St Edmunds', *Medical History*, II (1958)

Rowland Burdon, E., 'St Saviour's Hospital Bury St Edmunds', *Proceedings of the Suffolk Institute of Archaeology*, XIX (1927)

Rubin, M., *Charity and Community in Medieval Cambridge* (Cambridge, 1987)

Rubin, M., 'Development and Change in English Hospitals, 1100–1500', in *The Hospital in History*, ed. L. Granshaw and R. Porter (London, 1989)

Rubin, M., 'Imagining Medieval Hospitals', in *Medicine and Charity before the Welfare State*, ed. J. Barry and C. Jones (London, 1991)

Russell, J.C., *Dictionary of Writers of Thirteenth Century England* (London, 1936)

Russell, J.C., *British Medieval Population* (Albuquerque, 1948)

Rutledge, E., 'Immigration and Population Growth in Early Fourteenth-Century Norwich: Evidence from the Tithing Roll', *Urban History Yearbook*, (1988)

Rutledge, E., 'Landlords and Tenants: Housing and the Rented Property Market in Early Fourteenth-Century Norwich', *Urban History* (forthcoming, 1995)

Rye, W., *Carrow Abbey* (Norwich, 1889)

Saltman, A., *Theobald Archbishop of Canterbury* (London, 1956)

Saunders, H.W., *An Introduction to the Rolls of Norwich Cathedral Priory* (Norwich, 1930)

Serjeantson, R.M. and Adkins, W.R.D., eds *The Victoria History of the County of Northamptonshire, II* (London, 1906)

Shepherd, G., 'Poverty in Piers Plowman', in *Social Relations and Ideas: Essays in Honour of R.H. Hilton*, ed. T.H. Aston and others (Cambridge, 1983)

Shinners, J.R., 'The Veneration of Saints at Norwich Cathedral in the Fourteenth Century', *Norfolk Archaeology*, XL (1987)

Smith, R.M., 'Some Issues Concerning Families and their Property in Rural England 1250–1800', in *Land, Kinship and Life-Cycle*, ed. R.M. Smith (Cambridge, 1984)

Somerscales, M.I., 'Lazar Houses in Cornwall', *Journal of the Royal Institution of Cornwall*, new series, V (1965)

Spencer, B., *Medieval Pilgrim Badges from Norfolk* (Norfolk Museums Service, 1980)

Stirland, A., 'The Human Bones', in *Excavations within the North-East Bailey of Norwich Castle, 1979*, ed. B. Ayers (East Anglian Archaeology, XXVIII, 1985)

Stirland, A. and Bown, J., *Criminals and Paupers: Excavations at the Site and Churchyard of St Margaret Fyebridgegate, Magdalen Street, Norwich* (East Anglian Archaeology, forthcoming, 1996)

Talbot, C.H. and Hammond, E.A., *The Medical Practitioners in Medieval England* (London, 1965)

Tanner, N., *The Church in Late Medieval Norwich* (Pontifical Institute of Medieval Studies and Texts, LXVI, 1984)

Tanner, T., *Notitia Monastica* (London, 1744)

Thompson, A.H., *The History of the Hospital and the New College of the Annunciation of St Mary in the Newarke, Leicester* (Leicester Archaeological Society, 1937)

Thompson, B., 'From "Alms" to "Spiritual Services": The Function and Status of Monastic Property in Medieval England', in *Monastic Studies II*, ed. J. Loades (Bangor, 1991)

Thompson, S., *Women Religious* (Oxford, 1991)

Thomson, J.A.F., 'Piety and Charity in Late Medieval London', *Journal of Ecclesiastical History*, XVI (1965)

Tierney, B., 'The Decretists and the "Deserving Poor"', *Comparative Studies in Society and History*, I (1958–59)

Ward, B., *Miracles and the Medieval Mind* (Aldershot, 1987)

Watt, J.A., 'The English Episcopate, the State and the Jews: the Evidence of the Thirteenth-Century Conciliar Decrees', in *Thirteenth Century England II*, ed. P.R. Coss and S.D. Lloyd (Woodbridge, 1987)

Waxler, N.E., 'Learning to be a Leper: a Case Study in the Social Construction of Illness', in *Social Contexts of Health, Illness and Patient Care*, ed. E.G. Mishler (Cambridge, 1981)

Wells, C., *Bones, Bodies and Disease* (London, 1964)

Wells, C., 'A Leper Cemetery at South Acre, Norfolk', *Medieval Archaeology*, X (1967)

Williams, J.F., 'Ordination in the Norwich Diocese during the Fifteenth Century', *Norfolk Archaeology*, **XXXI** (1956)

Woodman, F., 'Hardley, Norfolk, and the Rebuilding of its Chancel', in *Studies in Medieval Art and Architecture Presented to Peter Lasko*, ed. D. Buckton and T.A. Heslop (Stroud, 1994)

Wormald, F., 'The Rood of Bromholm', *Journal of the Warburg Institute*, I (1937–38)

Unpublished Theses

Cullum, P.H., 'Hospitals and Charitable Provision in Medieval Yorkshire 936–1547' (York University PhD thesis, 1990)

King, A., 'The Merchant Class and Borough Finances of late Medieval Norwich' (Oxford University DPhil thesis, 1989)

Underwood, E.C.K., 'Fifteenth-Century Clergy in the Diocese of Norwich' (Tasmania University PhD thesis, 1993)

INDEX

Adam, Master (physician), 28
Albertus Magnus, 29
Albon, Richard, 74
Alexander IV, Pope, 98, 129 n.29
Aleyn, Lady (wife of Sir Robert), 67
anchorites and anchoresses, 48, 58
n.58, 104, 143-44
Anne of Bohemia, queen of Richard
II, 107
Appleyard, family of, 116
Aristotle, 28
Aswardby, Robert de, 148, 165
Attleborough, Mary de, 125
Avicenna, 28
Ayermine, William, bp., 119

Barnwell Priory, Northants., 98
Bastwick, Norf., 119
Bawburgh, Norf., 140
Beaufo, Adam, 63
Beaufo, Richard, bp., 61, 63, 65, 164
Beaulieu Abbey, Hants., 86 n.38
Bec, Theobald of, abp., 63
Beck, Anthony, bp., 119, 121
Beighton, Norf., 64
Bertram, Alice, 65
Bettyns, John, 105
Bitton, Thomas, bp., 33
Blickling, Norf., 63, 65, 146
Blofield, Norf., 64
Blois, Henry of, bp., 62, 64
Bothumsyll, Alice (sister), 125
Brakelond, Jocelin of, 142
Breccles, Richard de, 147, 165
Brentwood, Essex, 36
Breton, Matilda (leper), 49
Bristol, 24
Bromholm, Norf., priors and Priory,
98, 129 n.29, 140-41

Bronescombe, Walter, bp., 39
Brun, John le, 91, 165
Bungay, Robert de, 105
Burnham, Robert, prior, 71, 79
Bury St Edmunds, Abbey, 27, 75,
101, 139-40, 155. See hospitals.

Cailly, Agnes, 105
Cailly, Hugh, 105
Caister, Richard, 141-42
Calthorpe, Norf., 91, 104, 113
Cambridge, university of, 107-8.
See hospitals.
Canterbury, Christ Church Priory,
26. See hospitals.
Canterbury Tales, 136
Cantley, Norf., 119
Carleton, East, Norf., 119-20
Carrow Priory, Norf., 142-43, 164
Catton, Norf., 65
Catton, Richard de, 53
Chamberlain, Ralph, 54-55
charity, changing attitudes to, 10-11,
24, 66, 72-77, 82-83,
104, 127, 146-47, 153-60;
Christian teaching on, 13-18,
26-27, 38, 63-64, 94
Chaucer, Geoffrey, 44, 136
Chauliac, Guy de (surgeon), 36
children, education of, 69, 77, 94,
103, 122, 125, 131 n.56,
159-60, 165; mortality of, 20-21;
relief for, 19, 69, 92
Christ, Holy Blood of, 93; and
lepers, 38, 42-43; and poverty,
13-18, 26-27, 66-67, 98, 137, 139,
156-58; physician of souls, 15, 43,
46, 144
Colman, Alice (leper), 59 n.74

Colney, Norf., 120
Coltishall, Norf., 22, 24, 120, 146

Constance, council of, 146
corrodies, sale of, 74–76, 125, 153
Costessey, Norf., 113, 117
Cotton, Bartholomew, 94
Courtenay, William, abp., 66
Coventry, 24
Cressy, Isabel de, 113, 115
Creyforth, proctor of St Giles's, 53
Cringleford, Norf., 113, 120, 141
Cringlethorpe, Beatrice de (leper),
    52
Cromwell, Thomas, 83
Cusyn, John, 105

Danyell, John, 148, 166
Danyell, Walter, 148, 154, 166
David I, King of Scotland, 48
Derlyngton, John, 105, 108, 120–21
Despenser, Henry, bp., 66, 107, 109,
    145, 156
Dives and Pauper, 75, 127
Droxford, John, bp., 136
Dunwich, William, 102, 104, 115
Dynham, Oliver, 107

Earlham, Norf., 119
Eaton, Norf., 120
Edward I, King of England, 64, 145
Edward II, King of England, 22
Edward III, King of England, 22–23,
    155
Eleanor of Castile, queen of Edward
    I, 65
Erpingham, Norf., 104, 119
Erpingham, Sir Thomas, 74
Eton, Roger, 105
Everard, bp., 61, 63–64, 164

Farnham, Nicholas, bp., 103

Fastolf, Sir John, 120, 133 n.101
Fastolf, Richard, 14
Fastolf, Petronilla, 14
Feltard, John (leper), 39–40
Filby, Norf., 65
Fobbing, Essex, 120
food, contamination of, 21, 40–41;
    distribution of, 16–17, 30 n.11, 62,
    66–67, 82–84, 92, 98, 100, 125,
    158; shortages of, 11, 17–18, 22,
    100–1, 159

Galen, 28
Galtrehil, Norf., 65
Garzoun, Hugh, 148, 166
Gerberge, Sir Thomas, 116
Geoffrey, Master (surgeon), 28
Godale, Beatrice de, 105
Gogney, Joan, 88 n.62
Goldwell, James, bp., 47, 74, 105,
    107, 109, 111, 120
Goldwell, Nicholas, 47, 105, 107, 111
Grant, John le, 148, 166
Grant, Thomas le, 148
Gratian, 37, 94
Gray, John, bp., 65, 68, 140, 143
Gregory IX, Pope, 94
Gregory X, Pope, 64
Grey, Alice, 146
Grosseteste, Robert, bp., 93

Hales, Norf., 119
Hardley, Norf., 113, 117
Hawze, Richard, 125
Heacham, Norf., 59 n.74
Hecker, John, 111–12; family of, 116
Hedde, Isabel (sister), 74
Hekelyng, Robert, 74
Hellesdon, Norf., 65
Henry I, King of England, 41, 61,
    63–64, 80
Henry II, King of England, 61, 64

Henry III, King of England, 64, 69, 92–94, 96–97, 140

Henry IV, King of England, 38

Henry V, King of England, 145–46

Henry VI, King of England, 122, 142

Henry VIII, King of England, 64

Hethel, Norf., 119–20

Hethersett, Norf., 120

Hobart, Sir James, 116

Homersfield, Norf., 64

Horsford, Norf., 120

Horsham St Faith, priors of, 49, 122, 163

HOSPITALS, abuses in, 27, 46, 53–54, 67–68, 73–77, 99, 107–9, 111, 127, 135–36, 144–47.
burial facilities in, 14–16, 46, 50–52, 70, 104.
education in, 69, 76–77, 103, 159–60, 165.
episcopal involvement in, 46–47, 49, 61–67, 91–111, 113, 145.
finances of, 46–47, 70–72, 74–82, 109, 111–13, 115–17, 120–21, 123–24, 144–48.
functions of, 13–18, 62, 66–69, 98–103, 135–36, 140.
for lepers, 34, 41–54.
marginal situation of, 48, 52, 62, 114, 143–44.
patient care in, 24–26, 67–68, 102–4, 121–22, 125.
staff of, 69–71, 73, 80–81, 98–103, 115, 159–60.

HOSPITALS, Beaune, Burgundy, Hotel Dieu, 14; Basingstoke, Hants., St John, 135; Beck, Norf., St Thomas, 109; Beverley, Yorks., Holy Innocents, 75; Brackley, Northants., SS James and John, 129 n.25, 136; Bridgwater, Som., St John, 68, 131 n.56, 135–36; Bury St Edmunds, St Saviour, 75–77, 101, 142; Cambridge, SS Anthony and Eligius, 54, 147, St John, 68, 147; Carlisle, St Nicholas, 113; Dudston, Glos., leper house, 42, 45; Florence, S. Maria Nuova, 25, 31 n.39, 69, 73; Gloucester, St Bartholomew, 88 n.56; Harbledown (Canterbury), leper house, 45, 62; Hautbois, Norf., hospice, 142; Horning, Norf., St James, 142; King's (Bishop's) Lynn, Norf., St John, 130 n.37, leper house, 44, 48, 52–53, St Mary Magdalen, 14, St Mary Magdalen (Gaywood Causeway), 43; Kingston-on-Thames, Surr., leper house, 49; Kingston-upon-Hull, almshouses, 149; Launceston, Cornw., St Leonard, 43; Leicester, St Mary in the Newarke, 68, 103; London, almshouses, 154, leper houses, 48, St Bartholomew, 94, 128 n.17, St Mary Bethelehem, 54, 111, St Mary Bishopsgate, 17, 67, St Mary Rouncivalle, 149, 166, St Thomas Acon, 127, Savoy, 25; Messingham, Norf., SS Mary and Nicholas, 109; Nimes, Ruffi's almshouse, 146; Northallerton, Yorks., St James, 88 n.70, 103; Oxford, St John, 69, 97; Paris, almshouses, 87 n.48, Hotel Dieu, 25, 69, Les Quinze-Vingts, 21; Peterborough, St Leonard, 34; Rushford, Suff., St John, 142; St Albans, Herts., St Julian, 59 n.68; Sherborne, Dorset, almshouse, 71; Skirbeck, Lincs., St Leonard,

16–17; Southwark, Surr., St Thomas, 76; Thetford, Norf., SS Mary and Julian, 142; Tranent, E. Lothian, St Germanus, 67; Walsingham, Norf., hospice, 142; Winchester, St Cross, 62, 85 n.9, St John, 130 n.50; Windham, Suss., St Edmund, 101; Yarmouth, St Mary, 14, 130 n.37; York, leper houses, 48, 59 n.72, *maisons dieu*, 72, 149, St Leonard, 62, 75, 102–3, 113. See Norwich.
Hungerford, Mary, Lady, 68

Ingulf, prior of Norwich, 61
Innocent IV, Pope, 92–93, 98
insane, detention of, 54–55, 68
Intwood, Norf., 119
Ixworth Priory, Suff., 110
Jannys, Robert, 154
Jews, persecution of, 36–38, 40
John, King of England, 64
Jullys, John, 111, 146

Kempe, Margery, 38–39, 44–45, 54, 141, 156–57
Ketteringham, John, 71
Knot, Walter, 49
Knott, John, 65

Lanfranc, abp., 26, 45, 62
Langham, Norf., 64, 139
Langland, William, 19
Lateran councils, 18, 26, 36–37, 47
Lazarus 'the beggar', 14, 43
Lazarus 'the leper', 42–43
Legarda, Lady (wid. of William of Apulia), 41–43
leprosy, 16, 19, 24, 27, 33–59, 68, 98, 122, 134, 138–39, 141, 147, 163–64. See hospitals.
Limpenhoe, Norf., 119

Lincoln, Margaret, countess of (d. bef. 1266), 50, 59 n.65, 163
Lincoln, Margaret, countess of (d. bef. 1310), 50, 59 n.65, 163
Loddon, Norf., 119
London, 24, 52, 69, 83, 93, 101, 147. See hospitals.
Losinga, Herbert de, bp., 13, 26, 41, 45, 47, 61–63, 142, 163–64
Louis IX, King of France, 21, 93
Lovell, William, Lord, 136
Lucas, Isabel (leper), 53
Lyhart, Walter, bp., 109, 111, 148, 166
Lyon, Agnes (sister), 76

Marshall, William, 19, 25, 157, 160
Marsham, Norf., 63, 65
Matilda, queen of Henry I, 44, 61
Matilda, queen of Stephen, 61
Mercer, Hildebrand le, 143, 164–65
Mettingham, Suff., 158
Middleton, William, bp., 100
Milan, Lanfrank of (surgeon), 102
Monmouth, Thomas of, 37–38, 138–40, 164
Morley, Emma de, 65
Morley, Isabella, Lady, 158
Morley, Morell de, 65
Mortmain, Statute of, 65, 113
Mundham, Norf., 119–21
Munforth, Robert (pauper), 116

Narborough, John, 74
Newcastle-upon-Tyne, 81, 147
Newman, John, 74
Newton, Norf., 64, 120
Newton Flotman, Norf., 119
Nightingale, Joan (leper), 36
Norfolk, John, duke of (d.1461), 120
Norfolk, John, duke of (d.1476), 117, 132 n.75

Norfolk, John, duke of (d.1485), 141
Norfolk, Mary, countess of (fl.1351), 105, 119
NORWICH, antisemitism in, 36–38.
  Benedictine Priory: almonry, 26–27, 52, 61, 82–85, 92; archives, 9; finances, 71, 77–85; and hospital of St Paul, 61–66, 70–71, 73, 76–82, 164; infirmary, 27–29; library, 28–29; monks, 10, 25, 98, 104, 140–42; priors, 14, 47, 98, 139.
  Castle, 21, 27, 61, 63, 145.
  Cathedral of Holy Trinity, 91–92, 95, 97, 139–40.
  Cow Tower, 114–15.
  episcopal school, 103.
  Guildhall, 17–18, 159.
  guilds, 16–18, 72, 87 n.47, 149.
  heresy trials, 137–38.
  hospitals: Aswardby's almshouse, 148, 158, 165; St Benedict, 48, 50–54, 153, 163; Brichtiu's, 138–39, 153, 164; Danyells' almshouses, 148, 166; Garzoun's almshouse, 148, 153, 166; Grant's almshouse, 148, 166; Hildebrand's, 143–46, 153, 164–65; St Christopher, 149, 166; St Giles, Bishopgate, 9–11, 17, 22, 46–47, 53, 64–65, 67, 72, 74, 85 n.11, 91–133, 142, 146, 155, 158–60, 165; St Giles (lepers), 48–49, 53, 148, 153, 163; St Leonard, 39, 48, 51–52, 153, 164; SS Mary and Clement, 48–49, 153, 163; SS Mary and John, 142–43, 153, 164; St Mary in the Fields, 46, 91, 110, 145, 153, 165; St Mary Magdalen (Sprowston), 26, 34, 41–49, 153, 163; St Paul (Norman's), 9, 12, 26, 32 n.46, 53, 60–89, 103, 122, 125, 140, 142–43, 153, 159, 164; St Saviour, 147–48, 165–66; St Stephen, 48–49, 53, 153, 163.
  lepers of, 33–54.
  pilgrimage to, 138–42.
  population, 10–11, 22–24, 27, 40, 61, 142–48, 153–54.
  sick poor of, 18–28
  testators of, 17–18, 46–47, 101, 105, 122, 143, 145–49, 154, 158–59.
Norwich, Hildebrand de, 143
Norwich, Julian of, 144
Norwich, Katherine, wid. of Walter de, 158
Norwich, Maud de, 158

old age and poverty, 19, 20, 24–25, 29 n.9, 30 n.24, 67, 101, 122, 142
Ordyng, Elizabeth (sister), 125
Origen, 42
Ormesby, Norf., 63, 65, 80–81
Orreby, Sir John de, 105
Oxford, council of (1222), 37
Oxford, university of, 94, 96, 107, 109, 146. See hospitals.
Oxford, John, bp., 64

Paris, Matthew, 92–93, 96, 98
Paris, university of, 94. See hospitals.
Parys, Thomas, 49
Passion of St William the Martyr of Norwich, 37–38
Paston family, 81, 109, 117, 132 n.75
Peasants' Revolt, 136, 155–56
Peckham, Katherine (sister), 69, 77
Peterborough, Abbey, 34, 156. See hospitals.
Piers Plowman, 19
Philip V, King of France, 37
pilgrims, 16, 19, 24–26, 55, 62, 65, 67–68, 96–98, 135–43, 164

plague, effects of, 10–11, 17, 22–24, 33, 40, 81, 84–85, 101, 119, 121, 135, 142, 153, 155
Plymouth, 24
Pontigny, Abbey, 97

Porter, John, 74
Prat, Roger, 105
Preston, Thomas de, 105, 119
purgatory, 14, 18–19, 48, 58 n.56, 100, 157

Questiones Physicorum, 28

Raleigh, William, bp., 96, 97
Ravenser, Richard, 113
Reedham, Norf., 119
Reeve, John, 77
regimen sanitatis (regimen of health), 67–68
Repps, Norf., 119
Revelations of Divine Love, 144
Richard II, King of England, 107, 156
Ringland, Norf., 119
Rollesby, Norf., 119–20
Ruffi, Pierre, 146
Rye, William, 53

St Albans, Adam de (surgeon), 145
St Albert of Cringleford, 141
St Ambrose, 156–57
St Anne, 95, 105, 111
St Anthony of Egypt, 142
St Augustine of Hippo, 14
St Barbara, 17
St Benedict, 26–27
St Benet Hulme, Abbey of, 117, 142, 151
St Bernard of Clairvaux, 29
St Dominic, 94
St Edmund of Abingdon, abp., 96–97, 101, 129 nn.25, 28

St Elizabeth of Hungary, 73, 158
St Ethelwold, bp., 92
St Francis of Assisi, 44, 94
St Gilbert of Sempringham, 43
St Giles, 95–96, 100
St-Gilles, Provence, Abbey of, 96
St Hugh of Lincoln, bp., 44
St Helen, 104–5, 112
St Katherine, 104
St Leonard, 51–52
St Mary Magdalen, 42–43, 69
St Mary, the Virgin, 15, 16, 92, 95, 104–5, 111, 142, 145
St Michael, 17
St Neot, Cornw., 33
St Nicholas, 105
St Paul of Tarsus, 63–64
St Peter, 105
St Richard Wych, bp., 94, 96–97, 101
St Theobald, 142
St Thomas Becket, abp., 141
St Thomas Cantelupe, bp., 138
St Thomas More, 82, 138
St Walstan, 141
St William of Norwich (never canonised), 37–38, 41, 92, 138–42, 164
Salhouse, Norf., 120
Salmon, John, bp., 105
Salter, Thomas, 69
Schaerbeke, Alice of, 58 n.56
Scrope, Richard le, abp., 38
Secreta Secretorum, 29
Seething, Norf., 113, 125
Selot, John, 109, 117, 132 n.75
Setman, William, 59, 145, 154
sin and disease, 18, 36–40, 42–43, 45, 48, 54, 68–69, 96, 136–37
Sisland, Norf., 119–20
Skerning, Roger, bp., 104, 145
Skinner, Geoffrey (leper), 122
Smyth, John, 105, 120

Somercotes, Lawrence, 94
Soper, William, 111
South Acre, Norf., 35
Sparham, Norf., 39–40
Sprowston, Norf., 41–47, 49, 119, 163–64
Spycer, Hugh (pauper), 116
Stanford, Robert, 51
Stapledon, Walter, bp., 33–34
Stephen, King of England, 61, 142–43, 164
Stow, John, 83, 92
Suffield, Geoffrey (physician), 28
Suffield, Walter, bp., 48, 64, 66, 67, 91–109, 113, 116–17, 125, 134 n.118, 140, 159–60, 165
Swannington, Norf., 120

Taverham, Norf., 63
Thornage, Norf., 64
Thornham, Norf., 64
Thornham, Simon, 46
Thornton, Roger, 147
Thorpe, episcopal manor of, Norf., 41, 63
Thorpe St Andrew, 66, 119
Thurlton, Norf., 116, 119
Thurstan, 65
Thwaite, Norf., 119
titles, for ordination, 109–11
Torpel, Robert de, 34
Trefnant, John, bp., 66
Trowse, Norf., 120
Tybeham, Roger de, 105
Tytel, Thomas (leper), 53

vagrancy, legislation on, 25–26, 54, 136, 156, 159
Valor Ecclesiasticus, 82–83, 122
Veryes, John, 105

Walpole, Ralph, bp., 100

Walsham, South, Norf., 113, 119
Walsingham, Norf., 140, 142
Walsingham, Thomas, 156
Walton, Simon, bp., 92, 97–98, 145
Watchman, William the, 52
Watton, Norf., 125
Wellys, Henry (leper), 51
Wellys, Richard (leper), 52
Wendover, Richard (physician), 94, 102
Wendover, Roger of, 141
Westminster Abbey, 28, 82, 83, 93
Westminster, synod of (1200), 51

Wetherby, Thomas, 120
Weyden, Roger van der, 14
Whitewell, William, 97
Whittington, Richard, 69
Wickmere, Norf., 119, 120
Winchester, 23, 56 n.15. See hospitals.
Winchester, Roger, earl of (d.1264), 129 n.25
women, as carers, 25–26, 43–44, 69–70, 72–74, 76, 94, 102–3, 125, 130 n.52, 143, 158–59; diseases of, 20–21; relief for, 11, 19, 68–75, 80, 87 n.48, 106, 139, 154–55, 158–59, 164
Wrenne, John (leper), 134
Wroxham, Norf., 120
Wycliffe, John, 137
Wykeham, William, bp., 76

Yarmouth, 14, 28. See hospitals.
York, 20, 23–24, 72, 139, 149. See hospitals.
Ypres, poor relief in, 17, 19, 25, 136, 157